TEACH YOURSE

Philosophy of Religion

Philosophy of Religion

Mel Thompson

TEACH YOURSELF BOOKS

For UK orders: please contact Bookpoint Ltd, 130 Milton Park, Abingdon, Oxon OX14 4SB. Telephone: (44) 01235 827720, Fax: (44) 01235 400454. Lines are open from 09.00–18.00, Monday to Saturday, with a 24-hour message answering service. Email address: orders@bookpoint.co.uk

For U.S.A. & Canada orders: please contact NTC/Contemporary Publishing, 4255 West Touhy Avenue, Lincolnwood, Illinois 60646 – 1975 U.S.A. Telephone: (847) 679 5500, Fax: (847) 679 2494

British Library Cataloguing in Publication Data
A catalogue record for this title is available from The British Library

Library of Congress Catalog Card Number: On file

First published in UK 1997 by Hodder Headline Plc, 338 Euston Road, London NW1 3BH.

First published in US 1997 by NTC/Contemporary Publishing, 4255 West Touhy Avenue, Lincolnwood (Chicago), Illinois 60646-1975 U.S.A.

Typeset by Transet Ltd, Coventry, England.
Printed in Great Britain for Hodder & Stoughton Educational, a division of Hodder Headline Ltd, 338 Euston Road, London NW1 3BH by Cox & Wyman Ltd, Reading, Berkshire.

Impression number	10	9	8	7	6
Year	2004	2003	2002	2001	

CONTENTS

INTRODUCTION

People long to make sense of life; to find some key that will unlock its mysteries and enable them to understand themselves and their place within the universe. Faced with their own fragility and death, they seek courage or comfort. Longing to develop and create, they seek inspiration.

In this human quest for meaning, some take to philosophy, others to the creative arts, and others – in fact the majority of humankind – take to some form of religion.

Almost every profound aspect of life – from sexuality to artistic creativity, or from the emotional trauma of prolonged suffering or bereavement to the spontaneous expression of wonder at natural beauty – may become the raw material out of which a religious interpretation of life can be built.

But why? What are religious beliefs, and how do they relate to the rest of our understanding of life? Can they be justified rationally? Are they a mental springboard, launching us into a deeper exploration and appreciation of life, or a mental prison, closing our minds to reason and evidence? Or are they neither, but only our use (or misuse) of them makes them so?

These are just some of the questions we need to address: there will be many more.

What is the philosophy of religion?

The philosophy of religion examines the general ideas and principles upon which religion is based. It takes the truth claims that religious people make and tests them for logical coherence and meaning.

Logical coherence: Does this belief make logical sense? Does it fit the evidence? Does it accord with other beliefs that the person holds? If it is true, what implications does it have?

Meaning: Is the language in which this belief is expressed meant to be taken literally? If so, what evidence may be given for or against its truth? If not, is it simply a statement about the mental state or creative wishes of the person who makes it?

The philosophy of religion therefore looks at religious beliefs and asks if they make sense and if they are logically coherent. It does not simply ask if they are true, but probes deeper to ask:

- How can we know whether they are true or false?
- What sort of evidence can be given to support them?
- Why do religious people make these claims?

In other words:

The philosophy of religion takes religious beliefs and asks how they are to be understood, if they make sense, and if they fit with the rest of our knowledge of the universe.

Philosophy cannot show that a religion is either right or wrong. What it can do is to show that its beliefs are either logical or illogical, that its language is best understood literally or metaphorically, and the degree to which its beliefs are compatible with other beliefs that people might hold to be true.

Very few people adopt a religion for purely rational reasons. Indeed, if Richard Dawkins of Oxford is right, they may catch religion from their parents or from other people in the same way that they catch a virus! On the other hand, religious believers of all sorts claim to be rational. They claim that their religion makes sense – and it is this claim that the philosophy of religion puts to the test.

— Why study religion in this way? —

Those who have religious beliefs generally want to be able to share their faith with others, but they cannot do so except on the basis of a common language and set of ideas. Indeed, they cannot even think about their religious beliefs without using concepts and language that are the common currency of their age and society.

For the sake of personal integrity, it is also important that religious beliefs should to examined and tested out just like any other beliefs one might hold. The alternative is to have intellectual 'no-go areas', leaving religion unexamined, private and mute. Not only is that unhealthy for a thinking being, it is also contrary to the great religious traditions, all of which wish to comment on the world, passing on their message and values to society as a whole.

A believer therefore needs to take the philosophy of religion seriously. But what of the non-believer? Why study religion at all? Perhaps because it is an inescapable fact of life.

It is difficult to overstate the global importance of religion:

- Western politics, culture and ideas are largely shaped by the Judaeo/Christian religious tradition. Even for a person who claims no religious allegiance, his or her thought patterns, language and general concepts have all been shaped by religion, even where that shaping is no longer self-evident.
- Can one start to think about the Middle East without thinking of the culture and life of Islam? Or of the Indian sub-continent without Hinduism? Or the Punjab without Sikhism?
- Can one appreciate the self-understanding of people of the Far East without some idea of Buddhism, Confucianism and Taoism?
- The many tribal religions, the old Norse legends, the rich traditions of the Native Americans and the Eskimo peoples, the deeply natural religions of Wicca, of the Druids and of the many early pagan cults – all of these have contributed to the rich emotional, intuitive and artistic life of humanity.

In other words:

You cannot properly understand society, global or local, without some awareness of the part that religion plays and has played in it. Even the absence of a religion is itself a phenomenon worthy of exploration.

So, if religion cannot be ignored, how should it be understood and evaluated? Well, it can be evaluated psychologically, in terms of the mental health of its adherents, or sociologically, in terms of its effects upon society. But central to religion is the fact that it makes truth claims. It proclaims certain things to be so and invites people to assent to them. The assessment of those claims is the task of the philosophy of religion.

What is involved?

The philosophy of religion has emerged as a branch of Western philosophy, concerned with the examination of the truth claims of Western religions, particularly Christianity. It has been concerned with proofs for the existence of God, the problems of Evil and the possibilities of miracles, providence and the other questions relating to the idea of God's activity in the world, and particularly with the nature and status of religious language. In general it has been less concerned with the actual phenomena of religion, which have sometimes been left to the more specific disciplines of the psychology or sociology of religion.

Much of Western philosophy in the twentieth century has been concerned with language – with the meaning of statements and their logical or evidential proof or disproof. This has coloured the way in which the philosophy of religion has been approached – hence the concern with the validity of truth claims rather than with the phenomenon of religion.

Above all, the philosophy of religion is concerned with the rational aspects of religion. Now all philosophy is rational – it is the process of taking a careful look at some aspect of life and examining it in a logical way, exploring its dilemmas, attempting to clarify its ambiguities and resolve its apparent inconsistencies. In this sense, the philosophy of religion must be rational. But there is more to religion than the rational. Religion is to do with the heart and will as much as with the mind. Religious people believe *in* things, they do not simply believe them to be the case. People are committed to their religious views, holding on to them even in the face of apparently overwhelming evidence to the contrary. This in itself is a phenomenon to be taken into consideration.

But things should not be dismissed just because they are not capable of being justified rationally. Much of what is worthwhile in life is not rational – love, music, art, the whole world of the emotions. We need therefore to remain aware of the limitations of a rational approach.

Both Freud and Marx made the mistake of believing that once the psychological or political basis of religion was exposed, religion would wither and die – once it was explained, it would have no more power. Nothing could be further from the truth.

The power of religion is not the power of explanation, but of integration. People become religious when, through some moment of insight, they sense that their energies are harnessed and unified, their life is given new direction, their future is filled with a sense of hope. Many religions speak of the religious or spiritual life in terms of a journey – it is a process of self discovery and growth, a process which is fuelled by the sense of renewed energy and well-being which it provides along the way.

In other words:

Religion is a total experience, not just a set of propositions.

In his preface to the 1993 edition of *God and the Universe of Faiths*, John Hick, speaking of the inclusive recognition of the value of the spiritual traditions of other religions, asks:

> ❛ Why not simply accept that *the transformation of human existence from destructive self-centredness to a new centring in the ultimate transcendent Reality that we call God* is taking place in and through all of the great world traditions. ❜ (italics mine)

The italicised phrase here seems to be a good general indication of what religion is actually about. It describes what may be called 'salvation' or 'the spiritual goal.' Not every religion would use the term God here, but substituting the absolute or the transcendent still retains the general sense. The point is that it is human narrowness of vision that is regarded (from the religious perspective) as destructive, and from which humankind needs to be liberated.

That is the process; but the point is, do we need a rational understanding of religion in order to bring it about? The answer to that question is 'probably not'. After all, many people lead utterly transformed and spiritual lives without studying the philosophy of religion. On the other hand, if a religion does not give some adequate account of its central beliefs, it cannot integrate its insights into the overall view of life that people hold.

In so far as we ask questions, it is natural that we will ask them of religion. Philosophy of religion is unlikely to provide the ultimate insight into truth, but it can at least clear away some of the obstacles that the rational mind places in the way of such insight.

Comment:

Too often, religious argument has been carried on in a way that is rational but shallow, and has:

- caricatured a person's belief
- re-stated that caricature as a rational proposition
- shown that such a proposition is either meaningless or false
- therefore dismissed the original belief as unworthy of serious consideration.

The original religious intuition, expressed through the belief in question, is untouched by such an argument. The religious believer may appear to walk away vanquished, but continues to believe – for the power of that belief has been neither appreciated nor diminished. **By contrast, our task in this book is to try to probe beneath the superficial, to see what is both real and rational in religion.**

Whatever may be said about religion by philosophers, the phenomenon of religion will remain while people actually claim to feel its benefits. If religion did not actually give people a sense of purpose, it would not survive. And indeed, if it had not met a deep need, it would probably never have appeared in the first place.

The structure of this book

This book is the attempt to look systematically at what religion is and how it is related to our overall understanding of life. It therefore starts with the nature of religious experiences, and moves on to look at the language people use to describe them. Only then does it move on to examine the religious beliefs and arguments that are put forward in order to explain them.

So, for example, there is little point in looking at an argument for or against the existence of God, or about the possibility of miracles, without understanding the sort of experience that might be interpreted by someone as an experience of 'God'. That experience is the bedrock, and it is open to a variety of interpretations. A logical rejection of belief in God does not therefore deny the experience that the word 'God' sought to explain; indeed, a Buddhist may have had a very similar experience, and recognise it as being spiritually important, but without any attempt to use language about 'God' to explain it.

After looking at concepts and arguments about 'God', we move on to three topics that are central to a religious understanding of life:

- the nature of the self
- the idea of providence and miracles
- the problem of suffering and evil.

These last two are the positive and negative aspects of interpreting the world in the light of belief in God.

But there are two areas of life to which religious beliefs need to be related:

- One is science, which gives a view of the universe and a method of reaching conclusions about how the world is, based on reason and evidence. Superficially at least, this may appear to challenge areas of enquiry previously dominated by religion.
- The other is ethics, the branch of philosophy which examines the grounds upon which people make moral choices. Religion has a part to play in moral choice, so, although there is no scope in this book to explore ethics in general, it is important to set out how religion relates to it.

Note:

The philosophy of religion is largely a Western phenomenon, and has developed mainly in terms of the interaction between Christian beliefs and Western secular philosophy. This is reflected in the contents of this book, and there is no scope to include a full examination of the philosophical implications of other world religions.

This is inevitable, but a pity. In any case, to do justice to Buddhist or Hindu philosophy, for example, it would be important to set it against the broad background of Indian thought. Although some fundamental issues are the same (the problem of suffering and evil, for example), the ways in which the questions are asked and the answers formulated and defended will differ from religion to religion. However, where appropriate, references to religions other than Christianity have been included.

What this book aims to do

This book seeks:

- to introduce the key concepts in the philosophy of religion
- to set out some of the arguments that have be put forward both for and against religious beliefs
- to point out the limits of rational debate.

This last point is important. To attempt to make oneself believe or not believe something for emotional or social reasons is quite hopeless – one either believes it or one does not. On the other hand, one can have a deep conviction that something is the case, and yet be able to give little evidence to back up that belief.

While every intuition is a step beyond reason, reason quickly tries to colonise the newly acquired insight and to integrate it into a rational view of things.

- I just feel that I shall like this person or this place; later I shall find my reasons.
- If you do not offer me your friendship until you know all about me, we shall remain strangers.

Emotion may be warm; reason cold. **The philosophy of religion thrives on reason that has acquired a little warmth.**

Those who seek certainty, in the form of incontrovertible proof or disproof of religious beliefs, are likely to be disappointed. There is a point at which religious experience and belief go beyond the rational, beyond proof, beyond certainty. There is a point at which a person has to make a commitment, take a risk, in order to get further in the religious quest. Those fearful of such risks stay on the surface of things.

Perhaps one task within the philosophy of religion is to show why it is sometimes reasonable to step beyond reason and to allow the emotions and intuition to play a creative role.

1
RELIGIOUS EXPERIENCE

Starting with experience

If there were no religion, there would be no philosophy of religion. If there were no 'religious experiences', there would be no religion. Religion, unlike most philosophy, starts with the interpretation of experience, with trying to make sense of life as a whole, or of particular things that happen.

Relatively few people who belong to a religious group, or who would call themselves religious if asked, actually spend their days reflecting on the logic of believing in the existence of God. What they are actually doing is living within the ordinary world with a particular way of seeing things and a particular set of values to live by. They take part in acts of worship and feel 'uplifted'. They claim to be inspired; to have moments of insight. They find that, even when not engaged in specifically religious activities, they have experiences that tend to reinforce their faith – they see a beautiful sunset, or experience childbirth; they face their own death or that of a loved one; they fall in love. At all these moments, their experience is informed by and in turn informs their religion.

For reflection:

- You feel hot: they say you are running a temperature.
- You see stars: they point out that you have been hit on the head.
- You sense that the earth is moving beneath you: they say you are drunk, sexually over-excited, or have a disease of the inner ear.

The experience you have remains valid, even if the explanation given for it is proved wrong.

Therefore a religious experience is not invalidated by an argument showing that God cannot exist. The most such an argument could show is that the explanation you may have given of your experience is not logically coherent.

In general, you can argue for or against an interpretation or a proposition; you cannot argue for or against an experience, you can only seek to understand it.

A major feature of philosophy in general in the second half of the twentieth century has been the recognition that language is always used for a particular purpose and in a particular context and that its meaning is shown by its use. A philosophy of religion should therefore start where religion starts, with experience. It can then move on from that to examine religious language and beliefs – but it will have fundamentally misunderstood those beliefs if it takes them away from their religious context.

Towards the end of his book *The Varieties of Religious Experience* (1902) William James said:

> ‘ ... in a world in which no religious feeling had ever existed, I doubt whether any philosophic theology could ever have been framed. ’

In other words, however independent of actual experience some religious concepts may have become, and however rarefied a debate on them might appear, they owe their origin to the experiences of individuals and religious groups – experiences which those concerned have tried to describe, and whose descriptions have become the raw material of religious ideas and propositions. William James spoke particularly of ‘religious feelings’ – but are ‘feelings’ separable from the things that are experienced? And what is it about experiences that lead people to have ‘religious feelings’ associated within them?

So, before looking at the various forms of religious experience, we need to consider a few basic things about experience in general.

What happens when you experience something?

Your sense organs – sight, sound, smell, taste, touch – register something, and this information is conveyed to your brain. But this raw sensation does not remain in a 'raw' state for long. As soon as it is received, four things happen:

1 The experience is registered as pleasant, painful or neutral. Something that is physically damaging (cutting your finger with a knife) is registered as painful. This is an essential part of the body's survival mechanism – painful feelings are warnings of danger. A cool drink on a hot day will immediately register as pleasant, since it represents the satisfaction of a physical need. The response is automatic; largely outside conscious control.

2 But memory also plays a part. Something is recognised, and the memory of the last encounter influences how it is now experienced. When you meet a stranger, you do not know how that experience will turn out. (Unless of course, previous meetings with strangers have been significantly pleasant or painful.) You meet that same person for a second time and, although the actual sensations are the same, the whole experience is coloured by the first encounter. The person is now known, and his or her behaviour is anticipated.

3 The mind also starts to categorise what is experienced. It finds concepts and words to describe it. It experiences this thing *as* something. The more sensitive a person is to the thing experienced, the more sophisticated is this process of categorisation. A connoisseur of fine wines distinguishes a particular grape and vintage; a less fussy drinker registers is as either white or red, sweet or dry.

4 As a result of all this mental and sensory activity, the body evaluates the experience and responds accordingly. A friend is recognised – there is a feeling of pleasure, a smile, a sudden wish to rush forward and greet the person, a feeling of relaxed warmth. An enemy is recognised – there is a tightness in the stomach, a clenching of the fists and jaw. One prepares for fight or flight; the adrenaline pumps, for the body knows that action is needed.

This process of sensing, experiencing in terms of feelings, categorising and responding happens almost simultaneously and people seldom separate out the elements of the experience. Only when there is a mismatch between one process and the others does their separate functions come to light. If you register something as painful, but respond as if it were pleasant, the body objects.

Example:

You can't stand the sight of these people, but they are customers and you have to be polite. Your smile feels taut and forced, your muscles tense ready for a fight, but you smile and give a friendly handshake. The integrity of the experience is lost – response does not match feeling or categorisation – and the result is that the encounter is exhausting.

Every experience therefore involves sensation, interpretation and response.

What is religious experience?

Religion is a complex phenomenon. It includes beliefs about the world, particular values and attitudes associated with them, and ways of responding and living which reflect those beliefs and values. This being the case, religion is likely to influence and be influenced by everything that happens. Memory and ways of interpreting present experience are equally likely to be coloured by religion.

In practice, this means that – for a religious person – a quite normal experience (looking at a beautiful scene, for example) may be profoundly religious. A non-religious person (or, more strictly speaking, a person who claims to have no religion – you may want to consider the idea that everyone has a personal religion of some sort) would describe the same thing as inspiring, uplifting, or beautiful, but would not want to go on to associate that interpretation with anything overtly religious.

On the other hand, we should not minimise the fact that certain experiences are profoundly influential in a person's life – and these are most likely to be given the label 'religious'.

Although acknowledging that there may be a religious element in all experience, we may profitably focus on those more profoundly moving experiences that seem to bring about change in people's lives.

Where does the religious element come in?

If religion is to do with an understanding of life and responses to it, then it will influence the second, third and fourth parts of the experience process. It will matter less what actual sensations impinge on the body, and more on the way in which these are categorised, the way in which memory contributes to the feelings associated with them, and the responses that a person has to them. With this in mind, then, we can now turn to examples of religious experiences.

Throughout the history of the great world religions there have been accounts of experiences that have had a profound affect on the individuals concerned. Some famous examples:

- Siddhartha seeing four sights (an old person, a sick person, a corpse and a holy man) which were to lead him on a spiritual quest, and ultimately to becoming a Buddha, moved by the reality of life and death from which his comfortable and materialistic upbringing had tried to shield him.
- Moses at the burning bush, fascinated and awe-struck by a phenomenon which led him to a profound sense of the holiness of that place and also to the challenge to go back and lead the Children of Israel out of Egypt.
- The prophet Isaiah in the temple in Jerusalem, sensing the absolute holiness of God, and the moral failures of humankind ('Woe is me, for I am a man of unclean lips, and I dwell amidst a people of unclean lips, for my eyes have seen the Lord of Hosts.')
- Jesus in the desert, struggling with the temptation to misuse spiritual power for selfish ends.
- Paul on the Damascus road, having his views and his life totally changed; forced by a moment of insight to admit he was wrong and to take the side of those whom he had sought to persecute.
- Muhammad in the cave hearing the words of the Qur'an and being told to recite them.
- Nanak, entering the river to bathe, and emerging later as a religious leader with insights that were to make him the founder of the Sikh faith.

We can never get to the historical basis of these accounts, for they have come down to us as stories that already bear a heavy burden of religious meaning and tradition. But what they do indicate most clearly is that – for all these great religious leaders – these were moments of such significance and insight that the response to them involved a radical upheaval in their lives. These moments of insight and empowerment provide the key to explain all that followed.

But religious experiences need not always be so dramatic and they are not confined to those who are about to found a new religion! In general, religious experience involves:

- a sense of wonder
- a sense of new insight and values
- a sense of holiness and profundity.

A religious experience involves the whole of a person – mind and emotions, values and relationships – and seems to touch the most basic and fundamental sense of being oneself.

In other words:

A religious experience is one in which a person says 'this is who I really am', 'this is what life is all about', 'this is so wonderful that it makes everything else worthwhile'. But exactly how that experience is interpreted depends on the culture, ideas and language of that particular time and place.

Another common feature of the well-known religious experiences given above is that they were unexpected and powerfully disruptive for the individuals concerned. Muhammad was said to be terrified at the command to 'recite'. Moses was hardly taking an easy option to go back to Egypt from which he had already escaped in fear of his life. It is most unlikely that such experiences would have been induced artificially, at least on a conscious level. Their authenticity as experiences (irrespective of the religious interpretation given to them) is demonstrated by their unlikelihood and inconvenience.

— Induced religious experiences —

Some religious experiences occur unexpectedly, totally re-shaping the course of a person's life. But they are the exception rather than the rule. Far more common is the general 'religious experience' that occurs in the context of the worship, prayer or other rituals which are practised by followers of the world's religions. These experiences are deliberately encouraged, or induced, by their religious setting, words or ritual actions.

Note that although the experiences may be induced, they are not produced automatically. You cannot guarantee that two people attending the same religious event are going to respond in the same way any more than you can guarantee that two people listening to the same music are going to be equally moved by it. Following what was said above about the nature of all experience, it would be more accurate to say that religious rituals provide sensations and offer interpretations of those sensations in the hope that the people taking part will feel an appropriate religious response.

For example:

A gesture or a word may spontaneously lead a person to feel forgiven for some wrong they have done, able to regain their self-respect and tackle life with a clearer conscience.

In the induced equivalent of this, the priest may make a ritual gesture adding to it words of interpretation, suggesting that those who are present should feel that his gesture and words signify that their sins are forgiven. What cannot be guaranteed is that those present will **actually** feel forgiven. The total experience will therefore vary from person to person.

Some induced religious experiences look very strange indeed if viewed from the outside, even if it is possible to rationalise what is being done.

For example:

Members of one particular cult have been known to stand on one leg chanting "blue, blue, blue" in order to generate a blue shield to protect themselves from the evils of the outside world. It is possible to rationalise this:

- Standing on one leg requires constant attention to balance and this, in itself, helps to focus the mind.
- Chanting something over and over again can induce mental calm and a sense of wellbeing.
- Perhaps the mental image of the colour blue is particularly positive.
- Certainly, performing the otherwise silly action along with others will induce a sense of group identity and acceptance. It may also give a warm feeling of being on the inside of an experience from which the outside world is excluded – of being one of those who know, while the bulk of people remain ignorant.

One can see why such induced religious experiences might be quite powerful for those taking part, whilst recognising that for others they might appear quite crazy. We may be tempted to ask whether or not such activity could be regarded as valid or sensible. But here there are problems:

- By what criteria do you say that something is valid?
- If it is emotionally satisfying, if it reinforces a sense of community identity, can it be invalid?

Is waving a flag at a passing monarch, climbing a sheer rock face or collecting postage stamps a 'valid' activity? If people enjoy doing such things, is that not justification enough? Perhaps so, but what is being claimed about them? You are unlikely to find a stamp collector or rock climber arguing that his or her activity provides a key insight into the nature of existence. It is simply something to be enjoyed.

We may look at induced religious experience in the same way. If they claim to do no more than induce a sense of personal wellbeing, fair enough. If, however, it is claimed that some special knowledge of the world is achieved through them, then it is fair to look at any such claims and examine them rationally (and this is one of the tasks of the philosophy of religion).

On the other hand, we need to recognise that such rational examination may achieve little by way of agreement between the religious believer and the philosopher, since the believer is quite likely to claim that what is experienced goes beyond the rational and cannot therefore be assessed in terms of it.

We need to make a clear distinction between three things:

1 Experiences of personal religious significance. This would include moments of insight or commitment, and may have an importance for the person concerned that is quite independent of any rational explanations that are offered. (Even if a complete physical or psychological explanation for everything that took place could be given, **the event would still be religiously important**.)
2 Experiences which result from the deliberate cultivation of certain states – e.g. through meditation or worship, group activity or chanting. In this case, it is very often the case that the interpretation of the experience is suggested by the religious context within which it is induced. There is also a temptation to see such experiences as proof of the validity of the religion or cult through which they were induced.
3 A habitual way of seeing the world that may be described as religious, because its interpretation and values are given by the religion to which the person belongs. Thus, for example, a person who believes in a loving God will look at everything in life as having been provided for some loving purpose. A person who holds the Buddhist view of the interconnectedness of all things, will tend to view the welfare of himself or herself as bound up with the welfare of other people and of the environment.

Of these three, the first is largely independent of particular religions. It arises in people of any religion or of none. Indeed, it may have the effect of making a previously non-religious person review his or her own attitudes. This is particularly the case, for example, with near-death experiences. Having almost died and then been given life back, a person may well start to re-evaluate life and see everything quite differently.

The second is directly linked with religion. Because the experienced is induced and anticipated, it is coloured by the religion, and cannot really be regarded as independent evidence for the truth of that religion.

The third is not independent of religion (in that it is brought about as a result of reflecting on, or acting upon, religious teachings) but it is habitual and 'secular' in that it happens within the course of ordinary living, and not only on occasions which are regarded as overtly religious.

Prayer

Prayer is a feature of those religions which involve a personal relationship between individuals and a God or gods. It may involve:

- confession
- thanksgiving and celebration
- intercession (petitionary prayer)
- prayers for guidance
- acts of submission
- meditation.

Where these things are simply an expression of a religious commitment, they cause no problems for the philosophy of religion. Confession, thanksgiving and acts of submission logically follow from a belief in God. They are an appropriate thing for a believer to do whether or not God *actually* exists; it is enough that the person *believes* that he does.

Equally, meditation (in which a person quietly focuses his or her attention on a particular object or concept, allowing it to influence the unconscious as well as the conscious mind) presents no fundamental problems. Nothing is being claimed by the act of meditation – it is simply a process of encouraging a particular quality of mind. Neither do prayers for guidance create problems – they are simply a matter of the personal and voluntary orientation of the believer's life.

All the above forms of prayer can be understood in terms of human activity, and can be seen as valid in themselves, quite apart from any supernatural element.

The main problem comes with petitionary prayer, which raises questions about the existence and nature of God. If a person prays for something to happen, it is reasonable to want to know if, subsequently, the thing for which they prayed did or did not in fact take place.

- If it did, was that the result of the prayer, or would it have happened anyway?
- If it did not, was it that the act of prayer was done wrongly (e.g. with the wrong motive), and the desired result would have happened if the prayer had been done correctly? That there is no God to hear and answer the prayer? That there is a God, that the prayer was done in a way that he would find appropriate, but that God's will was not in line with what the person praying wanted? (This last option is usually covered by a 'nevertheless, thy will be done' clause in some prayers.)

But there is a moral and metaphysical dilemma here, which touches on matters we shall be exploring later in this book:

- If God is wise, just and omnipotent, he is willing and able to know and do what is best in each situation.
- To ask God to do something that he would not do anyway therefore implies that one is asking him to do something unjust or unwise!
- Belief in a wise, just and omnipotent God therefore renders all petitionary prayer unnecessary.
- To claim that a prayer has been answered implies that God's intended action has been changed, which means that either God was not originally wise and just, or that he has now been persuaded by the prayer to do something unwise or unjust!

To avoid such problems, a believer may claim that the purpose of petitionary prayer is not to change God's mind, but simply to remind the person praying of the crucial issues with which he or she should be concerned. In other words, to align one's mind with God's, rather than trying to align God's mind with one's own. **If this is the case, then petitionary prayer appears to be literal nonsense, but psychologically and religiously useful nonsense.**

In this section we have moved quite deliberately from an observation of religious experience to the sort of philosophical issues that such experience raises. The important thing is to ask what the person praying thinks he or she is actually doing. The question 'Do you think you can change God's mind?' asked of a praying believer, will set the context for the issue of God's existence, power, wisdom and justice. The philosophical arguments about these things arise, and are rooted in, people's experience of prayer.

Conversion

In *The Varieties of Religious Experience*, William James sees a conversion experience as leading to:

- loss of worry
- truths not known before
- the sense that the world appears to undergo an objective change.

In other words, a conversion implies both a new view of the world and a new and integrated sense of the self.

As we saw above, all experience involves interpretation. We experience everything *as* something. We also have a particular view (or 'blik') which is our habitual way of looking at the world. (We shall look at both these ideas again in Chapter 2, when considering religious language.) What happens when a person goes through the experience of a conversion is that he or she sees the world differently, interprets each thing with new significance, and responds accordingly.

As William James pointed out, this implies a change in the experience of the external world as well as a changed self-awareness. You test out the validity of a claimed conversion by seeing how the person subsequently responds to the world.

An example:

You tell me that you now love spiders. I release a particularly juicy specimen in the room. Do you still jump up on a chair and scream, or do you pick it up and stroke it gently? By your response shall your new 'blik' be judged.

Mysticism

A mystical experience is one in which a person has a sense of the underlying unity of everything, breaking down all conventional barriers between oneself and the external world, going beyond our normal awareness of the limitations of time and space. It can produce a very deep sense of joy, of 'being at home', of being at one with nature and of seeing a truth that cannot be put into words. There is a long history of mysticism in both Christianity and other religions.

Gregory of Nyssa, one of the theologians of the early Church, saw the human person as an icon of God – so that true knowledge of oneself brings with it knowledge of God. He thought that it was necessary to die to the senses (in other words to get beyond the particular things experienced) to see the 'logos' or divine word which lay beyond the whole of the phenomenal world.

This highlights two features of mysticism: that the ultimate (God, where that language is used) is reflected within the self, and that there is a principle of unity beyond the diversity of the things that we ordinarily experience.

Let us get a taste for the mystical side of religious experience through two lady mystics:

Hildegaard of Bingen was a 12th century abbess who led a community of nuns living about 25 miles south of Mainz. She was a most amazing woman, a composer of beautiful plainsong melodies, a poet, a visionary mystic and one who was passionately concerned about the environment. She was a prolific writer both on religious topics, and on natural history and medicine.

She described herself as a feather on the breath of God:

> ❛ Listen: there was once a king sitting on his throne. Around him stood great and wonderfully beautiful columns ornamented with ivory, bearing the banners of the king with great honour. Then it pleased the king to raise a small feather from the ground and he commanded it to fly. The feather flew, not because of anything in itself but because the air bore it along. Thus am I... ❜

Lady Julian of Norwich, a 15th century English mystic, had what she called a sequence of 'showings' (visions in which she believed that Christ showed her spiritual truths). In one of them, she sees the world as a cared-for whole.

> ❛ ... he showed me a little thing, the size of a hazelnut, which seemed to lie in the palm of my hand; and it was as round as any ball. I looked upon it with the eye of my understanding, and

> thought, "What may this be?" I was answered in a general way, thus "It is all that is made." I wondered how long it could last; for it seemed as though it might suddenly fade away to nothing, it was so small. And I was answered in my understanding: "It lasts, and ever shall last; for God loveth it. And even so hath everything being – by the love of God." ❟

Generally, mystics are all 'one-offs'. Mysticism is not something that can be organised. What is remarkable, however, is that mystics from very different cultural and religious backgrounds have a great deal in common.

> **Note:**
>
> There are many mystics whose writings are well worth exploring in terms of understanding this particular form of religious experience. In addition to those mentioned above, one might try St John of the Cross (1542–91) or St Teresa of Avila (1512–82) within the Christian tradition. Within Islam, there is the Sufi tradition of mysticism. Within Hinduism and Buddhism, meditation techniques aim quite specifically at overcoming the distinction between self and other – so much of what is termed mysticism in the Western traditions is central to these religions.

In a mystical experience, the distinction between subject and object is overcome: the person having the experience both sees something and becomes something at one and the same time.

But if the normal differences between self and world are overcome, there is the danger that the individual may be somehow lost or swamped within the mystical experience. However, mystics claim that the person is not lost, but that somehow the uniqueness of the individual is taken up into the experience, 'losing oneself in an abyss of love' (Bede Griffiths, 1989, p.253).

There is also a sense in which what is seen cannot be fully described, and it is this that has led to the general claim that mystical experience is ineffable (unable to be rationally articulated or understood). Meister Eckhart, c. 1260–1327, described God as being incomprehensible light.

In *The Varieties of Religious Experience*, William James gives four qualities associated with mysticism:

1 Ineffability (they defy description, and are quite different from ordinary experience).
2 Neotic quality (they are states of knowledge, even if that knowledge cannot be expressed; a kind of awareness that may be called 'revelation').
3 Transiency (they cannot be sustained for long).
4 Passivity (the person who has a mystical experience feels that he or she has received something, rather than done something).

To these, F C Happold, in *Mysticism: a Study and an Anthology*, Penguin (1970), added other qualities:

- a sense of the unity of all things
- a sense of timelessness
- a sense that there is an immortal, unchanging self, and that our 'ego' is not our true self.

William James also mentions two familiar features: a feeling of 'having been here before', and with it a sense of seeing something as familiar but also as seeing that familiar thing for the very first time as it really is – seeing it in quite a new way.

The problem with mystical experience, at least as far as a philosopher is concerned, is that it is difficult to know how one would either prove or refute anything that a mystic said. If what is being described is a mental state, then it cannot be contradicted, any more than one could contradict a person who honestly said that he or she felt unhappy. Claims can only be shown to be true or false if they refer to empirical facts that can be checked. The problem is that mystics do not generally make an absolute distinction between what is empirically 'out there' and the mental state through which they encounter it. From the mystic's point of view, what is seen is very much 'out there' rather than psychological, but it is an 'out there' which is encountered personally and not at all an 'out there' which is empirically defined.

Charismatic experiences

Charismatic experiences are those in which people are inspired and enthused, to the extent that they feel taken over by a spiritual power that comes from beyond but acts within them. Within the Christian tradition, there has been increasing evidence in recent years of powerful and emotional experiences. One particular group, which originated in a church at Toronto airport, experiences what has become known as the Toronto Blessing. People shake with laughter or collapse on the ground. They may cry out or wail. They go into trance states. The touch of the Pastor seems to release a power that the individual is unable to resist, and which plunges him or her into emotional and physical states that would ordinarily be quite out of character.

Within the faith community, these experiences are attributed to the direct action of the Holy Spirit and therefore a proof of the validity of the ministry of the church. External observers may try to explain the phenomena in psychological terms (perhaps as group hysteria), or as a form of hypnosis.

It is particularly difficult for the philosophy of religion to deal with charismatic experiences. This is because the experience itself is not rational; the person concerned is ecstatic, literally standing 'outside' himself or herself, having let go of normal rational controls. Like the mystical experience, the charismatic is one that, however powerful and transforming for the person having it, is not a source for reasoned evidence or propositions of any sort.

Revelation

Revelation is the term used for knowledge that, it is claimed, is given by supernatural agency. In other words, as a result of a religious experience, a person claims that God made something known to him or her.

We have already noted that religious experiences tend to be authoritative for those who have them. The 'revelation' is therefore proclaimed as being in some way superior to the knowledge given by reason; it is direct and immediate, not conditioned by the limitations of normal human awareness.

Note:

There are two ways in which the verb 'to reveal' may be used:

1 I may chip away the plaster from a wall to 'reveal' the brickwork underneath.

2 I may choose to 'reveal' something personal about myself to a stranger.

Religious experiences may claim to include revelations of both sorts.

- Where a person claims that (through meditation, for example) he or she has become more sensitive to spiritual things, it would be possible to say that religion had 'revealed' truths about life not previously known. This is the equivalent of chipping away conventional plaster in order to reveal a brickwork of deeper reality. The person practising the religion is the active agent in bringing this about.
- A person may believe that he or she has had a direct and personal encounter with God (or an angel, or some other spiritual being) in the course of which God has taken the initiative to 'reveal' something of himself. Examples of this are found in the scriptures of many religions.

Notice also that:

- The first of these does not require belief in any supernatural agent. It is just a way of showing that a person has been in a position to allow life to 'reveal' something that was not seen before.
- The second implies the existence of one or more independent, active, personal and supernatural beings.

In terms of the philosophy of religion, revelation raises several issues:

- Whatever the source of knowledge, something can only be articulated using words that have a commonly understood meaning. Once described or written down, a revelation therefore takes the form of descriptions and propositions that can be assessed rationally. On the other hand, that assessment is likely to reveal more about the limitations of concepts and logic than about the original 'knowledge' that they seek to articulate.
- Whatever rational assessments are made, the power of the revelatory experience is such that the person is unlikely to be convinced by criticism. Indeed, the 'revelation' becomes normative for critically evaluating the scope of human reason, not vice versa!
- The fact that something is known through revelation does not logically preclude it from being known by reason alone, unless what is 'revealed' goes directly against reason.

A distinction is made between *natural theology* and *revealed theology*. The former is based on human reason, the latter on the self-disclosure of God. The former can be assessed by looking at evidence and the logic of the arguments used. The latter provides its own authority for the person who has had the revelation. For others, it may be assessed by:

- seeing if what is 'revealed' is consistent with other religious beliefs
- seeing what the affect of the 'revelation' has been upon the person who has had it, and upon others
- seeing if there are any special circumstances which might lead a person to claim as a revelation something from within his or her unconscious mind.

Example:

A person arrested for a string of murders claims in his defence that he was commanded by God to carry them out. You may wish to ask:

- Is the command to murder consistent with other beliefs about God?
- What has been the effect of the murders? How does this relate to one's overall view of life?
- Does this person have a history of mental illness involving hearing voices (e.g. schizophrenia)?

But this last point raises another problem:

In schizophrenia, voices that originate in a person's own mind become disowned, split off, and therefore appear to come from some external speaker. Why not therefore consider all 'revealed' religion, involving belief in supernatural beings, to be a form of group schizophrenia – projecting outwards onto 'God' elements of the self or of society?

Mystics have sometimes claimed supernatural knowledge through visions and voices. St John of the Cross, a 16th century Spanish mystic warns (in *The Ascent of Mount Carmel*) against attachment to visions and voices, pointing out that they could come from the Devil as well as from God, and that there was a danger that they could give rise to pride. He also pointed out that one could not have a direct experience of God in this life, since God was not like other things, having no genus or species – and thus could not be encountered in the ordinary way. His own mysticism led him through the 'dark night of the soul', believing that God plunges human beings in darkness as a means of working towards 'illumination'. This view guards against claims to 'know' God in any literal sense.

Progressive revelation

Whatever the source of 'revelation', once a person describes what is revealed, he or she must do so in the language and thought forms of the day. Even if the revelation itself were valid for all time, the words used would soon become dated.

In other words:

- In considering a revelation one might ask: what must they have experienced to have expressed it like that?
- To identify a revelation with a particular set of words or concepts, rather than with the insight itself, is to kill it. To be devoted to the words and concepts used to describe a revelation in the past is a form of spiritual necrophilia!

But if words and concepts change, what happens to revelation? One answer to this is termed 'progressive revelation'. This is the idea that something is revealed for a particular age and may be superseded by subsequent revelations, which do not negate the earlier one, but bring it up to date.

For example:

- Christianity regards the Old Testament as a revelation which is made complete by the teachings of Jesus.
- Islam sees both Judaism and Christianity, in the form of a succession of prophets, as leading up to the final revelation given to Muhammad.
- Mahayana Buddhism regards the earlier 'Hinayana' tradition as an incomplete first stage, because people were not yet ready for the final form. This is made explicit in the Lotus Sutra.

The claim that the former revelation was partial and has been superseded is a good defence against changes in culture and language which render earlier beliefs untenable. We will need to think about such changes in terms of religion and science, since modern science reveals a world that is very different from that known at the time when the major world religions were 'revealed'.

In general, if earlier revelations are to be regarded as valid, there needs to be a recognition that all such descriptions will be partial and transient.

Some features of religious experience

In this section we shall look briefly at some features of religious experience through the work of thinkers who have been concerned to interpret them.

Schleiermacher

Friedrich Schleiermacher, writing at the end of the 18th century, was concerned to counter the view, prevalent at the time, that reason, aesthetic sensibility and morality between them were a sufficient basis for life, and that religion was entirely superfluous. He wanted to show that religious awareness was a profound and essential element in human life and culture. In his work *On Religion: Speeches to its Cultured Despisers*, he describes religious experience in this way:

> ‘The contemplation of the pious is the immediate consciousness of universal existence of all finite things, in and through the Infinite, and of all temporal things in and through the Eternal.’
>
> (p.36)

In other words, he sees the essence of religion as something that comes through immediate experience, not as the result of argument. It is an awareness, not just of the Eternal and the Infinite, but of every individual thing in the light of the Eternal and the Infinite, of every particular thing in the light of the whole.

He goes on, in an important passage, to show that the ‘sense and taste for the infinite’ underlies both science and art:

> ‘True science is complete vision; true practice is culture and art self-produced; true religion is sense and taste for the Infinite. To wish to have true science or true practice without religion, or to imagine it is possessed, is obstinate, arrogant delusion, and culpable error. It issues from the unholy sense that would rather have a show of possession by cowardly purloining than have secure possession by demanding and waiting. What can man accomplish that is worth speaking of, either in life or in art, that does not arise in his own self from the influence of the sense for the Infinite? Without it, how can anyone wish to comprehend the world scientifically, or if, in some distinct talent, the knowledge

> is thrust upon him, how should he wish to exercise it? What is all science, if not the existence of things in you, in your reason? What is all art and culture if not your existence in the things to which you give measure, form and order? And how can both come to life in you except in so far as there lives immediately in you the eternal unity of Reason and Nature, the universal existence of all finite things in the Infinite? ❞ (op. cit. p.39)

The key feature of his approach to religious experience is a feeling of unity:

> ❝ Such a feeling of being one with nature, of being quite rooted in it, so that in all the changing phenomena of life, even in the change between life and death itself, we might await all that should befall us with approbation and peace, as merely the working out of those eternal laws, would indeed be the germ of all the religious feelings furnished by this side of existence. ❞ (p.71)

Comment:

It seems to me that what Schleiermacher was saying, in the context of the 18th century, was that the essence of life is destroyed by being analyzed and compartmentalised into rational, scientific knowledge on the one hand, morality and artistic expression on the other; that religion embodies both and draws them together; and above all, in modern terms, that **religion is about taking a holistic view**.

William James

A classic study of religious experience is given in William James' *The Varieties of Religious Experience* (1902). James subtitled his work 'a study of human nature', and he took a psychological approach to his subject. He made no attempt to argue from his accounts of religious experiences to any supernatural conclusions but was simply concerned to examine the effect of religion on people's lives.

He looks at the 'healthy minded soul' (the person who is naturally happy and positive) and the 'sick soul' (the person who is depressed and negative). To the 'sick' person, the 'healthy' soul is blind and shallow, not facing the realities of life; to the 'healthy' person, the 'sick' person is diseased and unable to enjoy normal life. James comments, however, that the morbid and depressed attitudes range over a wider range of life than the 'healthy', and that a religion is more complete if it can take these things into account. He cites Buddhism and Christianity as religions which have a great deal to say about suffering.

In looking at responses to religious experience, he points to the unification of the self, the sense of there being a higher controlling power, and the loss of cares as a result of it. There is also the sense that the world has objectively changed, and that truths are known as a result of the religious experience that were not known before.

He describes the positive side of religious experience as a process of moving from 'tenseness, self-responsibility and worry' towards 'equanimity, receptivity and peace'.

For reflection:

There is a considerable body of research into the experience of those who have been very near death but have subsequently been revived. A common feature of these so-called 'near death' experiences is a sense of moving away from the trauma surrounding the life threatening crisis (e.g. the medical technology in a hospital intensive care unit) into a state of calmness; of moving towards light and of being welcomed.

As a result of their near death experiences, those concerned tend to speak of a new sense of values, of not being worried about trivia, of a loss of fear of death.

Such situations – whether or not they are interpreted religiously by the people concerned – illustrate the sort of psychological impact of religious experiences outlined by William James and others.

Otto

In his book *The Idea of the Holy* (1917), Rudolph Otto introduced the idea that religious experience is about the encounter with something totally other, unknowable; something awesome in its dimensions and power, but also attractive and fascinating. He outlined a whole range of feelings (creeping flesh; the fear of ghosts; the sense of something that is uncanny, weird or eerie) to illustrate this encounter.

Otto described the object of religious experience as *mysterium tremendum et fascinans*, to include the elements of awesomeness and fascination that it aroused. He spoke of this as an encounter with 'the numinous', based on the word 'numen', which he used to indicate that particular quality of awe-inspiring holiness.

Examples:

1 You watch a thriller or a horror film at the cinema. You know that you are safe in your comfortable seat, that all round you there are people dipping their hands into buckets of popcorn – and yet you are drawn into the film. You feel your heart beat faster, you gasp, you shudder. You want to look away from the screen, but you are drawn back to it. Your rational mind tells you all this is nothing but projected images. The parts are played by actors; nothing is real. But still it stirs up in you some very basic emotions.

2 You climb upwards through woods, and then suddenly emerge into the sunlight at the top of a hill. There is a sense of wonder, of space, of light. You look out over the expanse of countryside and back down to the point from which you began your ascent. It gives you a 'tingle' – not fearful, this time, nor irrational, but something which cannot fully be put into words. There is a sense of your own smallness in a large world, but even that fails to catch the exact feeling.

- An encounter with 'the holy', according to Otto, is something like those experiences. Like them, it cannot be fully explained, only experienced.

How can you describe the 'holy', the 'numinous'? The problem is that it can only be described in words that have an ordinary, everyday meaning. But such ordinary language, taken literally, cannot do justice to the special quality of that experience. Many words seem to describe the feelings and express ideas that were close to this experience of the 'holy' (goodness, wonder, purity, etc.) but none of them actually describe what is special about the 'holy' itself. A set of words that attempts to describe the 'holy' are (to use Otto's term) its 'schema', and the process of finding words by means of which to convey the implications of the holy is 'schematisation'. Religious language is just such a schema, whereas the 'holy' itself is an *a priori* category, and cannot be completely described by using other terms.

Otto's idea of schematisation (finding a cluster of words which angle in on the experience) is important for understanding the limitations of what can be done by the philosophy of religion. Philosophy examines the concepts by means of which the religious experience is schematised, but it cannot get back 'behind' them to examine the original experience itself.

In other words:

- The numinous, described by Otto, is the sense of awe and fear that arises as a result of an encounter with the 'holy'. Otto emphasised the **otherness** of religious experience, something that had not been attempted before.
- He also saw that religious experience gets 'schematised'.
- The philosophy of religion, because it deals in words, can only function within this schema.

Kierkegaard

Kierkegaard, precursor of the modern existentialist thinkers, emphasised that religious experience was a matter of personal commitment and value – a matter of making a choice, of taking a risk. He argued (see his *Concluding Unscientific Postscript* Book 1, Part II, Chapter 2) that a person could be in one of two situations:

- convinced in faith of the truth of Christianity
- not a believer as such, but interested in Christianity.

The difference here is not in **what is believed**, but in the **way it is believed**. Kierkegaard argued that what mattered was one's relationship to a religious truth. He went so far as to welcome the paradoxical nature of some religious claims, stressing that one can only have the absurd as an object of faith.

For reflection:

- If something is absurd, one cannot accept it rationally. To believe it takes an act of commitment.
- If something makes sense rationally, does that mean that one cannot also be committed to it in a personal way?
- Commitment to what is beyond rational proof is a common phenomenon: totally rational people would never fall in love or make war; shopping for the latest in fashion would be suspect; rock climbing, bungee jumping and stamp collecting would cease!

Kierkegaard's approach emphasises another key feature of religious experience: that **it involves a relationship between the thing experienced and the experiencing subject**. Once that relationship is taken away and the object is analyzed, it ceases to be 'religious'.

For reflection:

- Many religious experiences are actually of quite mundane things – what makes them religious is the way in which they are interpreted, the impact they have on the people experiencing them, and the depth or quality of the experience. **A superficial religious experience is almost a contradiction in terms.**

Kierkegaard's work is a reminder to us that intuition and risk play an important part in religion. They often provide a starting point for what develops into a serious commitment and new understanding of life. On the other hand, that should not imply that the rational is totally set aside for faith (as Kierkegaard sometimes suggests) since the rational mind continues to work within the new framework provided by the intuition and one's subsequent commitment to it.

Examples:

- You fall in love (intuition and risk), settle into a serious relationship (commitment) and subsequently reflect on why this particular relationship has become important for you (rational thought).
- You experience a particular religious event or encounter a religious group and suddenly feel that this makes sense of life and is right for you (intuition and risk). You become a member of the religion (commitment). You then take your religion deeper by examining it and testing it out against your general understanding of life (rational thought).

Buber

In *I and Thou* (1937) Martin Buber argued that we have two different kinds of relationships: I–It and I–Thou. I–It relationships are impersonal, what is encountered is seen in a detached, objective, functional or scientific way. By contrast, I–Thou relationships are personal. Imagine meeting a good friend – that encounter involves emotions and a personal sharing. Now imagine that the friend was a stranger for whom one felt nothing, and with whom one had had only the most superficial of contact; something has gone from that relationship. I–Thou has become I–It.

For Buber the relationship with God was an I–Thou relationship, he described God as 'the Eternal Thou'. What is more, he saw this Eternal Thou as present in every other 'Thou' that we encounter.

Tillich's criteria

Paul Tillich (see, for example, his *Systematic Theology*), writing in the 1950s, described two essential components of a religious experience: 'being itself' and 'ultimate concern'.

Being itself

When you encounter something, your senses distinguish it as having a particular size and shape, colour, sound, smell or texture. These things enable you to distinguish and describe what you see. They enable you to think and speak of it as one thing, or being, over against others.

In a religious experience, this is generally not the case. It is not just an experience of a particular being, but of 'being itself', or reality itself, encapsulated in this particular moment.

Suppose, for example, a person is religiously moved by a particular scene, perhaps a sunset. He or she feels momentarily that a real thing of value and meaning has been glimpsed, life will never be the same again, this single thing of beauty puts everything else into perspective. It could be described as an experience of God, but it is certainly **more than** the information about that sunset that a photograph could capture. Someone might argue that there was nothing religious about that experience – it was just a pleasant mixture of colours produced by the light of the sun on the clouds and upper atmosphere. The essential point is that – for it to be religious – it is not just an experience of that particular sunset; it must say something about the whole of life.

> *In other words:*
>
> For something to be a religious experience, it needs to be about 'being itself' (life itself; reality itself) rather than a particular being.

Ultimate concern

Everything we encounter has some place within our overall scheme of things. A stranger glimpsed for just a fleeting moment makes little impact on us; he or she does not dominate our lives. On the other hand, a good friend may have a lasting and profound impression on us.

A parent or child may shape our lives quite fundamentally. In a sense, each of these things has a place on a scale of 'concerns': superficial, important, essential.

Tillich argued that, for something to be genuinely religious, the concern must be ultimate. If a person attends religious worship because of lack of other entertainment, or because he or she is lonely and hopes to make new friends, or because of a love of ritual or music, it might be enjoyable and valuable, but it is **not** religious. It lacks that quality of ultimate concern. (In many ways, this follows the point made above in connection with the work of Kierkegaard.)

In other words:

Something is religious only if it encounters us in an ultimate way, challenging the very basis of our lives.

To sum up:

- for Schleiermacher, the Infinite is seen in and through the finite
- for Otto, an experience suddenly reveals its numinous quality
- for Kierkegaard, the experience is personally challenging and involves commitment
- for Buber, the Eternal Thou is encountered within every other Thou we meet; it is there whenever we relate in a personal way
- for Tillich, religion is a matter of our 'ultimate concern' and the only suitable object of that concern is 'being itself', not particular beings.

Of course, all of these thinkers have a great deal to say, and this section has merely touched on some key features of their work. But cumulatively, they build up a sense of what is involved in religious experience.

What can we know?

Non-religious interpretations

Any religious experience may be analyzed and 'explained' in terms that are not themselves religious. For example:

- Freud noted parallels between religious behaviour and those of his patients who had obsessional neuroses – e.g. those who were continually washing themselves, yet never felt clean. He called religion a 'universal obsessional neurosis'. Such a psychological interpretation may see religious rituals as repeated attempts to cleanse sexual guilt.

- Sociologists may point out the social function of religion. It may mark particular stages in life and acceptance of an individual into society. It may be a way of holding a society together and giving it an identity and sense of purpose.

But what do such interpretations achieve? There is an old quip: 'Just because you're paranoid, doesn't mean they're not out to get you!' This applies to all such non-religious interpretations. A religious ritual may be used by a society to affirm its identity or by an individual to overcome sexual neuroses, but that does not in itself provide an exhaustive explanation of the experience.

If, as was said earlier, the result of a religious experience may be a new way of looking at life, then we might well expect social cohesion and sexual health to follow. Having found such benefits, an individual or a society might want to induce those religious experiences again, through performing religious rituals. At that point, the reason for doing it may indeed be to get the desired benefit; but that does not imply that the whole meaning of the original experience is explained in terms of that benefit, any more than travel from one place to another is a sufficient explanation of a motor car.

Objective and subjective

The philosopher Descartes, in attempting to establish what he could know for certain, doubted the validity of all sense experience, but came to the famous conclusion that he could not doubt his own existence as a thinking being – *cogito ergo sum* (I think, therefore I am).

Since Descartes there has been a tendency in Western thought to make a fundamental distinction between mind and matter, subject and object, the world of thought and the world of experience.

When someone asks if your experience is subjective or objective, they imply that it is either:

- a record of external facts, gathered through your senses; facts that may be verified independently and which are not dependent upon your own feelings and attitudes (objective), or
- the product of your own mind or imagination (subjective).

But religious experience cannot be either exclusively objective or subjective. Something is experienced (objective), but what is experienced is a matter of interpretation (subjective). Two people could experience the same thing; for one it would be profound, moving and 'religious', for the other it could be a matter of little interest. **The subjective aspect of experience is just as 'real' as the objective.**

For example:

I listen to a boring talk. I may vaguely be aware of what the speaker is saying, but I am far more aware of my own boredom. Boredom is a major part of that experience for me, and it cannot be denied just because the person next to me is sitting forward in his seat hanging on every word.

Boredom, irritation and happiness are things of which we are certain. They are as real as any other part of our experience of life, although there is no external sense experience that corresponds to them.

Authority and response

Religious experiences are authoritative for those who have them. Their response to them may involve:

- worship and devotion (it is seen as 'holy')
- a change of lifestyle or values (it gives a new sense of priorities)
- a new understanding of life (although it may not be articulated, most religious experiences have this cognitive element).

The responses are justified with reference to the religious experience which produced them. There is a problem with this, however, because there is no 'objective' way of establishing the truth or importance of a religious experience. Thus it is difficult to prove that a response is reasonable and appropriate. How then can we establish the authority of a religious experience?

An example:

We return to the mass murderer who claims that he was told by God to kill his victims.

- Clearly, the experience of 'hearing the voice of God' is authoritative for him and he responds accordingly.
- How can you tell if that was a genuinely religious experience, or whether the voice he heard was the result of schizophrenia?

- If a schizophrenic claimed to have been told by God to love his neighbours and went about doing so, would that be accepted as genuinely religious?

From the above example, it would seem that there are two very different ways of validating a religious experience and therefore ascribing authority to it. From the point of view of a person having the experience, it is self-validating, and needs no external support or authority. From the point of view of other people, however, the validity or otherwise of a religious experience tends to be assessed in terms of its compatibility with non-religious, rationally established views of life.

Conclusion

- Religious experience can give a **new perspective** on life. Contemplating the impermanent nature of things, the Buddha said of the body that it was like the froth of a wave. Lady Julian of Norwich sees the world as a small round object in the hand of God.
- Then there is a **response**, a new sense of oneself and an experience of being changed, converted or enlightened.

In terms of the relationship between the experiencing person and that which he or she experiences, we may say that there are three distinct but essential qualities:

1 There is a sense of the 'otherness' of what is experienced. It is something 'holy'. It gives a tingle, a sense of wonder, a feeling that the ordinary mundane world is small, limited in its scope and values, cut off from something far richer. Isaiah in the temple sees himself as a man of unclean lips. Those who have near-death experiences may say that the ordinary things of the world will never worry them again.
2 At the same time, there is a feeling of dependence – that the ordinary world is in some way resting on or rooted in something deeper. The religious experience is not of something 'out there', but of something 'within' and 'deeper'.
3 The movement from the first to the second of these features continues into the third – a sense of being at one with the holy and the divine. Particularly with mysticism, as we saw above, but in all religions, there is the sense of God being within the self, or of the self being within God. There is, I believe, a Muslim saying:

‘Allah is nearer to a man than his own breath.’

One way of expressing all this is to say that life is *self-transcending*. A particular thing, person or situation, may take on meaning beyond itself, may reveal something of Life itself (Truth itself, Being itself).

We saw earlier how people could sometimes have ‘religious’ experiences which were actually experiences of something quite normal (like a beautiful scene) which a non-religious person would see quite differently.

One might argue that the more deeply religious a person becomes, the more he or she is likely to see many aspects of life taking on that self-transcending quality.

Let the last word on religious experience be with a poet rather than a philosopher. In Wordsworth's lines composed a few miles above Tintern Abbey he describes the energy of his earlier enthusiasm for nature and the way in which this has given way to something deeper:

‘For I have learned
To look on nature, not as in the hour
Of thoughtless youth; but hearing often-times
The still, sad music of humanity,
Nor harsh nor grating, though of ample power
To chasten and subdue. And I have felt
A presence that disturbs me with the joy
Of elevated thoughts; a sense sublime
Of something far more deeply interfused,
Whose dwelling is the light of setting suns,
And the round ocean and the living air,
And the blue sky, and in the mind of man;
A motion and a spirit, that impels
All thinking things, all objects of all thought,
And rolls through all things. Therefore am I still
A lover of the meadows and the woods,
And mountains; and of all that we behold
From this green earth; of all the mighty world
Of eye, and ear – both what they half create,
And what perceive; well pleased to recognise
In nature and the language of the sense,
The anchor of my purest thoughts, the nurse,
The guide, the guardian of my heart, and soul
Of all my moral being.’

Here, nature is experienced as self-transcending – leading the mind to that which is 'far more deeply interfused', and he can describe that experience as the 'anchor' of his purest thoughts. Here is the raw material of religious experience.

Where does all this lead?

In his book *An Introduction to the Philosophy of Religion*, Brian Davies introduces religious experience after a consideration of the traditional arguments for the existence of God. His purpose in introducing it is given thus:

> ❛ The question currently at issue is therefore this: does experience tell a reasonable man that God exists? ❜ (op. cit. p.64)

In other words, having established what God is, he asks if religious experience can be used as evidence of his existence.

This is definitely **not** the approach taken in this present book. The questions we have been considering are:

- What is it in experience to which people ascribe the term 'God'?
- What has given rise to such a concept?
- What sustains people's interest in it?

Whereas Davies therefore considers objections to admitting experience as a valid argument for the existence of God, we need not concern ourselves about this. Even though experience is always ambiguous (and thus two people may experience the same thing in different ways or a person may misinterpret what he or she has experienced) **it is nevertheless upon this fallible and ambiguous experience that all religion is based**.

It is also the case that beliefs and religions continue, not because some intellectual conclusion has been reached about their validity, but because people benefit from them. One could say (following a line of argument taken by William James) that beliefs do not work because they are true, but that they are true because they work.

Of course, religious experience remains a private affair until someone attempts to describe it. This leads into the subject of the next chapter – the nature of religious language. But, as we examine it, we should be looking for those theories of religious language which allow this self-transcending quality of the religious experience to emerge. In other words, we should be looking for self-transcending language.

2
RELIGIOUS LANGUAGE

In this chapter we shall be asking:

- How does a person's faith relate to the things he or she claims to believe?
- What is the nature and status of religious language?
- Can a claim to religious knowledge be shown to be true or false?
- What function does religious language perform, and what are its limitations?

The first chapter examined religious experience and responses to it. Clearly, once there has been some kind of religious experience, a person starts to explain or think about it, and does so using such languages and concepts as are available. This means that the experience, once described, starts to be filtered through language and coloured by it. We need to take this into account. People from different cultures are likely to experience things in a way that reflects their culture – for every act of awareness takes with it a set of presuppositions and ways of looking.

So it is vital, in looking at religious beliefs, to appreciate the role that language plays in formulating those beliefs.

Comment:

You could argue that there is no such thing as religious language. There is simply language that is used for particular purposes – in this case, to express or describe religious experiences, practices or beliefs. If the words used within or about religion did not have an ordinary, non-religious meaning, how could they communicate anything?

For example: revelation, transubstantiation, incarnation, the numinous: these words are part of religious language, and have specific religious meanings, but each needs be defined in terms of other words. To be effective, any such definition has to give the meaning of a word using words that are understood outside the religious context.

A private language?

Can there be such a thing as private language? You could mutter to yourself words that mean absolutely nothing to anyone else, and claim to know what they mean. But would that be a language? Language is about communication, and communication only takes place when two or more people use words and ideas that they have in common. If you devise your own language, you will not be able to communicate. Translating your private language will require you to use terms that others understand in order to give a shared equivalent of your private concepts.

There is a lot more that philosophers have to say on this matter, but for the purposes of the philosophy of religion, it is enough to notice that **religious language is used to express and communicate religion, and it cannot do this if it is private**.

Although this may seem obvious, it raises a whole range of questions. How does the 'religious' meaning of a word relate to its wider (non-religious) meaning? Do all words have a wider meaning?

For example, 'forgiveness' is a term used in religion, and it is understood because people know what it is to forgive and be forgiven in a normal human context. Thus the idea of a God who 'forgives' makes sense. But what of a word like 'God'? Does that have to be explicable in non-religious terms? If it can't be, does it have any meaning that can be communicated to a non-religious person? If not, does anyone actually know what anyone else means when they use that word?

Knowledge and description

Some forms of language used in religion cause no problem whatever. For example, take the statement: 'Catholic priests usually wear vestments when conducting Mass.'

The word 'usually' covers any special occasions where Mass will be celebrated informally without vestments, or where Communion is given in extreme circumstances and it would not be expected that a priest could put his vestments on. Other than that the statement is purely factual. As long as you know what the terms mean, you could easily get evidence to prove that it is either true or false.

The reason there is no problem here is that the statement is **descriptive**. The test of its truth is empirical – just check the facts.

But what if a person says: 'I have just witnessed a miracle'? The truth of this may depend on what that person means by miracle, on the reliability of their senses (since they could have been mistaken), and on the way they have interpreted what happened. Someone might hear all the details and reply 'I appreciate what you saw and how you understood it, but I would not have called that a miracle.'

The issue here is that the statement claims to give knowledge which depends on a person's interpretation of facts.

In other words:

A miracle is not just a miracle, it is always something else as well! Therefore a person who does not believe in miracles will seek an interpretation of that 'something else', be it an unexpected cure of a disease or avoiding an accident, in non-miraculous terms.

Let us examine two other statements 'I believe in God' and 'God exists'. These are by no means the same. The first can be right and the second wrong, or vice versa. Just because someone believes something, it does not mean that it is the case. The first is a description of what someone believes, the second is a claim to knowledge.

If religious people did no more than describe the observable features of their religion, and comment in a detached way on their own beliefs, there would be no problem. But they actually use language in a whole variety of ways: they pray, give thanks, hold moral discussions and make statements about the content of their faith. We will need to look carefully at the way in which language is being used in each of these situations, and ask if what is said simply amounts to a description of something religious, or a claim to factual knowledge.

Note:

Much of philosophy in the twentieth century has been concerned with language. Indeed, many philosophers have seen the whole task of philosophy as one of examining language – so that political philosophy, for example, is not about politics (it doesn't tell you which way to vote) but about the meaning of political language, for example, the question 'What is democracy?'

Faith, reason and beliefs

Once you reflect upon religion, you are involved with concepts, and use your reason to sort them out and relate them to one another.

- You can remember something without concepts, but you cannot think about it without concepts.
- You can paint a picture of something without concepts, but you cannot describe it without concepts.

As soon as religion gets beyond the area of personal religious experience, it encounters human reason. Once it does so, the result is language. The religious experience starts to be 'schematised' (to use Otto's term) in terms of concepts, ideas and beliefs.

Reason may contribute two things here:

- It may examine the logic of a statement. Does it make sense? If it does, fine. If not, are the words being used in an unusual way? Is there any other way in which the statement can be interpreted?
- It can look to see if this particular thing is compatible with the rest of a person's experience of life, and therefore come to a view about the likelihood of a statement being true or false. Which is more likely, that this is true or that I have been mistaken?

Experience, expressed through language, leads to propositions – statements about what is the case. The propositions that a person accepts as being true are his or her 'beliefs'. If you say 'I believe in God' it means that you accept the proposition 'There is a God' as being true.

In other words:

The philosophy of religion examines the logic and general coherence of religious statements and, by comparing such statements with other widely-held beliefs about life, assesses the appropriateness of accepting them as true.

'Believing in' and 'believing that'

Faith is a matter of personal commitment and trust. A person's faith is not to be equated with a list of the things that he or she claims to believe. It includes them, or course, but it is more than that, for it describes the way in which he or she relates to them.

Examples

- You can have faith in your doctor, but need understand nothing of medicine.
- You may study psychology, but that doesn't (necessarily!) make you schizophrenic or depressed.

This can be expressed in terms of the difference between **believing that** something is true and **believing in** something. If you **believe in** something, it implies commitment and trust. Believing **that** something is true simply means that you think the statement is correct, whether or not it is of any personal interest to you.

Example

Compare 'I believe that God exists' with 'I believe in God'. The former may be the logical conclusion of an argument, but does not imply that a person is in any way influenced by that belief. The latter implies that a person has a personal relationship with God, or at least believes that God in some way matters.

Experience 'as'

Whatever we experience, we interpret. Things are not just experienced, but experienced '*as*' something. This aspect of religious language has been clearly set out by John Hick (for example, in 'Religious Faith as Experiencing-As' in *Talk of God*, Royal Institute of Philosophy Lectures, 1969), and it follows the work of Wittgenstein in his *Philosophical Investigations* (see also below p.59).

It is best illustrated by the well known visual puzzles in which the same image can be interpreted in two different ways. These include a duck that appears as a rabbit, a young woman that is also an old crone and an ornate chalice that become the silhouette of two people facing one another. There is no evidence to decide between the interpretations, it is simply a matter of choice, but considerable mental effort is required to shift one's view from one to the other.

The implication of this is that the religious way of interpreting the world is one valid 'blik' (view), alongside others. A person who has such a religious blik will interpret what is actually experienced in the light of it.

A key question, however, is why do we experience things as we do? What makes one person see the duck and the other the rabbit? What makes one person a theist and another an atheist? Their experience of the world (the sense impressions they receive) may be the same, but they experience it differently.

To sum up:

Believing in something is not simply believing that it is true. Believing in something implies value and commitment, but also a particular interpretation, a way of seeing life (a blik). Unlike straightforward descriptions, statements setting out what religious people believe are therefore seldom simple matters of fact that can be checked against the evidence of the senses, and should not be treated as such.

— The rational and the non-rational —

There have been times when a rational approach to religion has been much in favour. So, for example, from the second to the fourth centuries of the Christian era, there were heated debates about Christian doctrine. It was the period during which the Creeds were formulated, and differences in wording (with the implied differences in meaning) were the cause of serious strife between members of different groups. Those who disagreed with the majority (or those with official backing) tended to be branded as heretics.

Similarly in the 13th century there was a flowering of interest in Greek thought, and Aquinas set Christian doctrine within a scheme of thought derived largely from Aristotle. In the 18th century, following the rise of modern science, there was once again a quest to present Christianity in a way that was acceptable to those for whom rational coherence was almost the sole criterion of truth.

The twentieth century also saw a quest for unambiguous rational truth. This time, following the effectiveness of the scientific model, there was an attempt to dismiss every statement whose truth or falsity could not be established either by logic or by reference to empirical facts. Language was there solely to picture the external world. All these, in their different ways, were attempts to emphasise the importance of being 'rational'.

Now, what does it mean to say that something is rational? Basically, the rational process is one in which conclusions are drawn from premises by a sequence of mental steps which can be followed, verified, and which others (provided they understood the meaning of the words used) would accept as being true – and true for everyone, not just for that particular individual.

Where then does this leave the complex web of elements that make up a religious experience? Can a religious experience be described in a rational way? Clearly, for there to be an experience at all there must be some empirical basis; for something to be experienced, the senses must be stimulated in some way. **A religious experience may transcend this empirical basis, but it nevertheless includes it.**

But, for an experience to be religious, it cannot be confined to that empirical basis, for otherwise it would just be a scientific description of what is seen or heard, with nothing to make it 'religious' or to convey anything of its importance and power. It is therefore crucial to recognise that religion can never be fully explained in terms of what is rational. There is generally a 'something more' that eludes description. This does not go against reason (which would make it 'irrational') so much as beyond reason – taking a step which cannot be proved by logic or evidence, but which a person feels compelled to make.

Comment:

Trying to understand a religion by rational means alone is rather like attempting to find a mate by means of a dating agency. It can sort out some of the basic groundwork for you, but unless you find with your selected partner some spark of emotion, some willingness to take a risk, a leap beyond what is reasonable, you are hardly likely to embark on the most passionate relationship of your life!

Religions vary in the importance they place on a rational approach to belief:

- Of all the religions, **Christianity** is the most credal. It attempts to define and explain what is to be believed. Although it accepts the non-rational (e.g. in mystical experience), it keeps it in careful check.

- **Islam** too is concerned that its key doctrines are accepted universally. To do this it has to present its views in a rationally coherent form: all Muslims are expected to believe the same things and to have the same confession of faith.
- When it comes to **Judaism**, there is more flexibility – with some basic tenets of belief, but also a wealth of rules for spiritual life, gradually being interpreted in terms of ever more general principles. Judaism is a rich tradition, sometimes rational, sometimes poetic, rooting the spiritual in the physical stuff of life and emphasising that spirituality is not simply a matter of the rational acceptance of beliefs, but a total way of life.
- **Hindu** religious traditions have a wealth of material that goes beyond the rational. This is seen in the great variety of its worship and in the colourful stories of its scriptures. On the other hand, Hinduism has not been without its rational, philosophical systems, for example, in the Upanishads.
- **Buddhism** too welcomes a balance between the rational and the non-rational. In this case, the rational approach is encouraged, and every follower is to test out teachings to see if they are able to be confirmed in his or her own experience. On the other hand, meditation and devotion, the chanting of mantras and ritual performances (especially within the Mahayana / Tibetan traditions) go beyond the rational.

For the purpose of our understanding of religious language, all we need to appreciate here is that religions present a balance between the rational and the non-rational. Without the former, nothing of the beliefs could be communicated. Without the latter, nothing of the power of the religion would be effectively conveyed.

Interpreting language

We now turn to various ways in which language is used and the criteria by which its 'truth' may be assessed.

A literal picture?

The most straightforward use of language is as a means of literally picturing the world and giving information about it. Each word I use stands for something in my experience. A statement like 'There is a tree in my garden' is true or false to the extent that a person who understands the meaning of the words 'tree' and 'garden' can go and check if it is so.

David Hume (1711–1776) in *An Enquiry Concerning Human Understanding* allows only two kinds of meaningful statement: abstract reasoning concerning quantity or number; experimental reasoning concerning matters of fact. In other words, all knowledge of the external world is based on sense experience – the 'matters of fact'.

Analytic and synthetic statements

It is possible to divide statements into two kinds – analytic and synthetic. An analytic statement simply explains the meaning of its own terms. The statement 'two plus two equals four' is analytic. You don't have to go checking examples in order to prove it correct! A synthetic statement refers to external evidence. 'The cat is outside the door' is synthetic. No detailed explanation of the meaning of 'cat' or 'door' can ever prove the matter one way or the other – you have to go and look.

When it comes to a theory of knowledge, you can divide philosophers into two groups, those (like Hume) who base all knowledge on sense experience, and those (like Kant) who base it on the structures of thought by which we are able to experience and understand things. These two groups are generally referred to as 'empiricists' and 'idealists' respectively. It is the empirical tradition of philosophy which has emphasised the literal picturing function of language – because empiricist philosophers want to relate everything that is said to the 'facts' as they can be experienced.

The most narrow view of what constituted a meaningful proposition was developed in the 1920s by a group of philosophers meeting in Vienna and known as the Vienna Circle. They produced a theory of meaning known as the Verification Principle. Their ideas were influenced by the earlier work of Ludwig Wittgenstein (1889–1951) who had set out a radical view of the limitations of what we can know in a book called *Tractatus Logico-Philosophicus*, published in 1921.

Wittgenstein argued that the function of language is to picture the world. Something is said to be true if, on observation of the reality to which the statement refers, it is found to be the case. It is false if the evidence is against it.

The principle is therefore that truth is established by empirical verification. Of course, there are statements that are analytic, and these form the basis of logic and mathematics, but they do not tell us about the world. Statements that give us information are synthetic and need verification.

Not everything can be checked. 'I saw your cat last night' is a statement that cannot now be verified. But it still has a basis in observation. What it means, in effect, is that if you had been where I was last night, you would have seen your cat.

This approach to language and its verification became known as Logical Positivism. The logical positivists claimed that the meaning of a statement was its method of verification. When I say something, I am giving information that could in theory be checked by going back and examining what was actually seen or heard.

They therefore went on to argue that those statements for which there was no means of empirical verification were meaningless.

Example:

If I say 'Fred exists', that statement is meaningful, because it would be possible to point out someone who has the name Fred.

If I say 'God exists', there is no evidence which I can offer, no observations which can make it true or false. Therefore, according to Logical Positivism, it is meaningless.

The work of the Vienna Circle was made widely known by A J Ayer with the publication of his book *Language, Truth and Logic* in 1936. The impact on the philosophy of religion was quite traumatic, for what Ayer and the Vienna Circle was saying was not just that God did not exist, but that all talk about God was meaningless:

> ‘No sentence which purports to describe the nature of a transcendent God can possess any literal significance.’
>
> (op. cit. p.115)

For Ayer, the statement 'God exists' cannot be either true or false, because there is no empirical evidence that can be produced to prove the matter one way or the other.

This did not threaten all language about religion. Much is intended to be taken literally and causes no problems. For example:

Some priests wear black robes.
Muslims do not drink alcohol.

The truth of the first of these may be shown by observation. The second can be shown to be true by looking at Muslim writings, or asking practising Muslims. As long the terms are understood, and there is evidence for what is said, there is no problem with this kind of *descriptive language*. The problem occurs once you try to get beyond such literal description.

In other words:

The whole empirical tradition in language was saying in effect that every word must picture something 'out there' which may be experienced. If there is nothing to which I can point (actually or at least theoretically) and say 'that is what it means', it is meaningless.

Of course, not everyone would want to claim that religious language was simply 'picturing' the world in quite this way. Many of the mystics and others mentioned in the last chapter would agree with Ayer – for their language was never intended to be taken literally; that would have been far too crude and limiting for what they meant by 'God'.

Note:

The logical positivists of the Vienna Circle originally proposed what is termed the 'strong form' of the *verification principle*. This claims that a statement is only meaningful if it is verifiable in terms of sense experience. It was soon recognised, however, that this was too limited. There were statements that could not be verified directly, but which nevertheless dealt with things that might be experienced, if circumstances permitted. This led to what is known as the 'weak form' of the verification principle: that, for a statement to be meaningful, it is necessary to know how it might be verified in terms of experience. It was this 'weak' form of the principle that A J Ayer expounded. He also accepted historical statements as meaningful, although it would be impossible to go back in time and verify them. It is enough to be able to say, in effect 'if you had been there, this is what you would have seen.'

A major criticism of the verification principle is that 'the meaning of a statement is its method of verification' cannot itself be verified. It is not analytic, so it cannot be shown to be true on logical grounds. Nor is there any piece of evidence that can count for or against its truth – a statement about what counts as factual or meaningful is not simply a picture of some sense experience. By its own argument it is therefore meaningless! In reply to this, logical positivists point out that the verification principle is not making a factual claim but simply a recommendation for the way in which words should be understood.

In many ways, the arguments of the logical positivists have not so much been refuted as bypassed. Towards the middle of the twentieth century, especially under the influence of later developments of Wittgenstein's work, there was a growing recognition that giving a literal representation of the world was a small part of the task of language, and that its many other functions (giving commands, expressing emotions, creating symbolic images, making jokes or caricatures) required a very different approach.

True or false?

In *New Essays in Philosophical Theology*, published in 1955, Anthony Flew presented a story (originally devised by John Wisdom) to examine the limits to which one could go in qualifying a statement whilst claiming that it was true.

In the story, two explorers come across a clearing in the jungle which has a mixture of flowers and weeds. One claims that there is a gardener who comes to tend it, the other thinks there is not. No gardener appears, so they set various tests to check for the presence of this invisible gardener.

In the end, the one explorer still thinks that there is a gardener – but an invisible, intangible, silent gardener who is insensitive to electric shocks and is in all other ways undetectable. The other, in despair, cannot see what the difference is between such a gardener and no gardener at all!

When all the literal language is stripped away, the gardener dies 'the death of a thousand qualifications'. Clearly, the same thing happens with God; what appears to be a claim that God exists in a very literal sense, is then qualified until nothing significant remains.

Several key themes have come out of this story and the discussions that followed its publication:

- Experience involves interpretation (as we saw in the first chapter). One explorer interprets the clearing as a garden, the other does not. Facts alone do not determine how something is interpreted.
- One's interpretation leads to a commitment. One chooses to see the

world in a particular way, and is committed to that view, and that influences the way subsequent evidence is assessed. The one explorer is reluctant to let go of the claim that there is a gardener because, for him, it has become a matter of faith rather than just a hypothesis.

- The story implies that what is 'real' is what can be described literally – since the 'gardener' dies the death of becoming less and less literally a gardener. But when applied to God, many believers would say that a God who existed in a literal way (along with other things that exist in the world) would not be the sort of God they are talking about. In the last chapter we saw, for example, that God could be described as 'being itself' rather than as 'a being'.

The limits of the literal

There are always problems when religious language is taken as literal. Here is the radical theologian Don Cupitt on literal language:

> ❛ The critics urge that we should always give straight answers and admit what we believe. But I am saying that there is no such thing as literal truth and no such thing as 'the real meaning' of any text. Church authority has in the past sought for power reasons to control religious language, but such control is 'the letter that killeth' and is death to religion. Religious terms do not stand for, label or copy religious objects. Religion consists in a change in the way in which we see everything, a change in our whole life. ❜
>
> (Don Cupitt: *Radicals and the Future of the Church* p.111)

Analogy

When the same word is used to describe different things, its use may be univocal, equivocal or analogical.

Univocal:

I wear white shoes and a white hat. The word 'white' is used univocally – it has exactly the same meaning.

Equivocal:

I may have apple tart for dessert. If it lacks sweetness, I may describe it as a little tart, in quite another sense. Neither relates to my colloquial description of that young lady in a short skirt! The 'tarts' are equivocal, having quite different meanings.

Analogical:

On a black night I may be in a mood that could (analogically) be described as 'black'. Or, to persist with the tart example given above, the one might be tasty and the other might look tasty – which would be an analogical use of 'tasty', unless of course you were intimately or cannibalistically univocal!

There are two ways of approaching the use of analogy in religious language – one based on reason and the other on religious experience.

On reason:

If you believe that God exists and that he is present everywhere, omnipotent etc., then it would not be appropriate to use the word 'good' of him in exactly the same way as you would of a limited human being. On the other hand, if 'good' were used of God equivocally it would convey no meaning. The only answer is to use analogy. The justification for it would be that, if God has created them, then the goodness of human beings is a pale reflection of the goodness of their creator.

On religious experience:

From the outline of religious experience in the last chapter, it is clear that univocal language does not do justice to the 'otherness' and inspirational nature of such experience. But, equally, people want to convey the meaning of what they have experienced. Hence, to use Otto's term, the original experience of the numinous becomes 'schematised'. Just as the original experience is based on, but goes beyond, the physical circumstances in which it arose, so the language by which it is described needs to be based on, but go beyond, any literal meaning. Hence the need for analogy.

Models and qualifiers

The language through which religious experience and insight is expressed will always be the common property of the culture within which it takes place. But words that are common property may have meanings which fail to do justice to the thing being described. 'It is a bit like this, but more so..!'

In *Religious Language* (SCM Press, 1957), I T Ramsey used the terms *models* and *qualifiers* to explain the way in which religious language differs from literal, empirically based language.

A 'model' is a form of analogy – an image that helps a person to express what has been experienced. For example, if God is called a 'designer', it does not imply that the believer has personal knowledge of a process of design carried out by God, simply that the image of a human designer is something like his or her experience of God.

On the other hand, having offered the 'model' it is then important to offer a 'qualifier' – God is an 'infinite' this, or a 'perfect' that. The model is therefore qualified, so that it is not mistakenly taken in a literal way.

In other words:

If 'God' is described as 'Eternal Father', 'father' is the model, with all the overtones that experience of actual fathers brings to the concept; 'eternal' is the qualifier, making sure that the idea of father is transcended.

- Without models, nothing would be communicated.
- Without qualifiers, nothing would get beyond a literal description of what is seen; it would not be religious.

Symbolism

What is a religious symbol, and how does it work?

We need to distinguish between a sign and a symbol. A sign is something that points to something else. It can be quite conventional (like road signs); you can change one sign for another, as long as everyone agrees what it stands for. By contrast, a symbol is something that expresses the power of that which is symbolises; it participates in it and makes it real. Symbols evoke the power of that which they symbolise.

Example:

A person waves the flag of his or her country: it becomes a symbol of patriotic feelings. Burning a flag is a great act of political defiance. It's not just a matter of burning a piece of cloth that happens to have a particular design on it; it's a sign of destroying the country and all that it stands for.

The theologian Paul Tillich held that religious symbols are the only means to pointing beyond individual beings to that which is 'being itself', for you cannot show being itself directly. Equally, he held that a symbol is religious if it shows a person's ultimate concern.

Religion is about particular things, situations or people which reveal 'being itself' and which become a matter of 'ultimate concern' for us. Now these things become symbols; they point beyond themselves. **They also give rise to symbolic language, because the description of them, if it is to reflect the original experience, must also move beyond the literal meaning of the words used.**

At the end of the first chapter, religious experience was described in terms of the 'self-transcending' quality of life. The religious symbol is the linguistic equivalent of this. It transcends its own literal meaning.

> **Note:**
>
> All of this would be quite anathema to those philosophers who follow a Postmodern way of interpreting literature. For them, the actual words and concepts are the reality, there is no other hidden world 'behind' them for the words to reveal. This is an enormous topic, beyond the scope of this present book, but one should be at least aware that the whole idea of language transcending itself to express something 'more' creates problems for some modern philosophers.

Myth

Myths are stories which express aspects of human self-awareness. Thus some of the earliest myths are about creation, or about the expectation of life beyond death or of the end of the world. They are full of symbolism (as defined above) and present a range of symbols in a narrative form. Myth should not be reduced to a literal form of language. In its literal meaning, a myth may or may not be true; that is relatively unimportant. What makes it a myth is the meaning that is conveyed through the narrative and the symbols it introduces. Myths, like individual symbols, or like poetry or fiction, can present many layers of meaning and have a power that is destroyed once they are taken apart and examined literally.

> **Note:**
>
> If you want to describe a moment of insight, you need to use words and concepts with which your hearers are familiar. You are starting

to 'schematise' the experience (to use Otto's term). You are also starting to place it within a particular language, philosophy and social setting.

Later, other people will be able to look at your description and, on the basis of the words you have used, compare it with the thoughts and insights of others. What they cannot do is to get back behind the schema and reconstruct the actual moment of insight itself.

Except, perhaps, when reading a description, someone suddenly gets a tingle of excitement. Something in them says 'Yes, that's exactly how it is' – not because the words are logically compelling or soundly based, but because of an intuition that this description is of an experience parallel to their own.

To sum up:

- We have moved from literal to analogical language, and noted the way in which models and qualifiers influence religious description, and also the way in which language, like experience itself, can become self-transcending in the religious symbol.
- We have also noted the way in which experience is 'schematised' in a particular language and philosophy and that description (since all experience is 'experience as') includes interpretation.
- But so far we have only looked at cognitive language – language that attempts to describe the object of religious experience and devotion. In fact, language performs many other functions, and to these we must now turn.

Cognitive and non-cognitive

Language can perform many functions. It can describe what it experienced; indicate a particular emotion; express a preference; give a command; make a request. It can be the exuberant expression of joy – yelled in words with no meaning – or a vehicle of the deepest grief, where a name of one who has died or is lost is repeated over and over, conveying a lifetime of shared experience and of sudden isolation.

Some of these uses of language are cognitive, that is, they convey information. Others are non-cognitive, in that they perform an action (e.g. give a command) or express an emotion or a preference. Some forms of language are described as 'performative' in that they effect something by being used. When you marry, or take an oath in court, or agree to buy goods in a shop, your words are performative.

Comment:

If all language were of the cognitive variety, we would become overloaded with information but get nothing done!

Religious language is not there simply to give rational definition of abstract entities. It is there to help, encourage and give expression to the spiritual life of religious believers, and most of that is non-cognitive.

To sum up this process:

- Religious experience/insight leads to faith.
- Faith may be articulated in terms of beliefs.
- Beliefs may be tested by reason for logic and compatibility with one another.

Language is the medium by which the first of these leads into the second and the third.

In other words:

Rational, cognitive claims are part, but only part, of religious language. The arguments and proofs put forward by the philosophy of religion are mainly concerned with these rational, cognitive claims. In terms of religion as a whole, they therefore have a significant but limited function.

The emotive theory

Sometimes we use language to express our own emotions and preferences, rather than to describe the external world.

A J Ayer, while arguing that religious language was meaningless since it could not be verified by sense experience, suggested that religious language actually expressed the emotions and desires of the person using it. In other words, what appeared to be statements about objective, external realities were, according to Ayer, subjective.

This approach is seen most clearly in the case of ethical statements. If I say something is good or right, there is no piece of external evidence that is the equivalent of the word 'good', and thus no way of proving that I am right. Therefore, all I am doing in saying that something is good is that I like it.

Example:

'Murder is wrong' does not mean that murders do not take place, nor does it mean that if I, like a detective, examine the details of a particular murder I will find evidence for 'wrong'.

The statement 'Murder is wrong' is not based on fact and cannot be verified with reference to facts. It expresses a personal valuation and choice.

'Murder is wrong' not only expresses emotions, but is also prescriptive, in that it prescribes a course of action which avoids murder.

In other words:

In emotive terms, 'This is good' means 'I like this'.
In prescriptive terms, it means 'I want you to do this'.

If we look back at the verification principle proposed by the Logical Positivists, we find that the emotive or prescriptive statements do not come within what they considered to be literally significant propositions. They are not part of a description of the world and therefore cannot be shown to be right or wrong with reference to facts. They are not 'cognitive'. Key figures in this approach include A J Ayer, mentioned earlier, and Braithwaite. They take what is sometimes termed a 'reductionist' view, that religious language is in fact (and can therefore be reduced to) a way of expressing moral commitments and setting out a policy for living.

A key question for reflection:

Does the statement 'There is a god' say something about external reality, or is it merely setting out a policy for living? If it does say something about external reality, how could it be proved or disproved?

Performative utterances

'Turn right!' is not a description; it gives a command. It does not so much reflect reality as seek to create it. Religion is full of such 'performative' utterances: 'I baptise you...' 'I ... take you ... for my wedded wife.' 'Let us pray.'

Can a performative utterance be either right or wrong? Is any evidence relative to it? The answer to both these questions would seem to be 'no'. A performative utterance is the most obvious example of the creative role played by language. Language is not simply a transparent, neutral and value–free way of describing the world: it plays a part; it makes a difference.

Language games

In his earlier work (*Tractatus*), Wittgenstein had set out a theory that saw the function of language as picturing the world. His opening sentence was:

> ‘The world is everything that is the case.’

Language therefore was to follow experienced reality.

But we have looked at the limitations of literal language, particularly from the point of view of religious experiences and ideas. We have therefore moved on to consider other uses for language, expressing a particular view, emotion or choice, and actually performing a task. Language is far more flexible and creative than the Logical Positivists realised. This was recognised by Wittgenstein himself. His later work (e.g. *Philosophical Investigations*), recognised that language is used in many different ways. To know the meaning of a word is to know how to use it. So the meaning of the word is given in terms of the context within which it is used. Wittgenstein saw language rather like a game that we play according to a set of rules. There are many different games (ball games, card games etc.) and there are no actions that they all have in common. What makes them all 'games' is the fact that they all follow rules. Learning a language is like learning a game – it is getting to know how to use the words.

In other words:

- For the early Wittgenstein, a word was like a picture; it stood for some external reality.
- For the later Wittgenstein, a word was like a tool; you discovered its meaning by the variety of ways in which it was used.
- Every kind of language is therefore a form of life, a game to be played out according to its self-contained rules.

Another important feature of Wittgenstein's later work, for the purposes of the philosophy of religion, is his recognition (in *Philosophical Investigations* paras 123–4) that 'philosophy may in no way interfere with the use of language; it can in the end only describe it'. On the other hand, changing one's description of a language game can have quite dramatic effects. D Z Phillips, a theologian who follows Wittgenstein's approach, argues that the statement 'God is love' is not a description, but a rule for how the word 'God' is to be used. This means that statements about religious belief are really descriptions of the grammar of the religious language game – and the implication of this is that something cannot be both a rule of grammar *and* at the same time a description of reality.

Comment:

Followed to its logical conclusion, this approach leaves religious language going round and round within its own self-contained game, for ever defining its own rules. I am tempted to ask 'What's the point? Why bother?' If religious language does not in some way get beyond itself to explore reality, how did it get started in the first place?

Finally, it is worth noting that for Wittgenstein (as earlier for Jeremy Bentham and Gottlob Frege) it is sentences and not individual words that are the primary bearers of meaning. **If you want to know what the word 'God' means, look at the sentences within which it is used.**

Language and truth claims

Unless we are going to end up like Phillips and consider all religious meaning in terms of the grammar of the religious language game, we are likely to want at some point to claim that something is true or false. In other words, we are likely to relate religious beliefs to a general understanding of the world.

In doing so, we need to distinguish carefully between existential statements, which may express religious commitment, wonder or values, for example 'Jesus is Lord', and apparently factual propositions, for example 'Jesus is the unique Son of God'. Of course, it can be argued that the latter is in fact just another way of expressing the former. Once expressed as a proposition, however, an item of belief becomes limited by the language used, and with it a whole set of cultural presuppositions. This creates a problem for the dialogue between religions. Can truth claims from different religions be compatible?

For example:

A Christian examining Buddhist ideas does so in the light of the central Christian experience and beliefs. From that perspective, Buddhist ideas are bound to be found wanting. But the same thing will apply the other way round. Ideas about sin and forgiveness, for example, which may be quite central to a Christian view of the relationship between humankind and God, are seen as unacceptable and positively harmful to the Buddhist. This is not to deny the validity of the experience of these things on the part of the Christian, but simply that, from a Buddhist standpoint, a healthy spiritual life requires the setting aside of what it sees as unskilful attitudes such as guilt.

To guard against this, it may be important to recognise that all truth claims are made in a particular context, using a particular language and set of ideas. In a different context, the same experience or conviction would have been expressed very differently.

However, where religious propositions are put forward, they are open to be assessed on the same criteria as scientific and other theories. In other words, we may still ask of a religious belief:

- Does it fit the evidence?
- Is it coherent as a theory?
- Is it the simplest (or most straightforward) theory which may be given to account for the facts?
- Is it fruitful in producing new ideas and giving meaning for personal existence?

(For a further examination of this see, for example, A Peacocke's *Theology for a Scientific Age.*) Such an approach does not rule out religious questions on a narrow dogmatic basis, but allows them to be explored alongside questions raised by science.

The limitations of language

All the major religions accept that there is a fundamental limitation to what can be said. Every attempt to define God will be limited, offering at best a partial image, not a full definition or description. The same could be said of Buddhist ideas of 'the eternal', or the 'uncompounded', which in that religion is set in contrast to this world in which everything is compounded and liable to change and decay.

It could be that the experiences of a Buddhist and a Christian may be similar, but the whole structure of thought and language that has built up within each religion will ensure that the resulting descriptions will be different and possibly incompatible. This reminds us of the limitation of any attempt to express the essence of religion.

For a mystic (see the first chapter), the sense of the transcendent is beyond language. The nearest language can get to describing mystical awareness is through symbols. Bede Griffiths, in *A New Vision of Reality*, points out that the intuitive mind is controlled by the right hemisphere of the brain, whereas the analytic and rational functions are controlled by the left. Clearly, mysticism is a right brain activity. He quotes Meister Eckhart as describing God as 'incomprehensible light' and Dionysius the Areopagite, a sixth century neo-Platonist mystic, as saying that the Godhead is beyond name, thought and imagination. The Divine is seen by mystics as something to which one can point, but which cannot be described.

Summary

Literal description of religious activity, the expression of religious emotions and choices, the performative language used in religious ceremonies: none of these create any significant problems. The controversial aspect of religious language occurs where it makes cognitive claims about that which transcends ordinary experience.

Western culture is dominated by literal language, particularly in the sphere of science. It is understandable therefore that religious beliefs are sometimes taken literally and examined as though they could be proved empirically, even if that was not the intention of those who originally formulated them.

We saw in the first chapter that religious experience occurs within the empirical world of sense experience but also transcends it. The language used to describe this similarly needs to be self-transcending, always pointing beyond itself.

3

GOD: THE CONCEPTS

Many philosophical and religious problems about 'God' arise from misunderstandings about exactly what that word is taken to mean.

For example, within Western religions, to speak of God as literally existing in a particular place, a being 'out there' in some way, external to the world, is to limit him; and a being so limited cannot be God. So we need to be clear that any argument about an external, separate entity (as one might debate the existence of some remote star in the galaxy) is **not** about the God of the Christian, Jewish or Muslim traditions.

I know ordinary things exist because I can define them, set boundaries to them, know what is them and what isn't. In other words, things are known to exist because they are limited – we can stand outside them and point to them. If God is infinite and eternal, he is everywhere all the time. It would not be possible to point to him, because it would not be possible to point away from him!

But if God does not exist in the same sense that individual things exist, does it make sense to say that he exists at all? We shall return to this question later.

Comment:

Other concepts give us similar problems:

- Does space or time exist? (Can you point to them?)
- Does 'reality' exist?

(Notice how these concepts form a kind of framework within which things are experienced. Might God be part of our framework?)

- Does 'love' exist?

(Even in the personal aspects of life, there are things that we might describe as real, or existing, but which defy definition. If love is something more than hormonal urges and acts of kindness, how is that 'more than' to be explained? Where would it be located?)

Even before we look at the arguments for his existence, it is therefore clear that God is not part of the universe. Nor is he outside the universe; for, if he is infinite, he cannot be outside anything. But we should recognise that much of what passes for belief in God in popular thought is, by the standards of the traditional concepts and arguments that we shall be examining, nonsense if taken literally.

Note:

Clearly, God cannot be either male of female, but for convenience he will be referred to as male.

That does not mean that you cannot employ symbolic and poetic language to express belief in God. But such language needs to be recognised for what it is, and not taken literally. Once taken literally, the god it refers to becomes a useless or dangerous idol. For the purpose of discussions about the existence of God, we need to have some basic definition of what the term 'God' means. Without some such definition we may argue at cross purposes. Here is one such definition, offered by R Swinburne in *The Coherence of Theism*:

> ❛ a person, without a body (i.e. a spirit), present everywhere, the creator and sustainer of the universe, a free agent, able to do everything (i.e. omnipotent), knowing all things, perfectly good, a source of moral obligation, immutable, eternal, a necessary being, holy, and worthy of worship. ❜ (p.2)

Some terms used of belief in God:

- Belief in the existence of God (in the sense that he has been described above) is **theism**.
- The conviction that there is no such being is **atheism**.
- The view that there is no conclusive evidence to decide whether God exists or not is **agnosticism**.
- An identification of God with the physical universe is **pantheism**.
- The belief that God is within everything (but not simply identified with the physical universe) is **panentheism**.

- The idea of an external designer God who created the world, but is not immanent within it, is **deism**.
- The literal identification of God with any individual thing or concept is **idolatry**.

For reflection:

- Anyone who claims that there is a possibility that God exists, denies God. A possible god is no God at all.

God as creator

In traditional theism, God is said to be the creator of the world, and to have created it out of nothing (*ex nihilo*). This is an important feature of theism, for it implies that God is not an external force working with matter or coming in to animate it, nor is he an agent over against other agents. Rather, he is the absolute origin of everything. There is no external material, no 'nothingness' out of which things can be made. Everything that comes into existence does so as a creative act of God – that is the implication of the idea of God as creator.

Now there is another side to this (which we shall explore again later): if there is no matter external to God through which he creates, then God cannot be **separate from** creation. You cannot say 'There is something of beauty', and then point to something else and say 'There is its creator.'

In other words:

To say that God is creator ex nihilo implies that everything is alive with his life. God has no 'other'.

Eternal

There is an important distinction to be made between 'eternal' and 'everlasting':

- Everything that exists within time can be thought of as having a beginning and an end. Even if it does not appear to change, it can still be said to be getting older. Now, something can be described as everlasting if its duration in time extends infinitely backwards into the past and forwards into the future. It is already very old and it will continue to get older indefinitely.

- If you want to describe a reality which is outside the ordinary world of space and time – the world in which all finite things can be said to exist – then it is 'eternal'. Terms like old, new, past and future cannot be applied to it. It is not part of the world that is known through the senses, for as soon as it becomes part of that world it is within space and time.

Within the tradition of classical theism (which originated from ideas in Greek philosophy and is found developed in the Christian tradition by Augustine of Hippo and Aquinas), God is definitely eternal rather than everlasting. He is not simply an ongoing part of the universe, but is beyond the whole process of change.

Note:

This is reflected in the religious awareness of Schleiermacher (see above p. 27) where he speaks of religion as a sense and taste for the infinite, and sees the eternal within every moment.

By contrast, Biblical language and much of the liturgy of the Church speaks of God in terms that suggest he is everlasting rather than eternal. He is described as being in the past, as guiding the course of events: the one who was, and is and is to come. Such a god is involved with the process of change; he is described as acting within the world. But action implies change and limitation, doing one thing rather than another, and it is difficult to reconcile this with the idea of an eternal God who is beyond time and space.

In other words:

- To exist is to be in time and therefore to age.
- To act is to make a succession of changes with the passing of time.
- Therefore, if God exists and acts, he cannot be eternal.

Philosophers who regard God as eternal generally see him as embodying the structure of reality, out of which emerges space and time and the world which we encounter with the senses. This is highlighted by the idea of creation out of nothing – not at some point in the past, but as a bringing into reality everything that exists here and now.

Those who emphasise the idea of a God who is, was and always will be active within the world, engaged in the unfolding of events, thereby imply that he is everlasting rather than eternal.

In other words:

- An everlasting God may be seen as a counter (although by far the largest counter, the greatest imaginable counter) moving within the board game of the universe.
- An eternal God remains the structure of the board game itself. That's fine, but you cannot throw dice and get him to move!

But note also that some writers use the term 'eternal' to cover both the idea of being outside time, and also being unending but within time.

Omnipotent

If God creates out of nothing, his power is not limited. If his act of creation is not something that took place in the past, but an ongoing feature of life, it implies that God brings everything about, without being limited by the material that he uses to do so.

In this sense, the idea that God can do anything (i.e. is omnipotent) is implied in the doctrine of creation. It would be illogical to call God the 'creator' in this absolute sense and then to say that there are things he cannot do.

There is one exception to this: God cannot be said to do anything which is logically impossible. Once the meaning of the terms is understood, 2 + 2 = 4. God cannot make 2 + 2 equal 5.

Omniscient

If God is omniscient, he knows everything. There can be two ways of looking at this:

- If he is eternal, existing outside time altogether, then his omniscience is timeless. His knowledge of past, present and future is simultaneous. It is not that he correctly guesses what will happen in the future, but that – for him – there is no future. His knowledge is eternally present.
- If he is everlasting, then he will know everything that has happened in the past, and everything that is happening in the present. He will also be aware now of those things in the present which will determine what happens in the future. In this sense, God might be said to 'know' the future, even though he hasn't been there yet!

The central problem with this for theists concerns human freedom and responsibility. If God knows what we think we freely choose to do, is not our freedom an illusion? Once someone knows that something is going to happen, then that thing is not a matter of chance, but inevitable. If it's not inevitable, then he can't know it – at best he can make a reliable guess.

In other words:

- If God is omniscient, he knows everything.
- He therefore knows that I will do X.
- Therefore I am not free to choose not to do X.

But some thinkers (e.g. Brian Davies in *An Introduction to the Philosophy of Religion*) would counter this argument by suggesting that God might know that at some point in the future I will freely choose to do X. In this case, my freedom is part of what God knows – therefore I remain free to choose.

But this seems to create a logical problem:

- I am free to choose if, and only if, there are at least two possible options at the moment of choosing.
- If God knows that I am free to choose, he must allow two possible outcomes.
- Therefore he cannot know which of those outcomes I will choose without denying me my freedom to make that decision.

An example might be: 'You can choose any colour you like, as long as it's red!' (No freedom) or 'You can choose any colour you like.' (Freedom, but I cannot insist that you choose red.)

One way out of this dilemma is to say that we freely make choices based on many factors, both conscious and unconscious. We do not fully understand these, and therefore do not fully appreciate why we make the choices we do. On the other hand, an omniscient God would understand all about us, and would therefore know exactly those factors (including our desire not to be predictable) which lead to our apparently 'free' choice.

An alternative approach (taken by Richard Swinburne in *The Existence of God*) is that omniscience implies that God knows all that it is *logically possible* to know. To know an undecided future event is logically impossible. Therefore an omniscient God would not know that, any more than he would know that 2 + 2 = 5.

Transcendence and immanence

When we looked at religious experience we saw that, although it took place in a particular place at a particular time, its meaning went far beyond them. An experience became 'religious' when it said something about the meaning and purpose of everything. The same was true of religious language; it had a literal meaning, but went beyond it. A religious symbol – whether an event, an image or a word – pointed beyond itself and yet in some way participated in the power of that to which it pointed.

When we come to descriptions of God, this 'self-transcending' quality of religious experience and language needs to be appreciated. God is said to be within and yet also beyond our ordinary experience and the words we use. The pair of words to describe this are **transcendence** and **immanence**.

The transcendence of God indicates that he is beyond any concept, language or experience. He cannot be limited or contained. A literal definition of God is nothing but an idol, however sophisticated that mental idol might be.

On the other hand, we have no means of apprehending or speaking about the reality to which the word God applies without using words that have a literal meaning, and which reflect the situation in which God is encountered. Since God is described as infinite, there is no place where he may not be found. Equally, if he is infinite, there is no way to experience him without simultaneously experiencing something else as well. He is therefore described as **immanent**, found within everything.

Theism, pantheism and panentheism

- **Theism** is the belief in a creator God who displays the qualities outlined in this chapter, and who is described as being encountered within but not limited to the material world. It reflects a balance of immanence and transcendence.
- If God were thought to be immanent but not transcendent, he would be identified with the material world itself. This is termed **pantheism** (literally: everything = God).
- Some philosophers and theologians use the term **panentheism** (literally: God within everything). Panentheism does not really add

anything to what is implied by theism, for the god of theism is already seen as immanent within everything. Panentheism is thus a reminder of the need for both immanence and transcendence. It is the philosophical equivalent of the Biblical idea that 'In him we live and move and have our being.' (Acts 17.28)

Example:

Although we are mainly concerned with the Western concept of God, it is interesting to note that the Hindu tradition maintains a similar balance. *Brahman* is sometimes thought of as an impersonal term for God, something like 'absolute reality.' But, in fact, Hinduism has two terms: *Nirguna Brahman* (the eternal, self-existent reality of God) and *Saguna Brahman* (the personal aspect of God, seen in his relationship with his creation). God is also described as *satcitananda* (sat = absolute or true; cit = mind or consciousness; ananda = bliss). Although there are significant differences between Indian and Western philosophies, there is this same sense that the divine is encountered within and yet transcends human experience. (To explore some of these parallels further, see, for example John Hick's *God and the Universe of Faiths*.)

Atheism, agnosticism and secularism

- **Atheism** is quite a difficult concept, because it is used to describe very different things. It may, for example, be used loosely for an attitude which opposes all religion.

Example:

You regard religious people as guilt-ridden, cringing whimps, afraid to take responsibility for their life or face the reality of their own annihilation at death. At best, you see religion as a set of fairy tales, acted out to make the feeble feel better about themselves. At worst, you see it as an agent of emasculation, preventing growth and maturity. You regard their 'god' as a fiction behind which the religious hide. You are therefore likely to call yourself an atheist. It does not mean that you deny that the word 'God' has meaning for them – indeed you are the first to point out that it is a powerful but harmful idea – what you mean is that you do not see what they call 'God' as an inevitable, correct or desirable interpretation of reality.

This situation is very different from that of someone who is religious, but who, confronted with the arguments for the existence of God, concludes that God cannot exist. Such a person may interpret God as a subjective attitude, a way of interpreting life, but not one that corresponds to any external reality. Yet this person, too, might be called an atheist.

To take it one step further, a theologian might conclude that in normal usage the verb 'to exist' implies that something may be located (to 'stand out' as a distinct thing) and therefore that God cannot be said to exist, since that would mean that he was not infinite. He might therefore deny God's existence in order to preserve God's essential qualities.

In other words:

There are two kinds of atheists: those who deny or oppose the reality with which religion is concerned, and those who explore that reality, but who deny to it any independent or objective existence.

Agnosticism is rather different. It is the claim that there is no conclusive evidence upon which one can decide whether God exists or not. Sometimes this may indicate indifference, as when a person replies 'don't know' to a political canvasser at election time. But, as with atheism, it may also be a position held for religious reasons. Most Buddhist traditions offer a view of the world and a spiritual path that does not depend upon belief in the existence of a God or gods. It does not positively deny their existence – indeed, it often refers to gods (and even more importantly to Brahma, the creative aspect of God within the Hindu tradition) – but regards belief in them as of secondary importance. It sees arguments about the existence of God as a distraction from one's spiritual path, and is therefore happy to remain agnostic.

Secularism is a phenomenon that exists over and above atheism and agnosticism. It is the view that the real concern of humankind should be with this world. It may take the form of a conviction that the scientific quest will eventually reveal all that humanity will ever want to know about itself and the world, or it may reflect a view that religion is an illusion and therefore a distraction from the reality of life. Often, it is simply a term used for a preoccupation with the mundane.

Nietzsche: God is dead

In *Thus Spoke Zarathustra* Friedrich Nietzsche (1844–1900) describes the prophet Zarathustra coming down from his mountain retreat and marvelling that the people he encounters do not yet recognise that God is dead.

Nietzsche saw that the world of his day was breaking away from all the former certainties and fixed structures of thought (which included the idea of God). He therefore proclaimed the death of God as an inescapable fact. God was no longer there; the world was drifting freely towards an unknown future.

He also saw that, in place of God, there had to be some goal. For him it was the appearance of the Übermensch – the 'superman' who would represent the next step forward in the progress that had led from the animal world up to humankind. Man is something to be surpassed.

In a way, one should view Nietzsche against the background of the 19th century. He was reflecting the shifting times within which he lived. His atheism was in part a rebellion against what he saw as the emasculating effect of the Christian religion – showing concern for the welfare of the least fortunate rather than promoting the welfare of the strongest and the leaders.

In a way, Nietzsche was calling for courage – courage to see the world exactly as it is and to affirm it. In his idea of 'the eternal recurrence' he throws out the challenge of being prepared to say 'yes' to living this same life, exactly as it is now, over and over again. This, he believed, was only possible for the 'superman'. For him, religion was an escape from the task of building the future, a failure to accept reality.

Nietzsche is a difficult but fascinating and challenging writer. All we can do here is note that it is not enough to get rid of God, one has to consider the implications – including what one puts in place of God in terms of an overall goal and understanding of life.

— Secular interpretations of God —

It is possible to argue that, while the idea of God may be an important one for religion, and while it may in fact be helpful in making sense of life, an explanation of it may be given in worldly (secular) terms.

Note:

- The fundamental issue is this: if there is a sufficient explanation of the idea of God in secular terms, is it not an unnecessary complication (in the absence of any other evidence) to claim also that he exists?

- A question to ask of any secular explanation is this: if the idea of God is effective (i.e. if people find it religiously satisfying, if it provides a useful way of interpreting the way the world is, or if it helps them to find meaning and purpose in their lives), does this explanation give a satisfactory account of that effectiveness?

Feuerbach

In *The Essence of Christianity*, Feuerbach (1804–1972) described God thus:

> ❛ God as a morally perfect being is nothing else than the realised idea, the fulfilled law of morality, the moral nature of man posited as the absolute being. ❜ (trans. Evans p.46)

In other words, God is a projection of the human moral idea. He is what the moral person would like to be, freed from all his or her limitations:

> ❛ God is the self-consciousness of man freed from all discordant elements. ❜ (p.97)

Individuals and societies are limited, they can never completely exemplify the ideals that are sought within religion. God is therefore a projection of those ideals; to believe in him is to believe in a moral order freed from all conflicts and limitations. He is a way of describing the highest aspirations of our own self-consciousness.

Marx

In his most famous passage, in *Introduction to the Critique of the Hegelian Philosophy of Right*, Karl Marx (1818–1883) says of religion:

> ❛ Religion is the sigh of the oppressed creature, the feelings of a heartless world, just as it is the spirit of unspiritual conditions. It is the opium of the people. The people cannot be really happy until it has been deprived of illusory happiness by the abolition of religion. The demand that the people should shake itself free of illusion as to its own condition is the demand that it should abandon a condition which needs illusion. ❜

The implications of this would seem to be:

- That religion may be effective: it serves as a consolation.
- That the happiness it offers is illusory, not real, since it does not

remove from people's lives those conditions which cause them to suffer.
- That people would be better freed from illusion, and that this can only be effected by the abolition of religion.
- That only once people are freed from illusion will they set about taking responsibility for abandoning those conditions which cause them suffering.

You may wish to reflect on these things again when we come to consider the problem of suffering and evil. As far as secular interpretations of God are concerned, we should notice that, whereas Feuerbach offered a positive interpretation of God as projection, Marx offered a negative one.

The reason it is negative is that Marx believed that real happiness is possible if people can change the conditions that cause them suffering, but that this is unlikely to happen until religion (illusory happiness) is abolished.

In this, Marx comes close to Nietzsche, since it is only in shaking off the emasculating restriction of Christianity that, according to Nietzsche, one is able to take the positive step of self determination and follow the path of the 'superman', accepting and affirming life just as it is.

Humanism

A modern humanist position on religion may be seen as a development of Feuerbach's view. But first, for a definition of humanism, here is what Professor Sir Raymond Firth has to say:

> ❛ My own assumptions are humanistic, based on the view that a central part of reality for people everywhere lies in the existence of human individuals in their social matrix, and that it is comprehensible only by human cognition and expressible only in human language. The universe holds many mysteries from the behaviour of quasars in space, to the sexual attraction between two persons. Many human problems are obscure, and the fate of individuals unpredictable. But I assume that whatever be the nature of the external world, there is no reality of another order beyond the world, no revelation of divine plan or divine values, no creative supersensible transcendent mind that can give meaning and sense to human experience and human endeavours. ❜
> (from *Religion: a Humanist Interpretation*, Routledge, 1996, p.9)

The key feature here is the denial of 'another order beyond the world.' Whatever the nature of religious experience and of religion generally, its explanation is to be found in secular terms. He is therefore able to say on page ten that 'religion is a human act.' Like Feuerbach, he sees ideas of God as an expression of human values:

> ❛ In the sophisticated major religions, for example, concepts of the divine, of 'ultimate reality', and of the extremes of knowledge, wisdom, morality and power associated with the divine, are just a summation of the absolutes of human imagination... It may seem harsh to say that God is an example of the fallacy of misplaced concreteness. But while at an abstract, figurative level the ideas of god, Yahweh, Allah, Brahma can provide spectacular symbolic expressions and penetrating thoughts upon the human condition, at bottom they are just essentially human constructs. ❜ (p.214)

His overall evaluation of religion is positive:

> ❛ To me as an anthropologist, each religion, even that which may appear to be intellectually not very sophisticated, contains some explanatory ideas about the world, some rituals as guides to conduct, serving as patterns for human relationships. Therefore I would argue that there is truth in every religion. But it is a human, not a divine truth. In every society the beliefs and practices of religion are modelled on secular beliefs, desires, interests, fears and actions. These are raised by religion to a higher power, given an alleged external authority and legitimacy, because in their abstract, figurative, often symbolic form they are ultimately an outcome of the human condition and an attempt to remedy its difficulties. ❜ (p.215)

This shows both a secular interpretation of ideas of 'God' but also the way in which religion itself emerges from human life and its aspirations. It also has implications for the nature of religious truth. Early in the book (page eleven) he compares religious truth with music:

> ❛ One does not speak of a musical composition as true... but as beautiful, powerful, aesthetically pleasing and emotionally satisfying. And so it should be with the imaginative creations of religion. ❜ (p.11)

One may ask two fundamental questions of this approach:

- What makes something aesthetically and emotionally satisfying?
- But also, why should one adopt humanist values as 'true'?

Professor Firth makes his humanist position clear by saying:

> 'Many of the values of these religious faiths are true values, in the sense that if honestly adopted, they make for a more viable social life – self-sacrifice, thought for others, avoidance of deceit, care for more vulnerable members of society, integrative meaning of rituals, strength in cooperation.' (p.215)

But why should these values be adopted? Why should they be any more true than, for example, the approach to social life that Nietzsche or Machiavelli might take: that the strong should not be restrained in order to benefit the weak?

Comments:

- The humanist position, as it is outlined with exemplary clarity by Professor Firth, does religion a great service by emphasising that concepts of God should not be taken to refer to a crude 'out There' entity. Religious experience is rather more subtle than that, and the language used to convey it should not be taken literally.
- Religion, as a response to the self-transcending nature of religious experience, is, of course, a human construct. It is an attempt to articulate, reproduce and live out what is perceived as of ultimate value.
- For a humanist, there are fundamental values which reflect an understanding of human life and its place within the universe. They are described as 'human' values, but they transcend any individual human being and any individual society. If they did not, they would not be used to judge the truth of human and social values as 'true'. The values themselves are not the product of society (if they were, they could not be used to judge society's constructs, like religion), but transcend it.

But the transcending of human experience by values that are encountered within individual situations, but are not limited to them, is exactly what religion is about. The point about the concept of 'God' is that it is an attempt to express that transcendence.

— A postmodernist interpretation —

Don Cupitt has argued for a radical and secular interpretation of Christianity. His philosophy is influenced by the movement known as postmodernism. In this, there is no external reality to which our words refer and against which they may be checked, but the words themselves form a closed system of signs. We live within a world of signs and words, and cannot step outside it, even if we try to express the object of religious awe.

His point is that the traditional and 'realist' view of God – God as some being or force or invisible reality that actually exists in itself separate from the ordinary things we experience – is not acceptable to thinking people today. This is not presented in a negative way, but in a positive one:

> ❛ A modern person ought to be spiritually strong and healthy enough to live and die without superstition. Nothing is hidden. Everything is just what it appears to be and there is no occult reality. The world is ours and there is nothing conspiring against us. There is only the manifest, the world of appearances which is best analyzed philosophically as a world of signs. There is only this beginningless endless flux, the human world of doings, meanings and feelings. ❜
>
> (Don Cupitt *Radicals and the Future of the Church* p.140)

The result of taking this view is that his religion is one that says 'yes' to life just as it is, affirms it in spite of its changes and suffering.

> ❛ ... I am advocating a religion of life in the sense of a spiritual discipline that enables us to accept and to say yes to our life as it is, baseless, brief, pointless and utterly contingent, and yet in its very nihility beautiful, ethically demanding, solemn and final. ❜
>
> (op.cit. p.143)

Comment:

In many ways, this comes close to the Buddhist view that spiritual happiness is possible and suffering may be overcome in spite of a realistic recognition of the limited and transient nature of life.

He refers back to Kierkegaard who, in his *Philosophical Fragments*, saw religious faith operating at the very point where life is experienced and choices made. In other words, Cupitt sees Kierkegaard as offering the first genuinely secular faith. If God can become incarnate in Christ and operate through the Holy Spirit, it implies that he is to be encountered within the human world, especially at moments of commitment and choice, not accepted as a theory or philosophical proposition. Don Cupitt opposes a dualism which separates appearance and reality. He argues that to follow Plato and make the present, particular thing no more than a pale reflection of some eternal 'Form' is to devalue it, and therefore to devalue the whole world of our experience; it is to be permanently looking **out and beyond** for real meaning, instead of looking **within and around**.

This point of view can be justified on the grounds that it is 'incarnational'. In other words, just as for the Christian religion, Jesus is believed to be the incarnate Son of God – God taking human form on earth – so the whole of God is thought to be brought within the experienced world, rather than being seen as in some way over and above it.

Cupitt also takes the view that gods are simply what they are within religion:

> ❛ The gods are just what people can be seen to be worshipping; they are our faith in them, and the things we say and feel about them and do for them. There is nothing extra. Gods have no existence outside our faith and practice. ❜
>
> (*The Time Being* p.35)

Comments:

- There is a problem here. People worship because they have some sense of what God is, some sense that there is *something* that they want to worship. Then along comes a theologian and says that 'God' means exactly whatever people worship. This leaves open the question as to why they should feel the impulse to worship in the first place!
- The 'nothing extra' means that there is nothing else to be pointed to, no separate entity over and above that experience of faith and worship. But the transcendent cannot be an 'extra'; it is not something within space and time; it is not a 'thing' that can be identified. If God is eternal, he is beyond all that.
- Once again, what sounds radical is really no more than a blunt statement of what has always been a part of classical theism. The danger, of course, is that the subtleties of theism are often masked by the crude caricature of belief in God that arises from taking language about God literally.
- On the other hand, the general approach of postmodernism is one that denies the reality of anything that lies 'beyond' the actual words or images of a cultural artefact. There is no creative genius, only the words that are written, no 'thing' that the artist wants to capture, only the image within which he has captured it.

An important feature of Cupitt's approach is that, for him,

> ❛ ... there is no pre-established harmony between thought and being. Nothing says either that there have to be answers to our questions, or that whatever answers there are have got to be accessible to us. Life is not obliged to make sense. ❜
>
> (*The Time Being* p.40)

This represents a radical departure for philosophy of religion, for much of the debate about God has taken the form of a quest for the single concept which can hold together the whole of reality. The ontological and cosmological arguments (which we shall look at in the next chapter) were just that – attempts to argue from meaning or from the structure of the cosmos to a single underlying reality. The assumption is that our thought is such that it can lead to an understanding of that which is beyond our immediate experience. Cupitt simply denies that this is necessarily so.

The Christian concept of God: the Trinity

We started this chapter with a definition of theism. Most arguments within the philosophy of religion work on the assumption that belief in God is simply to be equated with theism. Although this is largely true, it is not the whole story.

Judaism and Islam are strictly monotheistic religions. Neither will accept any direct representation of God, and neither will allow anything to be associated with God – indeed, the rejection of idolatry is fundamental to both religions, being enshrined in the first of the Jewish Ten Commandments, and the basic Muslim statement of faith that there is no God but Allah.

The Christian doctrine of God is more complex, and springs from the conviction of the early Christians that God himself was present in and through the life and activity of Jesus of Nazareth, and that the Holy Spirit of God had been poured out upon the disciples at Pentecost. Jesus, moreover, became seen as the Logos, the divine word or principle, through which all things had been created.

After a complex process of doctrinal debate during the early centuries, during which those who held minority views were regarded as heretics, the overall view of God that emerged was enshrined in the doctrine of the Trinity.

The term 'Holy Trinity' or 'Triune God' is taken to mean that God may be known in three ways, or under three aspects:

- As Father: creator of the world.
- As Son: saviour or redeemer, in the person of Jesus.
- As Holy Spirit: an in-dwelling spirit, giving new life to those who become Christian, and manifested in various qualities and activities.

On the other hand, growing from within the Jewish community, the young Christian religion wanted to emphasise that it remained monotheistic, and that the divine Sonship of Christ and the divine nature of the Holy Spirit were fully compatible with that.

Hence the formula that God as Trinity is **three persons but one God**. In Greek, the Trinity is represented by one substance (*ousia*) and three persons (*prosopa*). *Prosopa* may be explained by its use as the term for a theatrical mask – three images therefore through which the same being is encountered. When translated into Latin, the Trinity became three persons (*persona*) in one substance (*substantia*). The term *persona* (and the concept 'person' which derives from it) implies a greater measure of individual reality than did the Greek theatrical mask. The three persons are said to be co-equal and co-eternal. This is important for Christian theology. If it had been argued that the Father was **really** God, and that the Son and the Holy Spirit were somehow 'tacked on' as an afterthought, it would not have reflected the way in which Christians believe God can be known. To experience other people as members of 'the Body of Christ' and of the Spirit experienced within the lives of individual Christians implies, if the Son and Spirit are co-equal, that the **whole** of God may be known and experienced directly in one's own life and in the lives of others.

In other words:

It's not that the Christian religion claims that there is a God, and that the Holy Spirit may be taken as evidence in favour of his existence. Rather, the experience of the Holy Spirit **is** an experience of the whole of what God is, acting in this place and at this time. Similarly, Christians claim that they are members of the Body of Christ, and that he lives his risen life in and through them.

The implication of the doctrine of the Trinity is that, for Christians, the encounter with God is to be located in their present experience and relationships.

Since Christian theology and the philosophy of religion have sometimes been considered in isolation from one another, it is easy to see why religious experience (in other words, the operation of the Holy Spirit) was seen as little more than one further argument for the existence of God – a God who had been defined in philosophical terms. In fact, of course, from the Christian point of view, the operation of the Holy Spirit makes arguments for or against the existence of God redundant. (Or rather, that they may be useful for communicating the idea of God to non-believers, but are not necessary for those who already experience the operation of the Holy Spirit.)

Comment:

'Does Mozart exist?' is not a question to ask in the middle of a performance of one of his symphonies. There may be some historical arguments for or against the authenticity of a particular composition; but this performance, this present experience, is what Mozart is. If you enjoy Mozart, it becomes little more than an academic game to start arguing about whether Mozart exists. There are instruments being played; there are musical notes on sheets of paper; there is a conductor; waving his baton; there is an audience whose eardrums are helping to convert vibrations into electrical impulses; there is a great deal of recognition, memory and other mental activity going on. Where then is Mozart? Mozart is the whole thing: Mozart is vibrations of eardrums and the scraping of hair on strings; Mozart is a manuscript and a tradition of interpretation. You can discuss and analyze Mozart, but in the end you have to ask someone if they have experienced the symphony. If they have, then to that extent they know something of Mozart.

A similar argument can be applied to God. The effect of the Christian doctrine of the Trinity is to locate the encounter with him firmly within life's concert hall.

— Beliefs, language and religion —

So far in this chapter we have been looking at concepts by means of which people have tried to express their understanding of God. Language describing God cannot be taken literally, and so the task is to find a balance between concepts that are flexible enough to do justice to the very unique set of ideas that are being explored in terms of

'God', and finding some way of pinning belief down, at least to the extent that people can agree on what they are talking about.

In other words:

With no concepts, 'God' can mean anything. With concepts that are taken literally, or too rigidly applied to 'God', the living nature of the religious experience becomes lost.

For the philosophy of religion (as compared with, for example, the theory of knowledge) there is an additional problem. People often feel very deeply about religious issues, and may not be willing or able to examine various philosophical options with detached objectivity. How does the asking of philosophical questions relate to the needs of those who are actually practising their religion?

An example:

In 1994, The Reverend Anthony Freeman, an Anglican priest in charge of a parish in Sussex, England, was removed from his post by his bishop for publishing a book in which he claimed that God did not exist independently, but was a creation of the human mind, and that he did not accept the idea of life after death. He was against the idea of an all-powerful interventionist God (in other words, a God whom one might expect to come to earth and intervene in the ordinary way in which life works), and argued that there was nothing 'out there', and that even if there was, we could know nothing of it. He commented to a newspaper (The Telegraph, 29th July 1994, p.7):

> ❛ I think of myself not so much as an atheist but a Christian humanist. God is not a person, not a being at all, but the sum of our values and of our spiritual experience: the ideal. ❜

Response to the dismissal was mixed. Liberal Christians claimed that he should not have been removed for expressing his theological views, because such openness was to be welcomed. Others claimed that a person who did not accept what would be regarded as central Christian beliefs should not hold a position within the Church.

This situation raises a fundamental question. Is a study of the philosophy of religion compatible with being religious?

In the above example, the clergyman was expressing a view about the meaning of the word 'God' that would be quite acceptable within the philosophy of religion debate. His problem, however, was twofold:

- Can certain views ever be compatible with Church discipline? In other words, if you belong to a Church which is based on a creed, can you retain membership of that church if you do not accept those credal statements in a way that is in line with the majority of your fellow members?
- The more general question, and the one that is of particular concern to us here, is this: are some views of God incompatible with the forms of worship and devotion found in particular religious groups?

To make the last point more specific, we could ask: does the idea of God as 'the sum of our values and of our spiritual experience' work as an object of devotion?

This question implies that there should be a **pragmatic** test for religious language and beliefs. Do they work? Can a person think of God in this way and find an appropriate and emotionally satisfying way of engaging with that belief?

> **Comment:**
>
> The dilemma for organised religion is this: How can you convey religious truth in a way that enables it to be passed on, without at the same time restricting its meaning? How can you capture the essence of an experience and put it into words or ritual actions without it becoming fossilised?

Exists?

We have examined many of the concepts used to explain what people mean by the word 'God'. But the one thing that separates a believer from a non-believer (to divide people in a rather over-simple way) is whether or not they believe that there is something that corresponds to that word. Whatever else they have to say, believers generally accept that God **exists** and non-believers claim that he does not.

The next chapter will be concerned with the various arguments that attempt to show whether God exists or not. But before that, it is as well to set out as clearly as possible what we mean by 'exists', keeping in mind the various terms used of God that we have already considered.

If God is infinite, he cannot exist in the same way that everything else exists. Other things exist because we can isolate them and define them. We can set boundaries to them. We can say, in effect, 'Go and look there and you will see what it is I am talking about.'

An example:

You can say 'Life exists' because you can imagine a universe in which there is no life. But can you imagine no universe? Even the nothingness that you try to picture in your mind's eye is set within some sort of mental time and space. (The same thing happens to people who try to think about what might have happened before the 'big bang'.) So it makes no sense to say, 'the universe does not exist': it is not only unimaginable, but logically impossible – since the act of saying it is the action of a person who exists. Any statement implies the existence of the universe.

Fine, that proves that the universe exists. But so what? It simply implies that to say the universe does not exist is self-contradictory. The statement, 'the universe exists' is, in all practical senses, a redundant statement.

The next question is: does the universe exist independent of our minds? Clearly, our minds are part of the universe. The universe would not be the universe if it were 'out there' somewhere, separate from the minds that think of it. But, since it is not a matter of sense experience (we cannot see or touch 'the universe' without at the same time seeing and touching something else as well) our knowledge of this thing called 'the universe' must originate in our minds rather than through our senses. It is a term we use for denoting the sum total of all possible experience – everything that is, whether we are aware of it or not.

From the above, we may conclude that 'the universe' is a term used by the mind to give overall coherence to experience.

Now transpose that argument to the idea of God:

- God is said to be infinite.
- He is therefore within the mind of every person.
- Once the definition of God as infinite is accepted, his existence or otherwise cannot really be debated – for all such debates are about limited things that might or might not exist. God, by definition, cannot be such an optional thing.

- In this sense, to say that God exists is as limiting a statement as to say that he does not.

Think of the forms of religious experience described in the first chapter. Think of the overwhelming sense of the smallness of the self and the practically infinite dimensions of its world. If the word 'God' is used to describe such an overwhelming sense of the dimension of things, does it really make sense to speak of him existing or not, as though he were part of the world's furniture?

For reflection:

- 'God' is about the dimension and quality of what is experienced.
- 'God' is about universal coherence and a sense of purpose.
- 'God' is about ultimate values and commitments.
- 'God' is about 'being itself', rather than individual beings.
- 'God' is at one and the same time very personal and also universal.
- 'God' is the experience of absolute reality – a point of stillness and calm, a point of reassurance and warmth, a point at which the overwhelming superficiality of much of life is seen, a point of sudden insight into the nature of things, a point of moral significance, a point of new direction, a point at which the body may be flooded with energy.

The above statements are an attempt to sum up some of the ways in which religious experience has been translated into language about God. Notice however that none of them attempt to define God as a being separate from ourselves. Do they express something which can be said to 'exist'?

— Religious alternatives to theism —

Having introduced the idea of a pragmatic test for belief – whether a belief can be used in the context of religious devotion – it is worth reminding ourselves that not all religions require belief in the existence of God, and that there are forms of devotion which thrive without it.

- Four of the major world religions (Christianity, Islam, Judaism and Sikhism) are theistic.
- Hinduism appears to be polytheistic. In other words, a Hindu will accept the reality of many different gods and goddesses, each of which will reflect a particular aspect of life. This is how Indian

religion appears to the outside observer and how it is expressed in popular devotion. On the other hand, at a deeper level, there is the concept of Brahman (the ultimate reality) which underlies all the individual deities.

- Whereas in theistic religions, the personal and the ultimate aspects of the divine are held together and presented in the form of a single being, in Hinduism, the two levels remain distinct. At one level there are many personalities among the gods, and at a deeper level there is this single reality within which they all share.
- Buddhism is the only world religion which is non-theistic, in the sense that it does not require belief in God or in gods. It does not deny the existence of God, but regards arguments about the existence of God as irrelevant to the task of following a spiritual path towards enlightenment. There is worship and devotion in Buddhism, but this is a matter of showing respect and gratitude to a spiritual ideal, not paying homage to a deity.
- In popular Buddhist devotion there are many images of Buddhas and Bodhisattvas (enlightened beings), and in Buddhist scriptures there are many references to the gods. What Buddhism seems to manage to do quite successfully is to keep separate the emotional needs of worshippers for images that can act as the objects of devotion, and the more philosophical argument about the nature of reality.

The points made above are, of necessity, over-simplified and should not be taken as a final statement about the Hindu or Buddhist views of 'God'. They are introduced here in order to make two important points:

- That there are forms of religion which do not require belief in God. So belief in God is not a **necessary** feature of religion as such, even if it is central to the three Western faiths.
- That both Hinduism and Buddhism tend to make a distinction between popular devotion and philosophical belief. The former is a means of engaging the emotions in worship, but it is not seen as being the final word. A person may want to go beyond the use of such images and engage reality directly.

Basic beliefs

Some of those who believe in God are quite prepared to discuss religious concepts and will try to show that belief in God can be justified on rational grounds. Not all philosophers are happy with this situation. Alvin Plantinga, in a paper entitled 'Is Belief in God

Rational?' (in *Rationality and Religious Belief*, University of Notre Dame, Paris, 1979) argued that belief in God is quite beyond logical argument, and is a 'basic belief'.

Arguments for the existence of God may be useful – by showing that belief in God is neither impossible nor illogical – but they can neither establish nor undermine the basic belief, for such a belief expresses a fundamental commitment.

This approach is sometimes called a 'reformed epistemology', since it has parallels with the epistemology (theory of knowledge) that lay behind the arguments about faith, reason and knowledge of God that were set out at the Reformation, particularly by Calvin.

There is a strand of Protestant thinking that says that mankind is fallen and sinful, and that human reason cannot rise above that state to understand God. Knowledge of God can come only through God's own action (grace). Those who hold this view are unlikely to appreciate arguments about the nature of God or about his existence. If human reason is fallen, all such debate is likely to do more harm than good. This 'reformed epistemology' reinforces the argument presented in this book, that one needs to start with religious experience and the attempts to articulate it. Logic comes later and may be offered as a justification for, but not a complete explanation of, the beliefs that arise as a result of religious experience.

Perhaps that is why philosophers who take an atheist position find arguing with believers so frustrating. They know that, whatever arguments they produce, the believers will wriggle and then continue to believe just as before. The ground changes but the fundamental belief remains. That does not mean that the believer is necessarily being difficult or illogical, it is just that the 'basic belief' lies below the level of logical argument and touches an experience that is independent of subsequent interpretation.

Summary

The task of this chapter has been to point out that the concepts used to describe what is meant by 'God' make the apparently simply question 'Does God exist?' in actual fact far from simple. As might be expected of a philosophical approach, the answer you give to that question depends on what you mean by 'God' and also what you mean by 'exists'.

We need to keep in the forefront of our minds the subtlety of both terms if we are to appreciate the traditional arguments about the existence of God, to which we will now turn.

4
GOD: THE ARGUMENTS

Immanuel Kant (1724–1804) argued, in his *Critique of Pure Reason*, that there were three types of argument for the existence of God:

- based on reason alone
- based on the general fact of the existence of the world
- based on particular features of the world.

These are called the **ontological**, **cosmological** and **teleological** arguments, and he set about giving a critique of all three. He then introduced a fourth one, the **moral** argument.

We shall examine all four of these in this chapter, and will also add a fifth line of approach, based on religious experience.

Note:

In looking at the arguments, it is important to keep in mind the concepts of God outlined in the last chapter. The relevant question to ask may not be 'Does this prove that God exists?' but 'What sort of "God" does this argument present? Does this argument address what religious experience or organised religion mean by the word "God"?'

So, for example, pantheists have no problem with arguments for the existence of God:

- God is everything that exists.
- Everything that exists, exists.
- Therefore God exists.

The traditional arguments set out in this chapter are an expanded version of those found in the chapter on the Philosophy of Religion in *TY Philosophy*.

But what has this sort of argument achieved? It is just saying that, when the pantheist uses the term God, he or she means by it 'everything that actually exists'. It illustrates the meaning of a word, it does not argue for or against the actual existence of anything.

The ontological argument

The ontological argument is not based on observation of the world, or on any form of external evidence, but simply on the definition of the word 'God'. It says, in effect 'If you understand what God is, you understand that he must exist.'

The argument was set out by Anselm (1033–1109), Archbishop of Canterbury, in the opening chapters of his *Proslogion*. He is not putting forward the argument in order to be able to believe in God – that is never in doubt (indeed, the argument is addressed to God) – but because his belief in God leads him to understand God's existence in this particular way: a way which leads him to the conclusion that God **must** exist.

The argument is based on an understanding that God is *aliquid quo nihil maius cogitari possit* – 'that than which no greater can be thought'.

Note:

This does *not* refer to something that just happens to be greater than anything else. He has not lined up a whole range of things and happened to decide that God is the greatest of them. Rather, the phrase 'that than which no greater can be thought' expresses his idea of 'perfection', or 'the absolute', the most real thing (*ens reallissimum*).

In the second chapter of *Proslogion*, the argument is presented in this way:

> ❛ Now we believe that thou art a being than which none greater can be thought. Or can it be that there is no such being, since the fool hath said in his heart, 'There is no God'? (Psalm 14:1; 53:1). But when this same fool hears what I am saying – 'A being than which none greater can be thought' – he understands what he hears, and what he understands is in his understanding, even if he does not understand that it exists. For it is one thing for an object to be in the understanding, and another thing to understand that it exists ... But clearly that than which a greater cannot be thought

cannot exist in the understanding alone. For if it is actually in the understanding alone, it can be thought of as existing also in reality, and this is greater. Therefore, if that than which a greater cannot be thought is in the understanding alone, this same thing than which a greater cannot be thought is that than which a greater can be thought. But obviously this is impossible. Without doubt, therefore, there exists, both in the understanding and in reality, something than which a greater cannot be thought. ❜

In other words:

- When it comes to spending power, the real pound or dollar in your pocket will always be greater than the imaginary wad of notes!
- So something is greater if it exists than if it doesn't.
- If God is the greatest thing imaginable, he must exist. For if he didn't, you could imagine something greater – something with all his qualities, but which did actually exist.

One of the clearest criticisms of this argument was made by Kant (in his *Critique of Pure Reason*) in response to a version of it set out by Descartes (1596–1650). Descartes had maintained that it was impossible to have a triangle without having its three sides and angles, and in the same way it was impossible to have God without recognising that he must exist.

Kant's argument may be set out like this:

- **If** you have a triangle
- **Then** it must have three angles (i.e. to have a triangle without three angles involves a contradiction)
- **But** if you do not have the triangle, you do not have its three angles or sides either.

In the same way, Kant argued:

- **If** you accept that there is a God, it is logical to accept also that his existence is necessary (as opposed by contingent – something that happens by chance)
- **But** you do not **have** to accept that there is a God.

To appreciate the force of Kant's argument, it is important to remember that he divided all statements into two categories – *analytic* and *synthetic* (see the note on this, page 48):

- *analytic statements* are true by definition;
- *synthetic statements* can only be proved true or false with reference to experience.

For Kant, statements about existence are synthetic; definitions are analytic. Therefore, the angles and sides of a triangle are necessary because they are part of the definition of a triangle. But that says nothing about the **actual** existence of a triangle.

In other words:

For Kant, necessity is a feature of logic and definition (2 + 2 must always equal 4). When it comes to describing what exists, we depend upon experience (there may be four things, but there could have been five).

Kant gives another way of expressing the same idea. He says that 'existence is not a predicate'. In other words, if you describe something completely, you add nothing to that description by then saying 'and it has existence'. Existence is not an extra quality – it is just a way of saying that there is the thing itself, with all the qualities already given.

Norman Malcolm (in *Philosophical Review*, January 1960) pointed out that Kant's criticism failed in an important respect. You can either have a triangle or not, but (on Anselm's definition) you simply cannot have no God, so the two situations are not exactly parallel.

Anselm himself had already faced and answered a criticism of this sort. A fellow monk, Gaunilo, had challenged him, by raising the idea of the perfect island. He claimed that, if Anselm's argument were true, then the perfect island would also have to exist. Anselm rejected this. An island is a limited thing, and you can always imagine better and better islands. But he held that 'that than which a greater cannot be thought' is unique. If it could be thought of as nonexistent, it could also be thought of as having a beginning and an end, but then it would not be the greatest that can be thought.

This introduces another version of the ontological argument that he presented in the third chapter of the *Proslogion*:

> ❛ Something which *cannot* be thought of as not existing... is greater than that which *can* be thought of as not existing. Thus, if 'that than which a greater cannot be thought' can be thought of as not existing, this very thing than which a greater cannot be thought is *not* that than which a greater cannot be thought. But this is contradictory. So, then, there truly is a being than which a greater cannot be thought – so truly that it cannot even be thought of as not existing. ❜

In other words, Anselm claims that existence is a **necessary** part of the idea of God.

> ## *Note:*
>
> It is important to distinguish between logical necessity and factual necessity.
>
> - If 'God exists' is a logical necessity (i.e. if it is an analytic statement), then 'God does not exist' would be self-contradictory.
> - If 'God exists' is a factual necessity, it implies that it is impossible for things to be as they are if God did not exist, and therefore that it is actually not possible for there to be no God.

Now, Norman Malcolm's comment depends on this distinction. The necessity of a triangle having three angles is a **logical** necessity; but it is not **factually** necessary for there to be a triangle at all. (Which is similar to the point that Kant made in criticising this argument.)

But Anselm clearly thought he was arguing for **factual** necessity. In chapter four of *Proslogion*, he asks how the fool can still claim that God does not exist, and concludes:

> ❛ For we think of a thing, in one sense, when we think of the word that signifies it, and in another sense, when we understand the very thing itself. Thus in the first sense God can be thought of as nonexistent, but in the second sense this is quite impossible. For no one who understands what God is can think that God does not exist ... For God is that than which a greater cannot be thought, and whoever understands this rightly must understand that he exists in a way that he cannot be nonexistent even in thought. He, therefore, who understands that God thus exists cannot think of him as nonexistent. ❜

For Anselm, God is not thought of as an object alongside others; the word 'God' is not used as a name for something. Indeed, if God were an object, then the worship of him would be idolatry.

So what did Anselm understand by speaking of God as 'that than which none greater can be thought'? In another work, *Monologion*, he spoke of degrees of goodness and perfection in the world, and that there must be something that constitutes perfect goodness, which he calls 'God', which causes goodness in all else. This idea of the degrees of perfection was not new. Aristotle had used this idea in *De Philosophia*, and it is also closely related to Plato's idea of Forms. Anselm's idea of God comes close to Plato's 'Form of the Good' (see below).

So how does this affect the ontological argument?

- Imagine you have an assortment of apples. You can arrange them according to quality and size, absence of defects and colour. You can set them in rank order, but you will always be able to imagine an apple that is just a little better than any existing apple.
- Now imagine 'the perfect apple'. It has qualities that go beyond any one existing apple – and so, in that sense, it does not exist. But without that concept of the perfect apple, how would you be able to judge the quality of all the existing apples?
- If you tried to argue that 'the perfect apple' existed in the same way that the other apples existed, you would be following Gaunilo and his argument for the perfect island.
- By contrast, the argument in *Proslogion* chapter four underlines the fact that the existence of God, for Anselm, is *not* like the existence of other things. God is a unique but necessary concept. The word 'God' may be dismissed, but the reality which that word signifies for Anselm is something that he cannot deny.

So:

- 'The perfect ...' is in a different category from individual things.
- 'The perfect ...' is not simply the top of a series of individual things.
- God, for Anselm, is not an object, and therefore does not 'exist' in the way that other objects exist.
- Anselm's idea of God springs from his awareness of degrees of goodness in the world.

Plato's cave

In Plato's 'cave' allegory in *The Republic*, prisoners within a cave see only images reflected on the cave wall from a light that shines from behind them. They take these images for reality, since they have known nothing else. One prisoner, becoming free from his shackles, is able to turn and see first the objects casting the shadows and then the source of the light. He makes his way out of the cave, painfully blinded at first by the brightness of the sunlight beyond the entrance to the cave. He now sees reality, and recognises the shadows below for what they were.

For Plato, this image reflects a key feature of his understanding of reality: that individual things, like the shadows in the cave, are but imperfect copies of their 'form'. Thus we only know things to be trees because they share in the qualities of the 'form of the tree', the ideal concept by which individual trees are to be understood. Chief of these forms is 'The Form of the Good'.

Note:

One of the great debates in philosophy is whether individual things are 'real' and the ideal representations of them are merely intellectual abstractions, 'names' we give to groups of similar things, or whether those ideals or 'forms' are reality, and individual things are merely derivative.

- Common sense might go against Plato and opt for the first of these possibilities (sometimes called 'nominalism', since the abstract terms are merely 'names').
- Genetics might sway the argument the other way – since individuals are members of a species because (with certain variables, specified by particular chromosomes) they share a common genetic code. The genetic code comes first, and the individual is able to grow and become a member of his or her species only because of it.

The 'greatest thing' for Anselm is an intuition – but once it is recognised, it is seen as necessary, since he considered all lesser qualities to be derivative.

In her book *Metaphysics as a Guide to Morals*, Iris Murdoch claimed that the argument about necessary existence can only be taken in the context of this Platonic view of degrees of reality. She pointed out that the ontological argument is not simply a piece of logic, but something that points to a spiritual reality that transcends any limited idea of God. It is also something that goes beyond individual religions:

> ❛ An ultimate religious 'belief' must be that even if all 'religions' were to blow away like mist, the necessity of virtue and the reality of the good would remain. This is what the ontological proof tries to 'prove' in terms of a unique formulation. ❜ (op. cit. p. 427)

And this, she claims, is a necessary part of our understanding of life:

> ❛ What is perfect must exist, that is, what we think of as goodness and perfection, the 'object' of our best thoughts, must be something real, indeed especially and most real, not as contingent accidental reality but as something fundamental, essential and necessary. What is experienced as most real in our lives is connected with a value which points further on. Our consciousness of failure is a source of knowledge. We are constantly in process of recognising the falseness of our 'goods', and the unimportance of what we deem

important. Great art teaches a sense of reality, so does ordinary living and loving. ❞ (p.430)

Comments:

- If we think of the ontological argument simply in terms of 'existence is a predicate' then Kant was probably right, and Anselm wrong, for to say that something 'exists' is quite different from anything else about it.
- But Anselm's argument can also be taken to illustrate the belief that some idea of 'that than which no greater can be thought' is a necessary part of the way we understand the world.
- The ontological argument is about how we relate the ordinary, conditioned, limited things we experience to the idea of the perfect, the absolute and the unconditioned.

Where does that leave God?

- God's existence, if he exists, cannot be a matter of chance: it is either necessary or impossible.
- Equally, one might claim that 'that than which no greater can be conceived' is a necessary idea (even though we may not be conscious of it, or call it 'God').
- What seems certain is that God does not exist in the sense that other contingent, physical things exist. Whatever else he might be, he is not part of the world in that sense. But we knew that already, from the qualities ascribed to God in chapter three: God is simply not that sort of thing.

The cosmological argument

In his *Enquiry Concerning Human Understanding*, Hume said:

> ❝ ... we can never ascribe to the cause any qualities, but what are exactly sufficient to produce the effect. ❞

We need to keep this principle in mind as we turn to the cosmological argument – which is the attempt to argue from the fact of the world's existence to a transcendent creator. In seeking an explanation (if one is needed) for why the world is, one is not justified in positing a God with qualities other than those required for the purpose of creation.

It is, of course, possible to come at the question of the existence of the world from quite a different angle. Richard Swinburne, for example, starts with the idea of a personal God and then asks if such a God would have a reason for making the world the way it is. So, for example, in considering the fact that human beings can choose to understand the world and to act, he says:

> ❛ It is because it provides these opportunities for humans that God has a reason to create a world governed by natural laws of the kind we have. ❜ (*Does God Exist?* p.51)

Indeed, he can go on to say:

> ❛ God has reason to make an orderly world, because beauty is a good thing... ❜ (p.54)

Not everything is centred on humankind; Swinburne says that God's reason for creating animals is to enjoy their beauty (p.63).

If you start from such a view of a personal God who shares your views about giving individuals responsibility, about the moral challenge posed by suffering, and your taste in beauty, then it is, of course, possible to interpret the world to fit.

It is more of a challenge to start with the raw facts of the world as we experience it, and see if its existence requires belief in a creator. It might then be equally possible to conclude that the universe is 'just there' as a brute fact which requires no further explanation, or that any explanation would be beyond the understanding of humans, since their whole way of reasoning is part of the universe and cannot escape beyond it to get any other perspective.

The Kalam argument

There are two forms of the cosmological argument. The better known is that of Aquinas (1224–1274) which he set out in the first three of his famous 'Five Ways'. The other, known as the Kalam argument, was set out by the Muslim philosophers al-Kindi (9th century) and al-Ghazali (1058–1111).

Note:

For a fascinating discussion of cosmology and the Kalam argument, see W L Craig *The Kalam Cosmological Argument*, Macmillan, 1979.

The Kalam argument is that, looking back in time, the universe must have a first cause. It may be set out like this:

- Everything that begins to exist has a cause for its existence.
- The universe began to exist.
- Therefore the universe must have a cause.

This argument throws up a very basic question: if you have a sequence of events, each one caused by another that precedes it, stretching back in time – can that sequence be infinite?

Although a theoretical infinity (as used in mathematics) may seem a straightforward idea, actual infinities cause all sorts of problems. Infinity plus one, equals infinity; infinities cannot grow. Since the time of Aristotle, philosophers have argued that an actual infinity cannot exist. Even if it did, how could you know that something was infinite? It is not the same as being without discernible limit.

You can therefore present the Kalam argument like this:

- An actual infinite number cannot exist
- therefore the series of causes for the world being as it is now cannot be an **infinite** temporal sequence
- in other words, the sequence of causes must be finite
- therefore the world began to exist at some point in the past
- and there was a time in the past when one of two states was possible – that there should be, or should not be, a universe.

Al-Ghazali argued that when two states of affairs are equally possible the one that comes about must be willed by a personal agent.

Comment:

- A circle provides an infinite journey. The surface of a sphere provides for infinite movement in all directions.
- Therefore, it is possible to think of a universe that is limited both in terms of space and time, and yet appears infinite to those within it.
- Were I to travel far enough, I would return home: familiar to us now, but unthinkable to those who assumed the Earth to be flat and speculated as to what existed beyond its edge. Is the Kalam argument an attempt to speculate about what lies beyond the universe's edge?

Aquinas' versions:

From the age of five, Thomas Aquinas had been brought up in the

Benedictine monastery of Monte Cassino, but because of the war between Frederick II and the Pope, he moved to the secular university at Naples when he was 14, to continue his studies there. That was a crucial move for Aquinas, for the University of Naples taught the philosophy of Aristotle, and he was able to use Aristotle's ideas as an intellectual vehicle for setting down his own religious philosophy.

Aquinas presented 'Five Ways' in which he believed the existence of God could be shown. They are:

1 The argument from an unmoved mover.
2 The argument from an uncaused cause.
3 The argument from possibility and necessity.
4 The argument from degrees of quality.
5 The argument from design.

The fourth of these has already been considered, for a version of it came in Anselm's *Monologion*. It concerns the way in which we understand goodness and perfection – and moves from them to the idea of a source of goodness. In *Summa Theologiae* (Book 1 Chapter 1, 5:1) Aquinas speaks of goodness as *achieved actuality*. In other words, to be good is really the same thing as to exist. But he goes on to say that the word good retains the sense of value that is missing in the term 'exists'.

> ❛ Good... expresses the notion of value and perfection, and thus the notion of completeness. To be called good without qualification a thing must be completely perfect... to be good without qualification is to achieve complete actuality. ❜

If goodness is completeness, then within a world of limited, fallible things, goodness is likely to be rather lacking. Nothing will display perfection. (This is rather like the Buddhist idea that everything is 'unsatisfactory' – we can always look beyond what exists for something more, our craving for perfection in particular things can be a source of frustration.) For Aquinas, goodness and completeness are qualities that belong to God, and particular things share in them.

The last of the arguments – based on the idea of design – will be examined in the next section. For now, however, we are concerned with the first three, which are forms of the cosmological argument. Unlike the ontological argument, which was based on logic, Aquinas' cosmological arguments are based on the observation of the world.

The first may be presented like this:

- Everything that moves is moved by something.
- That mover is in turn moved by something else again.

- **But** this chain of movers cannot be infinite, or movement would not have started in the first place.
- **Therefore** there must be an unmoved mover, causing movement in everything, without itself actually being moved.
- This unmoved mover is what people understand by 'God'.

Although referred to as the 'unmoved mover', for Aquinas the 'movement' that he is thinking about is more a matter of change than of physical displacement. Everything that changes is changed by something else. His example is of fire causing something potentially hot to become actually hot. But the thing which does the changing must itself have been changed by something else. Now, we must stop somewhere, otherwise there will be no first change, and, as a result, no subsequent changes. This first cause of change, itself not changed by anything, is what he understands by God.

The second argument has the same structure:

- Everything has a cause.
- Every cause itself has a cause.
- **But** you cannot have an infinite number of causes.
- Therefore there must be an uncaused cause, which causes everything to happen without itself being caused by anything else.
- Such an uncaused cause is what people understand by 'God'.

A possible objection to this argument is that you might indeed have an infinite number of causes or movers. Instead of stretching back into the past in a straight line (with all the problems that the idea of an actually infinite number can cause), the series of causes could be circular, or looped in a figure of eight, so that you never get to a first cause, and everything is quite adequately explained by the one cause that comes immediately before it. But this image of circularity does not really help, for it is unlikely that Aquinas was thinking of a series of causes (or movers) stretching into the past. His argument actually suggests a hierarchy of causes here and now. This is the crucial difference between the Kalam argument and Aquinas's version.

Example:

Of the two versions of the cosmological argument, Aquinas' is the one which most closely reflects the actual nature of the cause of particular events. For example, I sit at a computer typing these words. What is the cause of this action?

- One might trace back the muscular movements to electrical impulses in my brain. In turn these physical systems might be related to oxygen, food and drink that I consume in order to maintain them.
- Beyond that there is the chain of causes that have put this computer on this desk, including those who have developed the software and hardware. This will touch on many lives of people I will never know.
- Then there is the publisher of this series of books and the whole tradition of reading and buying books
- to say nothing of the other chain of causes, linking thirteenth century thinkers like Aquinas to twentieth century writers.
- And then there are the causes in my personal history that have led me to the point at which I have chosen to write this particular book
- and gravity to keep me in my chair, and heat from the sun etc.

Causes grow exponentially. Each action has a theoretically infinite number of causes. Equally, each action may produce a theoretically infinite number of results. At any moment, we move within a seamless web of causality that goes forwards and backward in time and outwards in space.

Comment:

Everything is only fully understood in terms of the whole. But how is the whole to be understood? **That** is the cosmological question.

The third argument follows from the first two:

- Individual things come into existence and later cease to exist.
- Therefore at one time none of them was in existence.
- But something comes into existence only as a result of something else that already exists.
- Therefore there must be a being whose existence is necessary, and that all would understand to be 'God'.

This further unpacks the points raised by the second argument. There is no one thing in the universe which will account for the whole universe – for everything is limited both in time and space. To account for the **whole** universe, you therefore need to posit something beyond the universe.

Comment:

The problem we face concerns our imagination and the implication of the word 'beyond'. The universe is theoretically infinite – however large we imagine it, we can always imagine something more. Therefore, to imagine (in the sense of getting a mental picture of) a cause 'outside' the universe is simply to extend the universe to include that cause.

Our conceptual ability is limited to the picturing of actual entities. We can develop concepts that get beyond those conceptual limitations – e.g. a theoretical infinity – but when we try to integrate them into the rest of our thinking, we have to take great care.

'God' is a concept that has suffered from being visually conceptualised and therefore 'placed' within the universe in a way that is quite inappropriate.

Perhaps attempting to think about an uncaused cause beyond the world is something that our minds are not designed to do. The philosopher Kant argued that the whole notion of cause and effect was one of the ways (along with the concepts of space and time) in which our minds interpret the world – we cannot help but impose causality upon our experience. If Kant is right, then an uncaused cause is a mental impossibility.

A rather different objection to the cosmological argument came from David Hume (1711–1776). He based all knowledge on the observation of the world. Something is said to be a cause because it is seen to occur just before the thing that is called its effect, and the linking of cause and effect depends on the observation of them as two separate things.

But, in the case of the world as a whole, we have a unique 'effect', and therefore cannot observe its cause. We cannot get 'outside' the world to see both the world and its cause, and thus establish the relationship between them.

Nor, since this is the only world we know, can we say that in the case of all **other** worlds there was seen to be a cause, and that therefore there is likely to be one in the case of **this** world.

If, like Hume, you consider sense impressions to be the basis of all knowledge, then the cosmological proofs cannot be accepted as giving proof of the existence of a God outside the world known through the senses.

An important limitation

Aquinas was well aware of the possibility of taking this sort of argument in a crude way, and he was at pains to guard against using the argument to defend a simplistic idea of God. (In *Summa Theologiae* Book I Chapter 1 section 2:2), just before introducing the Five Ways, he says of the arguments that he is about to produce:

> ‘... any effect of a cause demonstrates that its cause exists: it could not occur unless its cause first existed. In such proofs the central link is not what the cause is (since we cannot even ask what a thing is until we know that it exists) but what the name of the cause is used to mean; and, as we shall see, what the word *God* means derives from his effects. God's effects then are enough to prove that God exists, even if they are not enough to help us comprehend what he is.’

So Aquinas never intended that his arguments should be used to **define** ‘God’ – merely to illustrate the existence of something to which that word could be applied.

To sum up:

Perhaps this last comment by Aquinas points to a balanced way of approaching these cosmological arguments. They do not **prove** that there is a God who is the uncaused cause or unmoved mover – for (as Hume or Kant would readily show) that is beyond the possibility of human reason. However, they do point towards the sort of reality that a religious person is thinking about when he or she uses the word ‘God’ – not a particular thing within (or, imaginatively, outside) the universe, but a reality which underlies and sustains everything. Not one cause among the myriads of others that determine every event, but that which lies within and yet beyond all of them.

The teleological argument

The teleological argument is concerned with the sense of a ‘telos’ (meaning ‘end’ or ‘purpose’) in the world. It argues that the sense of purposeful design we see in nature suggests that the world has a designer – God.

In *Summa Theologiae*, Aquinas links the idea of causation to that of purpose. First of all, he makes the point that causation gives things their perfections:

> 'Something therefore causes in all other things their being, their goodness, and whatever other perfections they have. And this is what we call *God*.'

Then he links this to the idea of purpose:

> 'Goal-directed behaviour is observed in all bodies obeying natural laws, even when they lack awareness... But nothing lacking awareness can tend to a goal except it be directed by someone with awareness and understanding; the arrow, for example, requires an archer. Everything in nature, therefore, is directed to its goal by someone with understanding, and this we call *God*.'

The best-known example of this argument is given by William Paley (1743–1805). He argued that, if he found a watch lying on the ground, he would assume (having inspected the way in which all the mechanical parts worked together) that it was the product of a designer. Indeed, if any one part were ordered differently, then the whole thing would cease to work.

He argued that the world is like that watch, each part of it designed so that it takes its place within the whole. If the world is so designed, it must have a designer.

A little earlier, Hume (in his *Dialogues Concerning Natural Religion*) had set the argument out and offered several important criticisms of it. In the dialogue, the argument is presented by Cleanthes:

> 'Look round the world, contemplate the whole and every part of it: you will find it to be nothing but one great machine, subdivided into an infinite number of lesser machines, which again admit of subdivisions to a degree beyond what human senses and faculties can trace and explain. All these various machines, and even their most minute parts, are adjusted to each other with an accuracy which ravishes into admiration all men who have ever contemplated them. The curious adapting of means to ends, throughout all nature, resembles exactly, though it much exceeds, the productions of human contrivance – of human design, thought, wisdom, and intelligence. Since therefore the effects resemble each other, we are led to infer, by all the rules of analogy, that the causes also resemble, and that the Author of nature is somewhat similar to the mind of man, though possessed of much larger faculties, proportioned to the grandeur of the world which he has executed. By this argument a *posteriori*, and by this argument alone, do we prove at once the existence of a Deity and his similarity to human mind and intelligence.'

Hume (in the guise of Philo summarising Cleanthes) makes the key point that matter cannot arrange itself:

> ❛ Stone and mortar and wood, without an architect, never erect a house. But the ideas of the human mind, we see, by an unknown, inexplicable economy, arrange themselves so as to form the plan of a watch or house. Experience, therefore, proves that there is an original principle of order in mind, not in matter. ❜

Before moving on to look at Hume's objections to the argument, we should pause to consider whether this assertion – that matter cannot arrange itself according to a design or purpose – is correct.

Evolution

Darwin's theory of natural selection provided an alternative explanation for design, and one that did *not* require the aid of any external designer. He argued that those members of a species whose characteristics were best suited to enable them to survive in their environment went on to breed. Those ill suited generally died off before doing so. This mechanical process of selection meant that whenever an advantageous characteristic appeared, those who displayed it had a natural advantage which they could pass on to a proportionately larger number of offspring. In this way a species could gradually evolve without the need for any external agency.

- What Darwin therefore appeared to offer was a mechanical explanation for what had previously been thought of as possible only through the agency of mind (in this case, the mind of God).
- Therefore Aquinas' and Cleanthes' assertion that an arrow requires an archer or that bricks can't self-arrange themselves into a house is challenged by natural selection.

Genetics

Within living things, damage occurs in a random way to the genetic information coded on DNA molecules, causing random mutations. Where such a mutant is beneficial, in the sense that it adapts better than those without the mutation, then the opportunity is there for a new form of life to develop. Life progresses because what is randomly produced subsequently takes advantage of its situation. This would be a more modern way of expressing Darwin's argument – but notice that the whole structure of change is now based on random genetic damage.

There has been considerable debate on the whole issue of random change and its implications, particularly since the publication of *Chance and Necessity* by Jacques Monod in 1970. He sees creative developments becoming possible through random chance.

A most determined exploration of this is found in Richard Dawkins's book *The Blind Watchmaker* (Longman, 1986). He illustrates the way in which random changes can lead to an amazing variety of apparently 'designed' forms. In recent years, there has been considerable interest in the ability of 'open' complex systems to self-arrange.

Hume's objections

Hume (in the guise of Philo) argues that our concepts of design are limited and cannot be applied to the world as a whole. He asks:

> ❛ Have worlds ever been formed under your eye...? ❜

In other words, the analogy between a designed object and its designer, and the apparent design in the world and God, cannot hold. We do not know what it would be like to design a world – so how can we be sure of a designer?

But Cleanthes continues:

> ❛ Consider, anatomise the eye, survey its structure and contrivance, and tell me, from your own feeling, if the idea of a contriver does not immediately flow in upon you with a force like that of sensation. ❜

In other words, common sense leads to the idea of a designer, in spite of the fact that one is not able to stand back and observe the act of designing.

Hume argues that a supposed cause need only be proportional to its effect. The world is limited, therefore it cannot be the basis for arguing for an infinite or perfect God. Also, when observing the world...

> ❛ ... it is impossible for us to tell, from our limited views, whether this system contains any great faults or deserves any considerable praise if compared to other possible or even real systems. ... Many worlds might have been botched and bungled, throughout an eternity, ere this system was struck out; much labour lost, many fruitless trials made, and a slow but continued improvement carried on during infinite ages in the art of world-making. ❜

A key feature of Hume's first comment here is that, even if you find that there is order in the world, all that it enables you to say is... that there is order in the world. It does not justify the leap from that sense of order to the concept of a God. This point is brought out clearly by Mackie in *The Miracle of Theism*, who says:

> ❛ The further postulation of a god... is a gratuitous addition to this solution, an attempted underpinning which is as needless as it is incomprehensible. ❜ (p.251)

He makes this point in contrast to Hans Kung (in *Does God Exist?*) who sees God as the 'ground and support of reality' and who says that:

> ❛ If someone affirms God, he knows why he can trust reality. ❜ (p.572)

Kung contrasts this basic sense of trust with an atheistic nihilism. By contrast, Mackie wants to say that you can have a basic trust in reality on intellectual grounds, and that humans make their own values. In other words, like Hume, he argues that you do not need to take a further step and go beyond what is required by the actual experience of an ordered world.

For reflection:

- Design is easy to see in retrospect, and with a selective view of the facts.
- Design is also easy to see if you make your own existence the centre and purpose of the universe. Design is less easy to spot if your species is about to be wiped out and replaced by another.

Hume makes three other important points:

> ❛ The world plainly resembles more an animal or a vegetable than it does a watch or a knitting-loom. Its cause, therefore, it is more probable, resembles the cause of the former. ❜

> ❛ ... we have no data to establish any system of cosmogony. Our experience, so imperfect in itself and so limited both in extent and duration, can afford us no probable conjecture concerning the whole of things. ❜

> ❛ I would fain ask how an animal could subsist unless its parts were so adjusted? ❜

For reflection:

Consider the last point made by Hume. In order to live, all the various parts of your body need to be working together. If you had no lungs, you could not breathe, and the rest of your body would fail for lack of oxygen. Without a digestive system, you could not get nourishment to provide the energy to maintain all your systems. Does this imply a careful designer?

You could argue that any creature that needs oxygen and nourishment is going to die quickly if it is born without lungs or a digestive system. Such creatures therefore cannot exist. This argument works by simple logic. In other words, thinking about the way in which things work together:

- Everything is as it is.
- If anything were different, everything would be different.
- Everything contributes to everything else.
- If everything else were different, everything would contribute differently.

Projected design

The philosopher Kant argued that our minds impose the concepts of time, space and causality upon experience. They are regulative concepts. We experience everything as having a cause and as existing in space and time because that is the way we look at life.

Now this has implications for both the cosmological and teleological arguments. We could argue that, if we see the universe as an ordered place, it is because our minds are predisposed to interpret events in an orderly way. Indeed, modern philosophers of what we generally term a 'postmodernist' approach would see the very act of talking or writing about the world as a process of creating order. Order and design are a feature of the world that we create with our words.

To sum up:

- Religious common sense tends to see the intricacies of nature as pointing to a designing and purposive creator – God.
- We do not have the evidence or the perspective to sustain an analogy between human creativity and the idea of a divine creator. As a logical argument, the teleological approach cannot be sustained.
- The most we can say is that the world appears to have order and purpose. But even that may be challenged on two major fronts:
  1 The observation of the way in which open complex systems appear to organise themselves may provide an alternative way

of looking at what we take to be 'design'.

2 The very ideas of design and purpose may be considered to be projections upon the external world of aspects of human creativity.

- For a person who already believes in God, the cosmological and teleological arguments may provide support for that belief. On the other hand, for the person without such a prior commitment, they are logically inconclusive.

The moral argument

If pure logic (the ontological argument), the fact of the world's existence (cosmological arguments) or the apparent design and purposefulness of the world (the teleological argument) cannot give definitive proof of the existence of God, where might one look for such proof?

It seems reasonable that the next step should be to examine those aspects of human experience which relate to religion. In other words, is there anything in the way in which people respond to the idea of God that can be used to prove that God exists?

There are two possibilities here:

- the experience of morality – both the sense that there are certain things one ought to do, and also the guilt that may arise when one recognises that one has done what one believes to be wrong
- religious experience itself.

We looked at the nature of religious experience in the first chapter, and will return to it shortly to see to what extent it can be used as a basis of proof for the existence of God. For now, we need to consider if there is a valid argument for the existence of God based on morality.

Where do moral rules come from? There are three possibilities:

- They may be God's commands (but this makes any attempt to argue from morality to the existence of God circular, so we may set it aside for now).
- Moral rules may spring from an objective look at human nature and the structures of the world in which people live. If there are such rules, they may well be absolute, since they would apply to all people at all times. Rules in this category may or may not require the support of belief in God.

- Moral rules may be the product of human society and human choice – as promoting general welfare and the need for co-operation, for example. Such rules are unlikely to be absolute. They are devised to meet the needs of a particular situation.

We start with the second of these options. Aristotle related morality to his idea of a final cause (a concept which we shall examine in chapter eight). Basically, he held the view that we ought to do that which would lead to our maximum self-fulfilment. Once we understand our true nature, we will act accordingly.

In other words:

Morality is rational and objective: it depends on our understanding of our own nature and goals, and does not depend upon any rules imposed upon us by a god.

Within ancient Greek philosophy there was a debate between the Stoics and the Epicureans on how morality related to happiness. On the one side was the conviction that to do your duty was the way in which you would achieve true happiness, and on the other was the idea that the pursuit of happiness was your duty. Both sides of this debate require some linkage between duty and happiness; the world is a rational place, and therefore, in some way, the one ought to result in the other.

This attempt to give an objective basis for morality was approached from a rather different angle by Kant.

Kant believed that the cosmological arguments could never prove the existence of God, but that, by getting rid of those arguments, he could make way for an understanding of God based on faith, rather than reason. He did this by examining the idea of moral experience, and in particular the ideas of virtue and happiness with which the Greeks had been concerned. He argued that, in an ideal world, they should follow one another, so that doing what is right (virtue) should ultimately lead to happiness. But, as we look at the world around us, it is by no means certain that virtue will lead to happiness. Why then should anyone be moral?

Kant started from the fact that people do actually have a sense of moral obligation: a feeling that something is right and must be done, no matter what the consequences. He called this sense of moral obligation the '*categorical imperative*', to distinguish it from a '*hypothetical imperative*' (which says, 'if you want to achieve this, then you must do that').

In *The Critique of Practical Reason* Kant explored the presuppositions of this categorical imperative. He asked, in effect: what do I actually believe about life if I respond to an absolute moral demand? (Not, what must I rationally accept before I agree with a moral proposal, but what do I actually feel to be true, rationally or otherwise, in the moment when I respond to the moral imperative?) He came to the conclusion that three things (which he called the *postulates* of the practical reason) were presupposed:

- freedom
- immortality
- God.

The experience of moral obligation implies that you are free to act (even if someone observing you claimed that you were not), that you will eventually experience happiness as a result of your virtue even if you will not do so in this life (as when someone sacrifices his or her own life for the benefit of others), and that, for this to be possible, there has to be some overall ordering principle which will reward virtue with happiness – and this might be called 'God'.

In other words, Kant is saying that you cannot **prove** the existence of God, but that your sense of morality implies the world is ordered in a moral way – and that, in turn, implies belief in God.

Note:

The link between morality and belief in God is not without its difficulties. There are some (e.g. Bertrand Russell in *Why I am Not a Christian*) who have argued that human maturity requires that we get rid of religion. They point out that a truly free rational choice is incompatible with religious concepts like sin and the idea of rewards and punishments. To obey out of fear, or in the hope of gaining some reward, is not the same as making a free, moral choice.

Set alongside Kant's argument, this highlights a recurring problem for the philosophy of religion. The concepts of God, as explored and refined by the philosopher, may be very far removed from the actual practice of religion and the way in which the divine figure is perceived.

Kant's God is an underpinning of a rational view of the universe. It is a postulate of the pure practical reason. It endorses the rational mind. But, as we saw in the chapter on religious experience, there is much in religion that is far from rational. Actual religion may not fit the neat package into which philosophy might wish to put it.

In looking at an objective basis for morality, let us return for a moment to Kant's argument. If the idea of one thing causing another is something that our mind imposes on external reality, it cannot be used as the basis for a proof for the existence of God. This was the reason why he rejected the cosmological argument. So:

- **If** our minds impose the ideas of space, time and causality onto our understanding of the world, **then** to argue from these things to something outside the world is impossible.
- Equally God, freedom and immortality cannot be **in** the world that we experience, but have to do with **the way in which** we experience the world.
- God is therefore a **regulative** concept (part of our way of understanding) not a **constitutive** concept (one of the things out there to be discovered).

Kant's moral argument amounts to this:

> If we know what it is to behave morally – to do what we believe to be right, even though it may be against our own immediate interests – then, in the very act of being moral, we presuppose the idea of God. This is not a God within the world of phenomena, but a regulative concept, an overall idea of a divinely guaranteed moral order, as a necessary way of interpreting and making sense of life.

Let us be clear about the second possible origin of morality – the idea that there is an objective moral order. It may be used as a way of introducing God as the upholder of a moral order (as in Kant), but equally it may be used by the atheist to show that there can be a rational basis for morality that does not depend on God.

The third option is that morality is a human construct, a product of the individual or society's needs for protection and regulation. This is a 'naturalistic' approach, and does not require belief in God. It is taken by, for example, Hume, and is widespread in modern thinking. It is particularly appropriate where there is a number of different sets of moral rules competing with one another, for example in multi-ethnic or multi-faith situations. Moral principles are seen as the products of particular social groups, and they may be changed by mutual agreement.

Summary:

- If you believe that there is an objective moral order, it may be used *either* to suggest that the world is created by a moral being (God), *or* to show that morality is well established on objective moral grounds and no idea of God is needed.
- On the other hand, if morality is a human product, no God is required to account for moral experience.
- On balance then, the moral argument cannot prove the existence of God. At most, it can illustrate the way in which the idea of God is used in practical moral situations.

The argument from religious experience

In chapter one, we examined some features of religious experience. We saw that a key feature was what was called the 'self-transcending' quality of an experience. In other words, something which could have been experienced in quite an ordinary way (and for which there might be a rational explanation) pointed beyond itself to reveal something about the meaning of life as a whole.

The various forms of language in chapter two mirrored this self-transcending quality: language which had a straightforward, literal meaning could also go beyond that meaning in order to express the religious dimension.

But can such religious experience by used as an argument for the existence of God?

Someone who has a religious experience may say simply 'I have experienced God.' In one sense, that claim is irrefutable, for you cannot argue that someone has not had the experience that they claim to have had. **If that's what they call 'God' and that's what they've experienced, then no further proof is needed.**

On the other hand, there may be various ways of interpreting what is experienced. One person may call it 'God', another may say simply that it is a sense of beauty, or grandeur. One person may feel that he or she has been encountered by a reality that is in some way 'out there', another may say that it is all psychologically generated, or the result of drink or drugs.

In *An Introduction to the Philosophy of Religion*, Brian Davies asks if it is possible to be mistaken about what one experiences. If so, then it must also be possible to be correct about it. So, if someone could be mistaken about an experience of God, they could also be correct. The implication of that, he suggests, is that knowledge of God through experience is at least *possible*.

But notice the presupposition of such an argument. It requires a prior knowledge of what God is. If you do not know what God is, then there would be no grounds for saying that an experience of him was either correct or mistaken.

In other words: **if** you accept belief in God on other grounds, then religious experience may help to confirm it. If you do **not** then religious experience shows no more than what a person means by 'God'.

There is an additional problem. Davies asks whether we can know if someone is experiencing God or something else (page 125–7). But there is a difficulty with such a question. How is it possible to experience God other than through experiencing something else as well? If God is infinite, he is not located in a particular place, nor does he have boundaries. Yet all sense data is of particular places – things are known only because they have boundaries. Sense data is the result of chopping up reality into segments: this is one thing; that is another.

So arguments about whether one has or has not experienced God all require prior knowledge of God. This follows from the general point that *all* experience involves interpretation (we experience 'as'). Prior beliefs influence what is experienced. A believer experiences 'God' – but is that a matter of sense data or of the interpretation?

In terms of logical argument, there is a further problem:

- In order to be able to say that a person has or has not experienced X, one needs to know what X is (i.e. to have information about X that is independent of the present experience).
- But in the case of God, there is no such unambiguous, independent or objective information. If there were, then there would be no reason to be debating whether or not there is a God!
- You could take the view that God is whatever a person chooses to call 'God'. If so, religious experience is a source of knowledge of God, but it remains convincing only for that individual, or those who accept or share in that experience.
- But that view will not satisfy a philosopher, who aims to understand the terms 'God' and 'exists' in such a way that the

proposition 'God exists' can be shown to be either correct, incorrect or meaningless.

- Religious experience can therefore only become the basis for an argument about the existence of God, once there is the common acceptance of what the word 'God' means.
- Once there is some agreement about definitions, a person may say 'I have experienced something which, although it is in itself beyond description, corresponds to what I understand by 'God'.

There are many descriptions of religious experiences from widely differing cultures. If you recognise in them some common core of experience, some reality to which they are all pointing, then you can say that religious experience contributes to your understanding of the meaning of the term 'God', and therefore to the reality to which that word refers.

On the other hand, if you feel that these experiences, however personally interesting for those who have them, do not point to a level of reality which is theoretically available to everyone, then you will remain unconvinced by any argument from religious experience.

Note:

In the cosmological and moral arguments, we started with data (the nature of the universe, or the experience of the moral imperative) and examined whether the existence of God was a possible or necessary inference from that data. We noted that the arguments themselves produced their own definitions of God – so that, even if internally consistent, they might not be externally persuasive (i.e. a person might say 'Yes I see why, if that's the way you see the world, you believe in God' without therefore wanting to speak of God themselves).

The same thing applies to religious experience, except that in this case the data that forms the basis of the argument is far more varied, and it is difficult to see how anyone could deny having some inkling of at least some of the different experiences that have been called 'religious'. But this wealth of experience brings its own problem: a wealth of possible interpretations and therefore a wealth of possible ways of speaking about 'God'.

William James concluded that religious experience could not support belief in an infinite God, but that through it one might experience a

> ❛ ...union with something larger than ourselves and in that union find our greatest peace. ❜

Summary:

The argument from religious experience may therefore be enlightening and persuasive, but it is not a logically compelling argument. For this reason, philosophers may not like it much. However, they need to recognise that, for religious people, it is probably the most persuasive of all arguments, because it relates God directly to those things of which they are already well aware.

Conclusion

In considering all the arguments about the existence of God, it might be worth keeping the whole exercise in perspective by reminding ourselves that 'God' is hardly the sort of thing which might or might not happen to exist. Of course, this was an important feature of the ontological argument, but it is relevant to consider it in the context of the arguments in general. The theologian Paul Tillich, in *Systematic Theology* (Vol. I p.262), says:

> ❛ ... the question of the existence of God can be neither asked nor answered. If asked, it is a question about that which by its very nature is above existence, and therefore the answer – whether negative or affirmative – implicitly denies the nature of God. It is as atheistic to affirm the existence of God as to deny it. God is being itself, not a being. ❜

This reinforces what has been implied throughout the ontological and cosmological arguments: that what is being claimed is not the existence of one entity alongside others, but a fundamental way of regarding the whole universe. It is about the structures of being itself (to use Tillich's term) not the possible existence of a being.

Of course, it is always possible to define God in terms of the intuition of meaning and value that comes through a religious experience. In which case you might want to say that to have no God is to imply that life has no overall coherence and purpose, no ultimate point of reference for values, no sense of absolute morality, no direction.

To assess whether a person believes in God or not would then be more a matter of listening to them speak of what their life is for, what they hope for, what they value.

On the other hand, if you adopt this personal and experiential interpretation of 'God', you will almost certainly fall foul of those who insist that God must exist in a way that is far more independent of human intuitions and values.

Worth a bet?

Perhaps the last word in any discussion of the arguments for the existence of God should go to Pascal. In his *Pensées* (section III number 233) he sets out his famous wager. He points out that you cannot decide the question of God's existence, therefore it is advisable to look at what you gain or lose by your belief or disbelief.

- If you believe in God and he exists, then you stand to gain infinite happiness as your reward.
- If you believe in God and he does not exist, you lose nothing.
- If you deny God's existence and he does in fact exist, then you lose your chance of infinite happiness.
- If you deny God's existence and he does not exist, you gain nothing.

Given these options, according to Pascal, for practical purposes it is better to bet on God existing!

So what has been achieved by the arguments?

- The ontological argument has highlighted the logical problems in speaking about God as 'that than which no greater can be conceived', and in the distinction between logical and factual necessity.
- The cosmological and design arguments suggest that there are features of the world which lead the mind to that which goes beyond experience. What is the cause of everything? Why is the world as it is?
- The moral argument suggests that we all have an intuition of God (along with freedom and immortality) every time we experience a sense of moral obligation.
- The argument from religious experience cannot be conclusive, since all experience is open to various interpretations, but it does keep us focused on the fact that there is an awareness at the heart of religion which struggles to find expression in beliefs, including belief in God. Arguments have a context, and that context is the religious experience and people's responses to it.

Even if these arguments are not conclusive, they have value in indicating the sort of thing a religious person is thinking about when he or she uses the word 'God'. For a believer, they may reinforce faith. For an agnostic or atheist, they are unlikely to convince, but can at least illustrate the real differences in perspective that belief in the existence of God implies.

5
THE SELF

Ask most people what they think religion is about, and they will say 'God'. But press the question a little further and you will find yourselves discussing human responses to 'God' – morality, worship, new attitudes to life, new ways of understanding and evaluating one's relationships with other people. In fact, if there were no personal response to the idea of 'God', then there would be no religion, only philosophy; for religion is not about analyzing concepts, but about responding to the deepest intuitions of meaning and purpose.

This being the case, religion is as much about the self as it is about God, for it is concerned with the relationship between the two.

This chapter will therefore consider three questions:

- Who and what am I? (We shall look at some theories about the relationship between minds, bodies and souls, in order to see what kind of 'self' it is with which religion is concerned.)
- Are we fixed or free? What has shaped us, and what can we do to change ourselves if we wish to do so? How does our freedom relate to our identity?
- Is there life beyond death?

Bodies, minds and souls

The study of the relationship between mind and body is generally termed 'the philosophy of mind' or 'philosophical psychology'. In this chapter we shall examine some of the theories that have been put forward, in order to see the implications they have for religion. When we consider the relationship between bodies and minds, there are three broad possibilities:

- that minds are unreal; there are only bodies
- that bodies are unreal; there are only minds
- that there exist both bodies and minds, distinct from one another, but linked together in some way.

The first of these it termed **materialism**, the second **idealism** and the third **dualism**. Of these three, dualism has a great variety of interpretations, and has dominated Western thinking. Materialism and idealism have been put forward largely in response to problems posed by dualism.

Some of the material here on mind/body theories may also be found in the chapter on 'The Philosophy of Mind' in *TY Philosophy*.

Dualism

Plato and Aristotle

For Plato, the body is physical and therefore has extension (i.e. it is located in space), whereas the self is that which thinks, and it has no extension. He thought of the self as a thinking being, and therefore distinct from the body and capable of living without it. So from Plato you have a radical dualism of thinking self and physical body.

Aristotle took a different approach. He considered the soul to be the 'form' of the body; it is what turns flesh, bone and all other components into a living individual. By the same argument, a dog has a doggy soul, and that is what makes it a dog. Matter takes shape and becomes animated: it gets a soul.

But a soul is one thing and a rational mind quite another; human beings have a soul or self that is capable of an intellectual life. Animals may have feelings and sensations, but only humans can reflect on them and grasp general principles as a result of them.

Crucial to both Plato and Aristotle is the mind's ability to grasp 'universals' (general terms, e.g. 'goodness' as opposed to individual good things). For the Greeks it was the rational mind that separated humankind from the beasts.

In other words:

Humans know general truths by considering universals, which sum up and interpret individual things. Through the ability to understand universals, people come in touch with eternal truths; without it they would be forever trapped in the world of their immediate experience.

Greek terms:

sarx – the physical body (flesh and blood)
soma – the organized body, with its activities and characteristics
psyche – the sensations and emotions (also found in animals)
pneuma – the rational, spiritual aspect of humankind; mental activity
nous – the thinking mind

In Greek thought there is no distinction between your inner state of consciousness and the thing of which you are conscious. In other words, suppose you experience something as cold, your experience is of the coldness of that thing. There is no separate thing called 'an experience of coldness' that goes on unobserved in your mind. They did not ask (as Descartes and later philosophers did) 'how does my experience of cold relate to the cold I experience?' For the ancient Greeks, the distinctive thing about humans was their ability to reflect on 'coldness' as a universal concept, not the location of some ghostly 'coldness' going on in their heads!

Note:

The important thing here is to note the distinction between psyche (in the sense of animal life, awareness, sensations etc.) and pneuma (mental activity):

- For the Greeks, sense perception was on the 'body' side of the body/mind dualism.
- Later, Descartes (in the 17th century) included in the 'mind', all the feelings and sensations that he could describe, but which he could not locate physically.

So, when we come to look at dualism, we need to be aware that, within Western thought, there have been two distinct forms – the pre-Cartesian form, with mental activity distinguished from the body and its sensations, and the Cartesian (i.e. from Descartes), where everything non-physical becomes part of 'mind'.

Aquinas

Aquinas followed Aristotle, in seeing the soul as that which *animated* the body, giving it form and life (indeed, Aquinas uses the Latin term *anima* for the soul):

> ‘*Animate* means living and *inanimate* non-living, so *soul* means that which first *animates* or makes alive the living things with which we are familiar.’ (*Summa Theologiae* Vol. II 75:1)

> ‘Now the soul is what makes our body live; so the soul is the primary source of all those activities that differentiate levels of life: growth, sensation, movement, understanding. So, whether we call our primary source of understanding mind or soul, it is the form of our body.’ (*Summa Theologiae* Vol. II 76:1)

So we have two distinct but compatible ideas:

- that the soul is what ‘animates’ the body and gives it form
- that reason is what distinguishes humankind from other species.

Note:

The term used for ‘soul’ in the Hebrew Scriptures (the Old Testament) is ruach. This can perhaps best be translated as ‘breath’. God breathes life into an inanimate body; he gives it breath. Your soul therefore, in Old Testament terms, is what makes you a living thing.

In the later Old Testament writings, there is more emphasis on an other-worldly destiny for the ‘soul’, a religious theme that was developed particularly in response to persecution and martyrdom. But in the earlier period, the emphasis is very much on this world. It is probable that this shift was under the impact of Greek thought where, as we have seen, there was more of a division of mind and body, with the former separable from the latter.

In the New Testament the Greek terms used for the self are as set out above. It is important to distinguish between sarx, which has a very physical and earthy connotation and soma, which is an ordered body.

The Greek influence is more clearly seen in Gnostic writings, where people are divided up according to their spiritual disposition, the most elevated of whom were the pneumatikoi (from pneuma) – the spiritual ones.

This is a huge and complex subject, and there is no scope to pursue it here, other than to note where the body/soul division comes. For most biblical writers, the soul is concerned with feelings and actions – with the whole process of living – it is not simply the rational mind.

Descartes

Descartes' starting point in the quest for knowledge, 'I think, therefore I am', implied a radical distinction between the world of matter, known to the senses, and the world of thought, known (at least in one's own case) directly. They are two different realms; distinct but interacting.

Descartes recognised that the mind is able to control the mechanical working of the body, and therefore needed to find some point of interaction between mind and body, because in all other respects he considered the body to be controlled by mechanical forces.

In other words:

I decide to move my arm (a mental act) and as a result my arm actually moves (a physical act). If the mental and the physical worlds are totally different, how is that possible?

Descartes suggested that it was done through the pineal gland – a part of the brain, sitting conveniently between right and left hemispheres, for which he could find no other function.

There is a danger of imagining the mind as some kind of subtle, invisible body, existing in the world of space and time, yet not subject to its usual laws of cause and effect. This, of course, is a rather crude caricature of what Descartes and other dualists have actually claimed. (It is also an important caricature, having been used by Ryle in *The Concept of Mind* (1949), a most influential book for an understanding of the mind/body issue, where he called the Cartesian view the 'official view' and labelled the mind 'the ghost in the machine'.)

The essential thing for Descartes is that mental reality is not empirical and therefore not in the world of space. The mind is not located in the body (it is **not** the same thing as the brain). He arrived at the absolute dualism between the physical world and himself as a thinking thing, simply because his own act of thinking was the one thing he could not doubt.

Notice how radical a change came about with Descartes:

- The 'Forms' of Plato were **out there in the world**, although they were capable of being understood by the rational mind. The Greek term used for 'Form' was 'idea'.
- The distinctive thing about human reason was that it was able to appreciate the 'idea' rather than just responding to the particular thing that confronted it.
- By contrast, for Descartes, 'ideas' were **in the mind**, not out there in the world waiting to be grasped. He saw them as **the contents of the mind**.

Descartes therefore introduced a radical dualism of mind and body, with all feelings, sensations and thoughts on one side (things known only to the person experiencing them) and the physical (publicly observable) body on the other.

This was *not* the mind/body dualism of the Greeks, nor of the Bible or of Christian belief. But this radical, 'Cartesian' dualism came to dominate the philosophical debate.

A note of caution:

We need to look at the way in which dualism, materialism and idealism are presented in the philosophy of mind, simply because they have influenced the philosophy of religion, and it is clear that some of the options are incompatible with, for example, ideas of immortality or free will required for a religious or moral response to life. But in doing so, we should keep in mind that the mind/body 'problem' presented here is largely a response to Descartes, and was not an issue during the formative period of any of the major world religions.

Various forms of dualism:

Interactionism

Descartes held that the body could affect one's state of consciousness and also that one's consciousness could affect one's body. The most obvious examples of this are the increased heartbeat when one is frightened or excited. Here the emotion gives rise to a physical change. Similarly, if the body lacks food or oxygen, the mind will become dull and muddled, and if the body is injured the mind may register pain, anger or fear to such an extent that rational thought becomes impossible.

At one level, therefore, interactionism is obvious – there needs to be some way in which minds and bodies interact in order to make sense of our experience.

Descartes, as we noted above, believed that the pineal gland was the point at which the mind and body acted upon one another. But this interaction itself is very curious, given the radically different natures of mind and body. The pineal gland is definitely part of the body – even if it was to Descartes a sensitive and mysterious part. How then could its physical nature respond to that which was not physical at all?

Having set up a great gulf between mind and body, he strains to establish their point of contact – it is almost as if Descartes realised that such a radical dualism could not account for the normal interactions between the physical and mental aspects of our experience.

But how exactly is this interaction to come about? Here are some theories:

Occasionalism

On the occasion of my being hit over the head with a cricket bat, there is a simultaneous but uncaused feeling of pain! The two systems (physical and mental) do not have a direct causal connection. The philosopher Malebranche suggested that whenever he wanted to move his arm, it was actually moved by God.

Pre-established harmony

The physical and mental realms are separate and independent processes. Each appears to influence the other, but in fact they are independent but running in harmony. This view was put forward by Geulinx, a Dutch follower of Descartes. It is also found in Leibniz, who holds that ultimately everything is divisible again and again until you arrive at monads – simple entities without extension, and therefore mental. These monads cannot act upon one another, for each develops according to its own nature, but a complex being comprises countless monads. How do they all work together to produce intelligent activity? Leibniz argued that there must be a pre-established harmony, organizing the otherwise independent monads. As far as human persons are concerned, Leibniz held that there is a dominant monad (a soul) and that God had established that the other monads that form this complex person work in harmony with it.

Note:

'Pre-established harmony' may seem one of the most bizarre of the mind-body theories, but in Leibniz it has a very specific purpose, and one which has important implications for both metaphysics and the philosophy of religion. Leibniz was concerned to preserve the idea of teleology (i.e. that the world is organised in a purposeful way) in the face of the mechanistic science and philosophy of his day.

If everything is locked into a series of causes, what room is left for a sense of purpose or for God? Leibniz's answer is that the individual monads of which everything is comprised do not actually affect one another. Rather, God has established a harmony by which they can work together.

Epiphenomenalism

If mind and body are not separate things interacting, then one of them must be the product of the other. Epiphenomenalism is the name given to the view that the brain and nervous system are so complex that they give the *impression* of individuality and free choice. Although totally controlled by physical laws, we 'seem' to have an independent mind. This is the closest that a dualistic view comes to materialism. The essential thing here is that mind does not influence the body – what appears to us as the mind is no more than a product of the complexity of the body's systems.

The various things that I think, imagine, picture in my mind are *epiphenomena*. They arise out of and are caused by electrical impulses that move between brain cells, but they are not to be identified with those phenomena themselves (i.e. they are not electrical impulses), rather, they are 'above' (epi-) those phenomena and produced by them.

Example:

Imagine a robot, programmed by computer. A simple version could be a source of amusement, as it attempts to mimic human behaviour. But as the memory capacity of the computer is increased, the process of decision-making that the programme makes possible is elaborated to the point at which it becomes so complex that the computer takes on a definite character.

In this case the character can be seen to be produced by the computer's memory: that is epiphenomenalism.

Double aspect theory

If mind and body are not separate things that interact, and if one is not the product of the other, there remains the possibility that they are simply two ways of looking at the same thing. This 'double aspect' theory was set out by Spinoza and is sometimes called the 'identity hypothesis'. According to this theory, ideas and brain activity are simply two aspects of the same thing. (Thinking is thus the **inner** aspect of which brain activity is the **outer** aspect.)

Comment:

There are many other things to which a double-aspect theory could be applied. Music could be seen as the inner, cultural aspect of which sound waves of particular frequencies are the outer, physical aspect. Without sound waves, no music. But music is not something **else**, caused by the sound waves. Music **is** the sound waves, but experienced and described in a different way.

Spinoza argued that everything is both conscious and extended; all reality has both a mental and a physical aspect. The mind and body cannot be separated, and therefore there can be no life beyond this physical existence. Spinoza also held that freedom was an illusion, caused by the fact that we simply do not know all the real causes of our decisions.

But is the 'double aspect' a matter of reality or of description? In *Philosophy and the Mirror of Nature* (an important book for anyone wanting to look further into these issues), R Rorty asks:

> ❛ How... do we know when we have two ways of talking about the same thing (a person, or his brain) rather than descriptions of two different things? ❜ (p.29)

And this leads on to one of the fundamental problems of speaking about the private sensations that people 'have':

> ❛ The neo-dualist is no longer talking about how people feel but about feelings as little self-subsistent entities, floating free of people in the way in which universals float free of the instantiations. ❜ (p.30)

Comment:

It seems that Rorty has touched on a major theme here: that, in a dualist way of describing feelings, an aspect of human experience (the feelings) are somehow detached from the act of experiencing them, and are allowed a separate existence. For example: I feel happy on several occasions, but I am then described as experiencing 'happiness' as though it were something separate from what I actually felt. Once that separate existence is accepted, there arises the problem of how to relate it to the body and to the original situations. This is another example of the issue about Plato's 'Forms' – is there a 'form' of a tree over and above all the particular trees? And are there feelings (like happiness) that exist independently of my feeling happy on occasions?

Materialism

You can avoid all problems of relating minds to bodies if you explain everything in terms of physical objects. For a materialist, the mind or 'self' is nothing more than a way of describing physical bodies and their actions, including their brain activity. We may experience something as a thought or emotion, but in fact it is nothing more than electrical impulses in the brain, or chemical or other reactions in the rest of the body.

Some situations tend to confirm this materialist view. If a person suffers brain damage, his or her character may be changed. In severe cases he or she may not appear to be a person at all, but merely a living body, devoid of all the normal attributes of mind.

Materialism takes what is called a **reductionist** approach to mental activity. A person is 'nothing but' a brain, attached to a body and nervous system, so the person is 'reduced to' these things.

Comment:

The 'nothing but' distinguishes materialism from other theories, for nobody would deny that, in some sense, a person is related to a brain, in the same way as a symphony is related to vibrations in the air. The essential question is whether or not it is possible to express a 'something more', if the materialist position seems inadequate.

When you see people waving to you, all you actually see are arm movements, caused by the contraction of muscles, produced by chemical changes, which are brought about by electrical impulses in their brains. Does that indicate that they are friendly? That they know you? That they have minds as well as bodies? That they have freely chosen to act in this way? That they have previously recognised you, had friendly thoughts towards you, and therefore decided to wave?

The act of waving is explained in terms of a material chain of cause and effect. That chain is, for practical purposes, infinite – it depends upon the whole way in which the universe is constructed. There is no point in that chain for some 'mind' to have its say. The world of sense experience is a closed system, and everything in it is totally determined. That is the materialist perspective.

Behaviourism is the term used for the rather crude materialist theory that mental phenomena are in fact simply physical phenomena. Crying out and rubbing a part of the body is what pain is about. Shouting and waving a fist is what anger is about. All mental states are reduced by the behaviourist to things that can be observed and measured.

Comment:

I can think before I speak, or before I write; but for a behaviourist there is nothing other than the words or the writing. To know a feeling, for a behaviourist, one must observe behaviour.

Ryle

A particularly influential form of behaviourism is 'logical behaviourism', which is based on our use of language, and this was presented by Gilbert Ryle in *The Concept of Mind* (1949). He suggests that to speak of minds and bodies as though they were equivalent things is a 'category mistake'. To explain what he means by this he uses the example of someone visiting a university and seeing many different colleges, libraries and research laboratories. The visitor then asks 'But where is the University?' The answer, of course, is that there is no university over and above all its component parts that have already been visited. The term 'university' is a way of describing all of these things together – it is a term from another category, not the same category as the individual components.

In the same way, Ryle argued that you should not expect to find a 'mind' over and above all the various parts of the body and its actions, for 'mind' is a term from another category, a way of describing bodies and the way in which they operate. This he claims is the fundamental flaw in the traditional dualistic approach to mind and body (which he attributes to Descartes and terms the 'ghost in the machine'):

> ❝ When two terms belong to the same category, it is proper to construct conjunctive propositions embodying them. Thus a purchaser may say that he bought a left-hand glove and a right-hand glove, but not that he bought a left-hand glove, a right-hand glove and a pair of gloves.... Now the dogma of the Ghost in the Machine does just this. It maintains that there exist both bodies and minds; that there occur physical processes and mental processes; that there are mechanical causes of corporeal movements and mental causes of corporeal movements. I shall argue that these and other analogous conjunctions are absurd; but, it must be noticed, the argument will not show that either of the illegitimately conjoined propositions is absurd in itself. I am not, for example, denying that there occur mental processes. Doing long division is a mental process and so is making a joke. But I am saying that the phrase 'there occur mental processes' does not mean the same sort of thing as 'there occur physical processes', and, therefore, that it makes no sense to conjoin or disjoin the two. ❞
>
> (Ryle, *The Concept of Mind*, Peregrine Books p.23)

Ryle is primarily concerned with language: his book is about what we mean when we speak about the 'mind'. When we speak about the mind of another person we are not claiming to have any privileged information about their inner mental operations; all we are actually describing are activities performed by the body.

An example:

If I say that someone is intelligent, I do so on the basis of what he or she has said or done. Descriptions of mental states depend upon information provided by physical bodies, activities and forms of communication.

- Think of a person you know.
- Consider exactly what it is you mean when you describe that person's personality or mind. Think of particular qualities that you would ascribe to him or her.
- Consider the evidence you could give to back up your view of these qualities.
- Consider what would have to happen in order for you to be persuaded that you were mistaken about him or her.

Clearly, we can get to know another person, but if Ryle is correct and there is no 'inner' self to be found, in what therefore does the personality consist? His answer is in terms of 'dispositions'. These are the qualities that make me what I am; the propensity to behave in a particular way in a particular situation; the sort of beliefs and knowledge that habitually inform my actions and words. If I say that someone is 'irritable' I do not mean that I have some privileged access to an 'irritability factor' in their mind, I just mean that, given a situation that is not to his or her liking, he or she is likely to start complaining, sulking, etc. In other words, the irritability is simply a way of describing a disposition.

Thus, for Ryle, the ascription of mental predicates (clever, etc.) does not require the existence of a separate, invisible thing called a mind. The description 'clever' indeed refers to the way in which something is done, but, equally, cleverness cannot be **defined** simply in terms of that action. What is clever for one person might not be so for another, and the mental description refers more to the way in which the individual person habitually relates to the world, and the expectation a person would have of him or her, rather than some special quality of an action that makes it clever.

Comment:

A child is 'clever' if it learns to stagger to its feet and totter a few paces forward before collapsing down on the ground again. The same is not claimed for the drunk who performs a similar set of movements. If Ryle wishes to dismiss the 'ghost in the machine' he must equally dismiss the 'ghost in the action', for mental predicates refer to, but are not defined by, individual actions.

Actors create problems. I may shout, cry, hold the afflicted part of my body; I may scream and roll on the ground, curl up, look ashen: people will say I am in pain. But none of these things is actually the pain I am experiencing. I may watch an actor performing all these things, but, because he or she is acting, I do not imagine that there is any actual pain. Yet, if being in pain is actually identified with those things (as Ryle implies), then the actor is in pain.

But what if (doing the reverse of the actor) you disguise your mental state by refusing to act as you would normally? What if you are angry and yet you persist in smiling?

Now 'angry', according to behaviourism, does not describe some ghostly feature of the person in question; it describes a series of actions – scowling, shaking a fist etc. The person who does not perform any of these things, but is nonetheless 'angry' is therefore said to have a **disposition** to do these things. To be angry means to *want* to do these things, even if you don't **actually** do them.

How then would you define 'angry'? Clearly, you would have to list an almost infinite number of possible activities. Another problem: if you speak about 'dispositions to act', you have to explain what a disposition is, and why on occasions it may be resisted.

Comment:

An itch may be a disposition to scratch, but if I resist that disposition, it implies that 'I' am in a position to consider options and make choices – and surely that sort of language presupposes exactly the kind of independent mental activity that behaviourism is trying to avoid.

Idealism

Idealism is the theory that everything we know is in the mind – that reality comprises ideas. Descartes came to the view that the only thing he could not doubt was the existence of himself as a thinking being. What of the external world? You know your own thoughts directly, but the external world is in fact no more than an inference from what comes to you though your senses .

Kant set philosophy on a sound scientific basis by making the 'outer' world of space and time part of the 'inner' world of the mind, since he argued that the mind imposed these concepts on its experience. The whole knowable world for Kant was one of phenomena (what we experience); we cannot know things as they are in themselves.

Example:

I may think that I am typing this book into a real, actual computer. I may feel my fingers on the keyboard. But does it really exist? What do I actually know? I know the feeling in my fingers and the visual experience of shapes on a screen – in other words, what I know are the *ideas*, the interpretations of experience that my mind puts together and calls 'my computer'.

Idealism may sound crazy. The difficulty (given the parameters of the debate set out by Descartes and Kant) is to know how to *prove* that it is crazy.

One idealist philosopher, Leibniz, has been mentioned already. He argued that everything could be reduced to monads, which were so small that they could not be considered as having a physical dimension at all, and were therefore thought of as mental. Another is Bishop Berkeley (1685–1753).

An obvious question to ask of idealism is this: 'If everything is in the mind, how is it that we see the world as an orderly place? How can several people see exactly the same thing at the same time? If things only really exist in terms of my perception of them, do they cease to exist when I look away?' Berkeley's answer to this is that our experience is of things holding together and having continuity because God is always there observing them.

In other words:

I only know that something exists when I am there to perceive it. If it continues to exist, independent of any observer, there must be an omnipresent observer – God.

To sum up:

We can therefore sum up the broad philosophical debate about minds and bodies in this way. Either:

- everything is material and mind is an illusion;
- everything is mental, and the material body is an illusion;
- there are both minds and bodies, distinct by reacting on one another, or
- there is something fundamentally wrong with looking at bodies and minds in this way. (In which case, Ryle's approach may be more in line with your thinking.)

Knowing our minds

How do we define 'mental'? Clearly, for Ryle, 'mental' is simply a way of describing a particular form of behaviour; but is that adequate? In the case of my own mind, I do not need to observe my behaviour. So what is it that I know?

One approach to this is to say that we each have privileged access to our own mind. I may think about something, or may feel a bodily sensation or emotion, and I just *know* what that is. Nobody else can tell me that I do not feel a particular pain, or that I am not really happy.

An example:

If I'm happy, I'm happy. Someone else may comment 'You're not really happy, you're just drunk!' But that solves nothing. He or she may observe the circumstances in which I claim to be happy, but at most they are the cause of my happiness, not the happiness itself. They might then say 'You're just pretending to be happy!' That won't do either. What they actually mean is that I am lying about my emotions. If I'm only pretending to be happy, then happiness is certainly not what I'm experiencing. Unless, of course, pretending is what makes me happy. In which case, my happiness may be neurotically motivated and perhaps rather warped – but it is happiness nonetheless. In the end it just comes down to this – I know what I think and feel; I have immediate access to that information, and nobody else does.

So a useful working definition of mental might be 'that about myself to which I have privileged access'. I could declare that there are parts of my anatomy to which I wish to claim privileged access: I may not want anyone looking at my big toenail, or sections of my brain. But the fact is that both my brain and my toenail are observable. Whether I allow it or not, they are theoretically in the public domain.

By contrast, mental events are not observable. Someone may comment that my description of being happy corresponds to electrical activity in particular parts of my brain, but that electrical activity, even if it is the physical cause of what I experience as happiness, is not the same thing as happiness.

At various times, philosophers have used different ways of describing the mental. We have already looked at the important feature of their non-observability and the privileged access that each of us has to our own mind. There are others. The following list is given by Rorty (p.35):

1 ability to know itself incorrigibly (privileged access)
2 ability to exist separately from the body
3 non-spatiality (having a nonspatial part or 'element')
4 ability to grasp universals
5 ability to sustain relations to the inexistent ('intentionality')
6 ability to use language
7 ability to act freely
8 ability to form part of our social group, to be 'one of us'
9 inability to be identified with any object 'in the world'

Notice how important for religion some of these are. **2** links with ideas of life after death, **3** and **9** mean that it is not part of 'this world' with its physical limitations, **4** means that it can grasp general concepts – love, justice, truth – which form an important part of religion. (Imagine trying to express religious ideas without the use of these universals!) **5** (intentionality) is the ability to imagine something which does not exist, to contemplate it, and perhaps to create it. We have a relationship with our ideas, hopes and dreams. Without that ability, faith and hope would have little meaning.

Joining souls to bodies?

Richard Swinburne (*Is There a God?* p. 90), having looked at the problems associated with the relationship between brain events and mental events, outlines what he sees as the theistic answer to the problem:

> ❛ But theism can provide an explanation of these things. God, being omnipotent, is able to join souls to bodies... he can make the souls in the first place and choose to which brain (and so body) each soul is to be connected when foetal brain events require a soul to be connected to the brain. ❜

Now this is typical of Swinburne's approach. Finding a problem that cannot be solved scientifically, he simply says, in effect, 'What if there is an omnipotent God? He could do that!' Therefore, in the absence of any better or simpler explanation, this is a reasonable one to hold.

But this begs many questions. What might it mean to 'make souls' in the first place? What is a soul like if not joined to a body? What can it mean to say that the one is joined to the other?

Notice that Swinburne takes a thoroughly dualist view of souls and bodies, one that has only come into the philosophy of religion since Descartes.

Previously, as we saw above in the case of Aquinas (following Aristotle) the soul was very much the *animating* aspect of the body. An animated body is a body with a soul; but to pretend that this means there is a separate thing called a 'soul' which needs to be hooked onto the body, is to create an unnecessary separate entity from the animated body. (Rather like Ryle's argument described above about the colleges and the university.) A thinking, willing, feeling, acting body, is one that already has the soul – it is already animated.

Identity and freedom

A new sense of 'oneself' is a feature of much religious experience; a religious conversion is about a life transformed. Whether through their moral rules, or in the process of confessing faults and receiving forgiveness, the rituals of organised religion look for the free choice of individuals to respond to 'God' or the spiritual path, and thus to enable their lives to be transformed.

A religion that claimed to make no difference would not survive for long. People want to understand what life is about, and to change their lives for the better – this is the impetus of much religious life. This aspect of religion requires us to consider the nature of the individual and his or her freedom to make and act on choices. Without the idea of a free self, morality makes no sense. Equally, a religious response makes no sense if we are mere puppets with fixed natures. In the earlier part of this chapter we set out some of the options for looking at 'selves' in terms of minds and bodies. Before assessing these for their implications for freedom, let us examine a very different approach to personal identity.

The postmodern self

According to the 'postmodern' movement in philosophy, you cannot get beyond the language and signs by which people communicate: there are no hidden meanings – everything is as it is perceived to be. We live and express ourselves within a world of words and images, and we cannot get beyond them. Don Cupitt, a radical Christian theologian, explores the nature of the self from a religious perspective but within this overall postmodern view of the world.

> ❛ People are what they look like and what they say; they are the text of their own lives. ❜
>
> (*The Time Being*, Don Cupitt, SCM Press 1992, p.35)

In other words, you live on the surface of your life and you are the communicative signs that link you with the rest of the world.

In this case, is there to be any view of the self other than what a person actually reveals? Is there any sort of continuity holding together all the various things a person says and does throughout his or her life? What makes me me? Cupitt's view is that the distinctive thing is the network of communication within which a person lives and acts.

What counts in the end is not found in some analysis of the self (of the sort that we have described above) but rather in the way that the person has related to the rest of the world.

> ❛ The question about the self, then, is going to come out like this: your life will have been worth living if one day a decently plausible story can be told about how you gave it for a cause. ❜
>
> (op. cit. p.45)

Now although this sounds unlikely at first glance, in practice it is exactly the way people are presented. Take the example of a cinema film. A character is presented and one can identify with him or her – one can get involved, and be moved emotionally by what happens on the screen. Yet all that is known of the person acting are the words and images portrayed. There is no other way to get to know the character. Yet our knowledge of a character in a film does not seem to be radically different from our knowledge of other people. Soap opera actors become part of viewers' daily lives, they seem to be as 'real' as anyone else.

The same could be said of the way of summarising a person's life. Funeral orations speak of the person's links with the rest of the world – relatives and friends, organisations, causes supported. Qualities are described in terms of typical actions – he or she was always someone you could trust, or someone who would help generously in situations of need.

This presentation of the self – and it is the stuff of which all biographies are made – does not require any privileged information. It is merely an examination and presentation of the surface of things; of the empirical evidence. 'He was a kind person' does not mean that there is some mysterious other ghost of a person who is seen to have the quality 'kind', it just means that the observation of the actions merit that description. The person is not first 'kind' and then, as a result, decides to do certain acts of kindness – they do those acts of kindness, and that is what causes them to be called 'kind'. In many ways, although coming to it from a postmodern route, through the sharing of the surface of things and the signs by which life is constituted, this is not too far removed from Ryle's criticism of the 'ghost in the machine'.

The essential difference between Ryle and, say, Cupitt, is that whereas Ryle comes from a tradition which is basically reductionist, seeing the physical as the only reality, Cupitt and others of the postmodern viewpoint see language and communication as the basis of reality. A person is therefore a series of events, of communications, given coherence only by being presented together. But of course, such a presentation is always open to question, for it could have been told otherwise:

> ‘A person is only a story, and stories are inherently ambiguous.’
> (op. cit. p. 46)

The self, for postmodernism, is therefore a temporal procession of events, it is not an external fixed entity of any sort. This is not new. Hume's view of the self (coming from an empirical standpoint) is much the same. According to Hume we are:

> ‘.. a bundle or collection of different perceptions, which succeed one another with an inconceivable rapidity, and are in perpetual flux and movement. The mind is a kind of theatre, where several perceptions successively make their appearance; pass, re-pass, glide away, and mingle in an infinite variety of postures and situations.’
> (*A Treatise of Human Nature* Book I, Part IV, Section VI)

And this view has an even older history, for it is a key feature of the Buddhist view of the self. In Buddhism, all things are interconnected, you are the centre of a web of causes and conditions that stretch to the ends of the universe. You are at every moment totally dependent upon things other than yourself. There is no separable, permanent ‘you’ to be found.

This is not a negative view of the self. In fact, Buddhism claims that the false notion of a fixed self is the cause of much of the world's suffering. Rather, it recognises that everything is in a constant process of change, and that we have a choice – either to recognise and adapt to that flow of changes, using every situation creatively, or to fight a losing battle to keep ourselves fixed and intact, a battle which will certainly be lost when we die. By concentrating on the present moment and present experience, reality for Buddhists is ‘eternal’ – beyond the changes of the world of *samsara* – and therefore touches on a level of stillness, non grasping and happiness which is termed *nirvana*.

Comment:

There is, of course, far more that one could say about the Buddhist idea of the self. It is mentioned here in order to put the ‘postmodern’ self into perspective. Although it raises many problems for Western religion, the postmodern approach is neither totally new, nor incompatible with fundamental religious experience.

Freedom?

What makes us do what we do, and how does this relate to bodies and minds? We know two things:

- At any moment, the various parts of my body (including my brain) work according to the laws of nature. Also, I can trace back a theoretically infinite succession of causes of any bodily activity. I do what I do, physically, because of what the whole of the rest of the universe does and has done.
- At any moment, I am aware of making choices, of moving my limbs, or speaking words that will influence the actions of others. As a thinking, living, acting self I set up chains of causes that theoretically extend to infinity in all directions. The rest of the world will be as it will be partly (even if that part is infinitely small) because of my action.

Neither of these things can be denied: the first because it is the basis of all science and all common sense; the second because it is the basis of all human experience. Any view of the world that does not take these into account is going to be rather limited.

The issue of freedom and determinism occurs at many points in the philosophy of religion: personal freedom and the nature of the self; miracles; science and religion. We need to ask in what ways the self is determined.

The first thing to be clear about is that science, in considering causal connections, will always seek (but never actually achieve) an exhaustive explanation for every event. In other words, science will always give a reason why something happens, or, if it does not know the reason, it will still assume that a reason will eventually be found.

Hence, from a scientific and materialist point of view, freedom is always an illusion. It represents a point of indeterminacy, which it is science's task to whittle down by successively accurate explanations.

In terms of the self, there are two areas of science that attempt to give explanations of human activity: psychology and sociology. Psychology seeks to formulate the principles that lie behind human attitudes and actions. Faced with the freely chosen action of an individual, it seeks to show psychological causes (perhaps in terms of early experience, or established patterns of relationships) to 'explain' the choice. Although it is not generally set out in this way, the ultimate goal of psychology is therefore a total explanation – people would be shown to be acting in conformity with their deep psychological motives.

Following the same line of reasoning, many features of religion, including the free choice of individuals to take part in it, may be related by sociology to the needs of society, and therefore to the conscious or unconscious pressure to conform to religious social norms.

Comment:

The crucial thing to consider here is whether psychology, in giving an explanation for human dispositions and behaviour, has thereby removed freedom from the individual. If you hold that it offers an exhaustive explanation for all human choices, then there is little scope for religion to make any difference. At most, religion (as in Freud's view of the 'universal obsessional neurosis') would be seen as the product of needs, the origins of which are explained by psychology. On the other hand, if you see these psychological theories as explaining the influences on individuals and groups, but that those influences are only a partial limitation of human freedom (after all, we always act within limited spheres), then there will still be room for religion to 'make a difference'.

Of course, if the identity hypothesis is correct (the 'double aspect theory', see above p125), there is no freedom. Brain activity, like all physical processes, is limited by physical laws and is in theory predictable. But if mental events are simply another aspect of these physical events, they must also be limited by physical laws. If all my action is theoretically predictable, how can I be free?

Kant, on the other hand, held that we could be both phenomenally conditioned and noumenally free: as we are in ourselves, we experience freedom, but from the point of view of an observer (for whom our actions are 'phenomena') everything we do is causally conditioned and therefore predictable.

In other words:

I know I'm free; you perceive I'm not. I can choose anything I like: the better you know me, the more likely you are to predict my choice correctly.

Freedom: West and East

For Western religions, human freedom is important, since it is necessary for moral responsibility. Although God is described as omnipotent and omniscient, he is said to allow human freedom, even though he could overrule it, if he chose. Of course, if God *did* overrule freedom, people would become little more than puppets, and the whole idea of religion in terms of personal choice, insight and response to God would be meaningless.

In Eastern thought, the issue is presented rather differently. The concept of *karma* in Indian thought refers to the results of morally significant action. One's actions today will have an effect on what happens tomorrow. In this sense, freedom is limited by past karma, and, for this reason, karma is sometimes presented as fatalistic. On the other hand there has to be a measure of freedom in order for there to be any present action that can generate karma. Particularly in Buddhist thought, this leads to a creative awareness of freedom working within the conditions that exist at any given moment – and a factor in those conditions (and also in one's ability to respond to them) will be the result of one's past action or karma.

Life beyond death

In *Phaedo*, Plato argued for the immortality of the soul on two grounds:

- That the body was composite, and was therefore perishable, whereas the mind was simple, and therefore imperishable.
- That the mind had knowledge of the universals, the eternal forms (such as 'goodness itself') rather than individual events and objects. Because it related to the eternal realm (the forms being immortal, because not limited by particular instances), the soul was itself immortal and able to survive the body. In other words: truths of reason do not change or die, therefore reason is the link between human life and the eternal.

Few people today would wish to take up these arguments in the form that Plato presented them. But they persist in two widely accepted features of the mind/body question:

- That the mind is not within space/time and not material – and thus that it should not be identified with its material base in the brain.

- That the mind functions through communication and is not simply limited to the operations of a single particular body, i.e. the mind is not subject to physical limitations, and is related to transpersonal communication.

For a materialist, it is difficult to see how there could be life after death. The most that could happen is that the same material that composed the first person could be brought together again to form another person. And in that case, how could you establish an identity between the two?

Clearly, the various forms of dualism are more compatible with the concept of life after death, although there is the general problem of what continuity there could be. What would it be like to be a mind without a body?

In considering these things, we need to take into account two important distinctions: the first is between 'eternal' and 'everlasting' when applied to the self; the second concerns the difference between immortality and resurrection. By way of comparison, we will then also look briefly at Eastern concepts.

Eternal and everlasting

In considering concepts of God we looked at the two senses of 'eternal'. On the one hand it could refer to that which was **beyond time**, and on the other it could be used in the sense of 'everlasting', in other words, existing in time but of **endless duration**.

When considering 'life after death', we come up against the same issue:

- Is 'eternal life' timeless? If so, it implies that there is an aspect of ourselves that is outside time and space. Schleiermacher (see p.27) took this view when he described the immortality offered by religion as being at one with the infinite. In this sense, eternal life is not something that you get later on, but something that you have **now**. The difference between that and everything else you may have now is that it is not subject to change.
- Does 'eternal life' mean a life of endless duration? If so, did we have that life before our birth into this one? The Hindu concept of reincarnation implies that the self is neither born nor dies, so that, for example, in killing the body the warrior does not kill the true self.
- If endless duration is thought of as an endless continuation of something which has had a starting point in time (at our birth),

the self is a very unusual concept – it is something that can come into existence, but cannot go out of existence again. It is subject to change (at least as far as this present life's experience is concerned) but cannot change to the point that it ceases to be itself.

Attached to this last option are questions about the nature of personal identity and eternal life. Is the self that can move on into an endless life after this one, an expression of the last state that the earthly self achieved? If so, eternal life (or heaven?) is going to be rather a sad place, populated by the elderly and dying. Or is there some point in life which is the definitive self that will inherit eternal life? If so, how can such a point be determined, since there is no point between birth and death when we stop changing?

Traditionally, eternal life has been associated with relationships, in the sense that people might be reunited with those they love in heaven. The small, innocent child my grandfather knew (and might conceivably want to meet again) is the same person that a grandchild of mine would know only as an elderly bore! What can identity and relationships mean in a situation of eternal life?

The ever-changing self takes a theoretically infinite number of forms. Each person with whom, in this life, it has a relationship, also has a theoretically infinite number of forms, and so on. We know, recognise and relate to one another in a situation of constant change. How could we relate, and with whom, if there were no changes?

And this brings us back to questions about the nature of the self, and the fact that everything we know as 'self' now depends upon our physical body and environment.

A personal comment:

How can we imagine eternal life?

As a child, I had a recurrent nightmare in which I died and found myself flying forward over the surface of an absolutely flat, featureless world. On and on I flew, with that same drab world rushing past on either side. Then I suddenly realised that this movement was everlasting: it would never come to an end. I used to awake rigid with fear. (Clearly, part of my problem was the naive idea that my 'self', a self of flesh and bones and definite features, could be projected into a timeless and directionless environment.)

The nightmares only lifted when, pondering the nature of time and eternity, I realised that the same featureless world must logically have been there for me before my birth. I tried to imagine myself as baby moving backwards through such an emptiness – but somehow the fear had gone, for this was something that must *already* have happened. How then could I fear it?

Clearly, I should fear a timelessness after my death as little as the timelessness before my birth. We have come into being and will pass out of being. What you go to is what you have already known, so what is there to fear?

At the age of eleven or so, I had enough to fear at school, without coping with eternity – but at least, the attempt to reduce eternity to a quasi-extension of present experience, with all its attendant feelings of being lost and isolated, was over. **Whatever eternity is, it is bound to be familiar. Perhaps that is why those who have near-death experiences tend to feel that they are entering a place of light, warmth and emotional positivity.**

Resurrection?

One problem raised by the idea of life after death is that of personal identity in the absence of a body. After all, what does it mean to be a person? If by 'person' you mean someone with whom you can have a relationship, who acts and speaks, then it is difficult to see what it could mean to say that a person exists after the death of his or her body – since the body is required for most of what passes as human personality.

This problem may be addressed by the idea of resurrection – that there can be another life at some point after death, in which one's body is restored, or one is given a new body. Here, of course there is no problem with identity, because there is a body through which to express it. Or is there? Hick (in his book *Death and Eternal Life*) raises this point by way of a story about a man who dies suddenly in London but who then, at the moment of death, appears in New York with an identical body, complete with all the memories that the London man had up to the point of death. He then asks, is it the same person?

Perhaps one might extend this question in terms of cloning. What if it were possible to create (before or after death) a body identical to one's own? This body, with its brain identical and living, would have the same characteristics and memory as oneself. Would it therefore be oneself? Could there be two of you? If so, then the idea of receiving an identical replacement in the future for the body that has died (as in the idea of resurrection) makes sense. If not, then what might be resurrected would not be oneself. One further extension of this is to ask to what extent one belongs to one's surroundings – and that, taken out of those surroundings, even if supplied with an identical body, one would be a different person.

Reviewing these issues in *An Introduction to the Philosophy of Religion*, Brian Davies concludes that death followed by resurrection is a logical possibility. This is an important step in the philosophy of religion – for if something is logically impossible, then there is no point in continuing to ask if it can actually be the case. On the other hand, just because something is logically possible, that does not imply that it is in fact the case. One might argue, for example, that it would not be sufficient to reconstruct an identical body, but that (in order to be truly oneself in this future resurrected life) one would need to have an identical world within which to express oneself.

But what is this saying? Something along the lines of: 'If there were an identical world to this one, in which I had an identical body and memory, then I would be the same person I am now?' Surely, this is simply a long-winded way of saying 'I am the person I am now'? In an identical world, I would be an identical person. That may be true, but it is simply a tautology – for the idea of an identical world and an identical body implies an identical me. It therefore asserts nothing about what may or may not be the case.

An example:

If I had a twin brother or sister, I would be one of a pair of twins. In examining me, there is no reason why I could not be one of a pair of twins. Therefore it is logically possible that I am a twin. In fact, I'm not. Logical possibility has a purely negative function. It can show what cannot be the case, but it can't say what is in fact the case.

There remains the fundamental problem of *which* body a person might receive post-death in order to be himself or herself. After all, the physical body is constantly changing. If personality implies relationships, at what age might I be considered the definitive 'me' for the purposes of physical resurrection?

Comment:

Relationships are only possible between entities of similar size and complexity. I can stand and wave. This will be interpreted as a gesture of welcome by another human being. Animals may not recognise the gesture but at least they will know that I am there, and take appropriate avoiding action if they fear me. On the other hand, I may wave in the night towards the Milky Way. It will not respond, since it is of a totally different order of magnitude.

Equally, the millions of microscopic organisms that live in my mouth and gut will not respond. They are not aware of being part of me. Indeed, are they part of me? Should they to be thought of as beings in their own right?

Individual cells will be growing and dividing, replicating themselves perfectly (I hope!) and digesting nutrients that the blood carries to them. They benefit from the dinner I have eaten, indeed they depend upon it, but they are unaware of me and I am largely unaware of them.

Time matters as well. Some things live and die so fast we have no time to mourn them. Our galaxy is at this moment eating another smaller one, yet that meal is being eaten so slowly that humankind's existence is as nothing to it.

All this is by way of emphasising that identity and relationships are features of creatures of a particular complexity and a particular time and space. If 'mind' is indeed separable from its physical matrix, if it loses the sense of time and place that nurtured it during what we know of its life, then there is little reason to think that it is something with which we could ever communicate.

Reincarnation

In Greek thought, as mentioned above, there is life before birth, as well as after death. If the soul is everlasting (as opposed to eternal) there seems no reason why it should not become embodied more than once, with a complete memory loss between one incarnation and the next.

In Hindu thought, the *atman* (or self) is eternal and also everlasting, so that it may be embodied many times. In the Gita, the most popular of all Hindu scriptures, Krishna says to Prince Arjuna, as he prepares for battle, that he can neither kill nor be killed. All he can do is slay the body.

Taken literally, one might imagine a simple succession of bodies, each becoming the vehicle for the soul. On the other hand, in the more philosophical tradition of Hindu thought, the eternal nature of the self implies that it can also be identified with all that exists.

> ❛ He who sees all beings in the self, and his self in all beings, he loses all fear. ❜ (*Isa Upanishad* 6)

It is important to get a balance between the literal sense of a soul taking successive incarnations, and the overall sense in the Upanishads (the more philosophical – rather than devotional, cultic or narrative – tradition within Hindu literature) of the self (Atman) being at one with the whole of reality (Brahman). In a way, the recognition of this oneness means that, with the dissolution of this body, the self is still 'at home' in a world teeming with life. Whether thought of literally, or in terms of a spiritual and emotional perspective, reincarnation is an expansion of the self whilst recognising that a self is always linked to the physical for its expression.

Re-becoming

The Buddhist concept of 're-becoming' is different from Hindu reincarnation in that there is no fixed, eternal *atman*. There is no 'thing' that can pass from life to life. This is simply an extension of the Buddhist view of the self within this life – a person does not have a fixed identity, but is constantly changing in response to conditions. Personal qualities and identity are ascribed in conventional language and may appear to be permanent, but ultimately all is subject to conditions and therefore to change. The idea that a self can be detached from its surroundings and continue an independent existence makes no sense within the overall Buddhist view.

In Buddhism, the process of influence that one life might have on another is based on the idea of *karma* – the working out of the effects of one's ethically significant actions. An image used to describe this is that of one flame lighting another. Nothing passes over from the first flame, but its presence ignites the second.

Some Buddhists take the idea of re-becoming in quite a literal sense – continuing the process beyond death into successive lives in a way that is similar to Hindu reincarnation. The Buddha himself refused to say what happens to an enlightened person after death, so Buddhists may choose to remain agnostic about the details of any such process.

Near death experiences

There is considerable evidence for the sort of experiences that people have after they lose consciousness and come close to death. Those who have survived such situations often describe themselves as floating and moving down a darkish tunnel towards light at the end. There is often a feeling that all will be well once they move out into that light. They may feel emotionally positive, may encounter people they have known, or religious figures, like Jesus or Krishna. They may also experience themselves as floating above their body, looking down on it as it lies on the field of battle or in the hospital operating theatre – recognising what is happening, but quite calm and detached.

A person who believes that there is life after death, and that the mind is separable from the body, will see these 'out of body' experiences as evidence for that belief. In terms of the emotions, it is interesting that the response to having recovered from a situation in which one has come close to death and had just such an experience is a loss of fear. Death is no longer seen as a threat.

There are medical hypotheses to account for some of these experiences. A shortage of oxygen to the brain may be an explanation for a situation where the centre of the visual field is an expanding disc of light – giving that experience of floating down a tunnel. Similarly, it is argued that, when someone is unconscious, the brain, starved of normal stimuli, is likely to create its own setting – something that does not correspond to any external state, but which feels as real as any other to the person experiencing it.

In terms of religion, near death experiences may therefore be considered as neutral. They happen to anyone, religious or not. They do not necessarily make the person who has them religious, although they do have the effect of taking away the fear of death. What is more, they may be taken either as proof of life after death, or as phenomena created by a brain in the last stages of its life, starved of oxygen and external stimuli.

Comment:

How you interpret near death experiences will depend largely upon your own presuppositions, and in any case they do not have the form of a logical proof one way or the other, fascinating though they may be.

Some conclusions

Some of the key features of religion rely on the free choice of individuals. Morality implies freedom, and any theory of the self that is incompatible with freedom will make nonsense of moral life.

Equally, a theory which identifies a person totally with a particular part of the physical world – the brain, for example – will imply that there is no possibility of that 'person' having any form of existence beyond the physical and temporal period of their bodily existence. Life after death then makes no sense.

What is less clear, however, is the value of the sort of dualism that Descartes introduced, and which has caused so much philosophical debate. It may not be wise to hold as 'mental' both the sensations which we receive and also the thoughts we have about those sensations. For one thing, the sensitive aspect of the self is very closely linked with the physical body and its environment, whereas the ability to reason (as in the earlier tradition) is a distinguishing mark of humans, and involves a process which is not limited to the world around us.

It is curious to reflect that many of the problems that concern the meaning of 'God' recur here in terms of the meaning of the self. 'God' and 'Self' function as a pair of concepts, and how you see one will influence how you see the other.

6

CAUSES, PROVIDENCE AND MIRACLES

Causes

In order to understand the religious problems associated with providence and miracles, it is necessary to reflect on the nature of change and causation.

When we looked at Aquinas' arguments for the existence of God, we saw that he held God to be the 'uncaused cause'. In other words, he looked at that which lay behind and was the cause of everything else, including the theoretically infinite number of lesser causes, and said that all would understand such an 'uncaused cause' to be God. God then, through the agency of lesser causes, sustains the whole world.

A similar argument was developed by Aquinas and later by Paley to the effect that God was the designer of the universe, on the analogy of human designers (an analogy of which Hume was critical, as we saw in chapter four). The argument focused on the apparent existence within the world of a sense of purpose and design, which was taken to indicate the existence of a designer.

Cause and purpose were thought (by Aquinas and others) to exist 'out there' in the universe – in other words, they were part of the world as we experience it. This was challenged by the philosopher Kant. In what is probably one of the most important turning points in the whole of Western philosophy, Kant (in his *Critique of Pure Reason*) argued that space, time and causality were not features of the world 'out there', but were necessary features of the way in which our minds understand the world. In other words, we impose the idea of causality on our experience. Everything has a cause, because we give it one – just as everything exists within time and space because that is the way we experience things.

Events and interpretations

When we reflect on Aquinas on the one hand and Kant on the other, we see two different processes at work:

- From Aquinas and others, there is the sense that causes are universal, everything has a cause which in turn has other causes. It is therefore natural to seek an overall cause – not just to start but to sustain the whole process.
- The act of experiencing the world is one in which our minds have a positive and creative role to play. What we understand depends upon the way in which our minds work and analyze the experiences they receive. When we talk about causes and about purposes, we are talking about how we experience things, not necessarily how things are in themselves. This is the central theme of Kant's philosophy.
- Taken together, these two processes show that, whatever facts about the world there are to be known, we can understand them only through a filter of mental operations, and those operations lead us to seek causes, whilst at the same time forcing us to recognise that we can never say, absolutely and definitely, that we know what caused any one particular thing. We will never be able to give an exhaustive explanation of the cause of anything, since the overall interlocking series of causes is theoretically infinite in extent.

For reflection:

Throw a stone into a lake and watch as the ripples radiate out across the smooth surface of the water. Now throw another stone and another. The older ripples keep moving outwards, but are now crossed by other, younger ones, and more, and more... Eventually you see the whole surface of the lake crossed and recrossed by ripples as they are reflected back from the shore.

Keep throwing stones. The surface is far from smooth now and your stones hit the water obliquely as they cut into ripples which are themselves crossed by other ripples. And now the ripples from new stones are distorted and lost almost at once.

Now take a small plastic duck and throw that into the water. Watch it bob about. Now ask yourself: Which of the stones I threw into the water is the cause of this or that particular movement of the duck? Clearly, by now, every stone has contributed something to that movement.

In logical arguments, we may be tempted to see causation in terms of a single series of events, each neatly and exclusively causing the next. In reality, that is never the case. Only the whole lake and every stone that has every been thrown into it will explain the movement of the duck. The causes of its movement aretheoretically infinite.

Chance and necessity

Once something has happened, the rational mind analyses the factors that have brought it about and then declares that it was necessary. It does not matter that it was not predicted, the point is that (with the benefit of hindsight) it is possible to see causes that were operative, and thus to see that no other outcome was possible. In this sense, everything is seen as necessary, or determined.

On the other hand, we are never in practice able to know all the causal factors at work at any one time. We cannot say, therefore, that we have evidence for the necessity of everything. It is possible (and, at the sub-atomic level, it is indeed the case) that a system of random chances operates at some point – spreading a sense of chance into an otherwise determined universe.

We are also aware of the experience of choice, we may place a bet on a race, or buy a lottery ticket. We believe that the result is not yet determined, and also that we are free to make a choice. If there were no freedom, and no chance that depended upon our exercising that freedom, then many common features of the world would become meaningless – for much of what we do depends upon unpredictability.

Example:

I play a game of chess. Strategies are planned, choices are made, both players are free to work out how best to guess and inhibit the choices that the opponent is likely to make. We are free to play the game, to win or lose, and it is that freedom (and the ability to manipulate it) that constitutes the skilled player.

On the other hand, every move on the board is carefully defined. I am not allowed to move my bishop sideways, but only diagonally. I may move only my own pieces, not those of my opponent. My pawns move forward, but cannot retreat.

Now it is possible that an observer, noting every move of the game, will conclude that there is no personal skill or freedom of choice involved – for every move has followed very carefully defined rules. There has been no breaking of rules, and therefore no freedom.

It may be argued that no two games are exactly the same, but our rule-bound observer will rightly comment that the differences do not depend upon flouting the rules, but simply in the sequence of movements that are made within those rules.

Am I free to win, or is the game determined?

In the case of the game of chess, the matter is fairly straightforward. We are free to move, but only within the predetermined rules of the game. Those rules may inhibit us, but also provide the structure within which we may exhibit our creativity and freedom.

When it comes to the ordinary events of life, the matter is more complex because (unlike the game) we do not know the extent of the rules under which we are playing. We are often surprised to find that there is something which we can or cannot do, because some other factor has come into play.

Example:

I decide to go for a stroll. It pours with rain. I am determined that the changed circumstances will not inhibit my freedom to walk, and stride off through the rain. A moment later, I am knocked over and killed by a car, which is being driven too fast in restricted visibility because the driver wanted...and so on.

I act within a network of circumstances that are caused by factors that are beyond my knowledge, and some of those factors are the 'free' choices of other people. Yet I still think of myself as free to act.

Science and causation

Modern science reveals that the apparent orderliness of nature is (at least in part) the product of randomness at the sub-automic level. Complexity and order emerge at a higher level out of a sequence of random events at a lower level. This suggests that we do not need to posit a single law-giver to account for order, nor are we entitled to examine occasions when the law has been set aside for some higher purpose. Orderliness and disorderliness occur simultaneously, and complex entities come into being whenever apparently chance events create the right conditions.

Of course, just because something has a causal explanation does not mean that God could not be active within it. The idea that divine causality *excludes* ordinary physical causality would imply that God operates as one cause alongside others in the space-time structure of the universe. On the other hand, if God's activity is thought to be present everywhere, then its absence or presence would not be noticed, for it would have no characteristics of its own. To say that God caused it would be no different from saying that it took place.

In Richard Dawkins' book *The Blind Watchmaker* (Longman, 1986) he shows that random changes can lead to an amazing variety of apparently 'designed' forms. This has implications for the traditional teleological argument for the existence of God. It also has implications for any system where the patterns observed in nature are taken to be the products of inflexible 'laws'.

Quantum theory also contributes to this issue, for it shows that a minute physical change in one place may lead to vast changes somewhere else in the universe. Everything is linked to everything else. Everything is thus conditioned by everything else.

The implication of this is that, if I am free, the choices I freely make will contribute to the sum of conditions in the universe which will, in turn have effect on everything that happens in the future. My freedom will therefore appear as part of a causal network the moment after it has been exercised.

Note:

Some of these issues will be considered again in chapter eight: 'Religion and Science'.

Providence

The definitions of 'provide', 'providence' and 'providential' in the Concise Oxford Dictionary hint at the problems that these words cause for religious belief:

- 'To provide' comes from the Latin (pro–videre: to see on behalf of) and means 'to make preparation' for someone's welfare. So, if God 'provides' for people, he sees their needs and makes preparations to help them.
- 'Providence' is 'foresight, timely care; thrift; beneficial care of God or nature'. The problem with this, from the perspective of the philosophy of religion, is the 'God or nature' option. How can you tell which is doing the providing? Are God and nature mutually exclusive benefactors? If nature provides, the religious person will ascribe such providence to God. If God provides, how can he do this except through nature?
- 'Providential' is defined as 'of or by divine foresight or interposition; opportune, lucky'. If something happens at an opportune moment, you are lucky. Someone who believes in God will say that it was not luck at all, but the foresight of God.

Providence, then – the belief that God provides what we need – arises from an overall view that nature expresses God's purpose (as in the teleological argument, see p.102). If God is omnipotent and loving he might well be expected to provide for his creation. But a major problem with such 'providence' was set out by Hume in his *Dialogues*...

> ❛ Health and sickness, calm and tempest, with an infinite number of other accidents whose causes are unknown and variable, have a great influence both on the fortunes of particular persons and on the prosperity of public societies; and indeed all human life, in a manner, depends on such accidents. A being, therefore, who knows the secret springs of the universe might easily, by particular volitions, turn all these accidents to the good of mankind and render the whole happy, without discovering himself in any operation. A fleet whose purposes were salutary to society might always meet with a fair wind. Good princes enjoy sound health and long life... One wave, a little higher than the rest, by burying Caesar and his fortune in the bottom of the ocean, might have restored liberty to a considerable part of mankind. There may, for aught we know, be good reasons why Providence interposes not in this manner, but they are unknown to us; and, though the mere supposition that such reasons exist may be sufficient to save the conclusion concerning the Divine attributes, yet surely it can never be sufficient to *establish* that conclusion. ❜ (*Dialogues* Book XI p.74)

In other words, we do not have evidence to suggest that God (via nature) benefits the good and frustrates the evil. 'If God acts providentially, why does he not...?' is a question we will need to consider again in the chapter on evil and suffering.

General or specific providence?

As we have seen already, and will examine again under 'Religion and Science', it is possible to interpret the world as purposive, designed specifically to enable intelligent human life to develop. If any of the basic features of the universe were other than they are, then we would not be here (this is sometimes referred to as the 'anthropic principle').

In general terms, therefore, one might argue that God's providence is shown in all the laws of nature, and in the universal constants which have determined the way in which the universe has unfolded.

You do not need to have a religious viewpoint to see that certain species might have a better than even chance of survival. A secular interpretation of the opportunities afforded by 'chance' allow that survival may not be random, but that life is able to 'tame' chance, breaking down the very improbable into the less improbable. (In other words, we know how to take our chances when they arise and capitalise on them – making our evolutionary success more likely.) This 'taming' of chance is set out by Richard Dawkins in *The Blind Watchmaker*.

A religious person will want to go one step further. John Polkinghorne, in commenting on Dawkins' view of 'tamed' chance, says:

> ❛ Dawkins is emphatic here, partly because he wishes to counter creationist claims that the evolution of life is so improbable that only divine *intervention* (that is, action against the natural grain) can explain it. He and I hold common cause in that, but I am still deeply impressed by the anthropic potentiality of the laws of nature which enable the small-step explorations of tamed chance to result in systems of such wonderful complexity as ourselves. It would not happen in 'any old world'. That the universe is capable of such fruitfulness speaks to me of a divine purpose expressed in the given structures of the world. ❜
>
> (*Science and Providence* p.39)

So, for Polkinghorne, it is the general structures of the world that are providential. But here we meet the dilemma implied in the dictionary definition. Do the structures of the world **reveal** divine providence? Or is it the providential structures of the world that give us the **illusion** that there is (beyond them) a divine providence? In other words, we are left with the old choice: God or nature.

There seems to be no way of proving that we are entitled by the evidence to say more than that, since the universe is such that we have evolved, its laws facilitate that evolution. But surely, that is a tautology!

In other words:

If the world did not favour our evolution, we would not be here to think any such providential thoughts! Those not favoured are not here, and their perspective (that the universe did not 'provide' for them) is not taken into account.

We are the lottery winners, for whom the chance falling of the numbers has brought unexpected wealth. We see the whole of life summed up in this glorious, infinitely unlikely and therefore providential event. The millions of losers are unlikely to see it in quite the same way.

For someone who believes in a personal God, such general providence is unlikely to be enough. There need to be moments when providence becomes quite specific – moments when, contrary to the way the world usually works, things seem to act together in a uniquely purposeful way.

The history of religions is full of accounts of what are believed to be specific providential acts. They are generally termed 'miracles'.

Miracles

Hume defined a miracle as a violation of a law of nature, and we shall see later how this definition led him to the view that there could never be sufficient evidence to show that a miracle had taken place.

Note:

Hume's approach should be seen against the background of the philosophy and science of his day. He assumed that laws of nature could be established on the basis of the weighing of evidence, and that, once established, they would not be refuted by a single piece of evidence to the contrary.

Today, the attitude towards the process of developing and refining scientific laws is rather more subtle, as we shall see in chapter eight.

The most obvious feature of a miracle is that it is unexpected. It appears to go against the natural course of events. If we wish to avoid Hume's simplistic 'violation' of a law of nature, there would seem to be at least two other possibilities:

- that a natural process has been unusually speeded up or slowed down
- that a natural event is perceived as a miracle because of its timing i.e. it happens at exactly the right moment.

The first of these (e.g. the slowing of the movement of the sun to allow time to stand still, as in one Old Testament 'miracle'), is hardly likely to be well received by the sceptic, since the speed of change is an inherent part of an event. If I were told that a sapling had shot out of the ground and become a fully grown tree in a matter of minutes, the story would seem no less unlikely because a sapling normally grows into a tree anyway, given time. The whole event would still be contrary to all that we expect.

The second (synchronicity) enables a unique occurrence to take place without appearing to violate any natural law. In other words, if an event itself is not out of the ordinary it may still be regarded as a miracle if its timing is right. Thus, receiving a legacy from a long-lost relative at the same time as a final demand for payment of some impossibly large debt may seem miraculous. Not that it has happened, but that it has happened *now*, is the remarkable thing.

For reflection:

Every event is the result of a unique combination of circumstances. That something is unique does not make it a miracle.

These considerations pre-date Hume by many centuries. Aquinas distinguished between those things that are called miracles because they are thought to be impossible in terms of nature alone, and those which, although they could happen in nature, are unlikely to happen in this particular way and with this particular timing. For example, it might be possible for someone to recover from a particular disease, but not to do so instantaneously.

Religious requirements?

Let us go beyond Hume's definition for a moment to consider the religious requirements that turn an absolutely unexpected and unpredictable event into a miracle. The essential point to recognise here is that to call something a miracle is to make an *interpretation*. A person who believes in God will only call something a miracle if the apparent purpose achieved by that event is in keeping with his or her understanding of God's character.

In other words:

An act of mischief, however remarkable or unique, is unlikely to be called a miracle. An act of healing, on the other hand (even if there might be a rational explanation) may well be claimed as a miracle.

So miracles depend on interpretation. Let us take a situation which might or not be called miraculous:

- A plane crashes. Three hundred and ninety nine people die and the four hundredth is brought out alive from the wreckage. For that one person, his or her survival may be described as a miracle by friends and relatives. But the *total event* is a tragedy.
- But how do you know what that person will go on to do? Suppose the person who survives becomes a mass murderer. Is his or her survival in the plane crash then to be considered a miracle or a further disaster? If he or she had died then, the victims of the later crimes would be alive and well.
- But what of those victims? Suppose... and so it goes on.

The point we need to establish here is that to speak of anything as a miracle implies an interpretation and a value judgement. And that, in turn, requires a selective consideration of facts (we can never know the whole story).

Someone who believes in God and in providence may well say that, if we knew the whole story, we would see that everything has happened for the best. In which case, a miracle is a point at which something important within the overall story is suddenly and unexpectedly seen to happen here and now, cutting across what would be reasonably anticipated in the light of a partial examination of the facts.

In examining miracles (as all else) Brian Davies asks if the account of a miracle is logical and coherent. In many cases he would argue that it can be. But the point is that a person who does not wish to accept that something is a miracle is just affirming that there can be a non-miraculous explanation of that event, even if that explanation is not available to us at the moment.

Let us look at two examples of recent events that have been called miracles and consider the essential features of each of them:

Example 1:

In July 1995, a Roman Catholic priest suffered a severe stroke and was not expected to live. A fellow priest took the 300 year old mummified hand of an English martyr and placed it on his forehead while he was in hospital. The hand, apparently hacked from his body in 1679 when he was hanged, drawn and quartered, has long been regarded as able to bring about miracles. The priest recovered.

- There is no absolute claim that a miracle took place, nor that the hand worked some kind of magic. Due recognition is given to the work of the medical staff in bringing about the priest's subsequent recovery. The hand was described by the priest who placed it on his colleague's head as 'a link with a very holy man who died for the Catholic faith'. It is also recognised that there are other cases of people making a swift recovery following a stroke.
- The response of another priest was that, being a man of faith, he would not be surprised if a miracle had taken place, but would not jump to that conclusion. Equally, people may attest that asking saints for their help in times of trouble can aid recovery and some would want to link this with the use of relics.
- As it is presented here, the situation is very different from that in the Middle Ages, when relics were much sought after and were regarded as having spiritual powers what worked in a way that we might be tempted to call magical.

There are three additional factors to be taken into account:

- That we do not necessarily know the outcome of a particular medical condition. People do make unexpected recoveries.
- That medical care is taken into account. In other words, spiritual help and medical care are not regarded as alternatives – but as collaborating to produce an overall effect.
- That there is the element of psychological or personal response to the relic – in other words, the fact that the relic is revered may add, through the attitude of the person being healed, or those praying for him or her, to the overall effect. It is not a mechanical process.

Having said all that, the point remains that there is no proof that could be offered for a cure being directly linked to a relic. In practice, the more cures that come to be associated with the relic, the more 'empirical' evidence there would be for some special agency being at work – for association is taken to become evidence, even where the mechanism brought about by that association is not known. (There are many cases where scientists will say 'This works, although we do not know yet why it does so.')

Example 2:

In Naples, three times a year, people gather in St Clare's Basilica for a ceremony during which it is hoped that dried blood, believed to be that of St Gennaro who died in 305, will spontaneously liquefy. This 'miracle' is anticipated on a regular basis, and is seen as a good omen. It was first observed in 1389. On occasions, it does not take place and the mood of those present becomes sombre.

No explanation is given for the liquefaction, although spectroscopic examination of the substance confirms that it has the nature and properties of blood. Spontaneous liquefaction would go against the known 'laws of nature', and therefore, on a narrow definition, this would count as a miracle. One problem here is that, unlike the first example where someone is healed, there seems no particular reason why this phenomenon should take place, nor why it should be in itself of any religious significance.

Compare the second example with other unusual situations. In terms of the structures of the universe, a 'black hole' defies those 'laws of nature' which apply to the more limited range of conditions found on Earth. According to Hume's definition, a black hole might therefore qualify as a miracle – but then, black holes do not form part of a religious view of the world, so nobody is likely to call them miraculous.

Going against known scientific expectations is therefore not in itself sufficient cause for something to be called a miracle. For that to happen, there has to be some overriding sense of providence or spiritual assurance.

In the case of healing, the religious significance is obvious. The implications of the liquefaction of St Gennaro's blood is that the saint is believed to be active and willing to come to the aid of the people of Naples. Indeed, it is claimed that, when their football team is having a difficult time, the crowds of supporters are heard to chant for the saint to come to its aid!

Comment:

Whatever arguments might be presented by philosophers or theologians, there is little doubt that in the popular religious mind miracles are seen as events for which there appears to be no rational or scientific explanation. A fascination with the unknown, or the bizarre, is very common, quite apart from any religious connotations it may have. Film makers, television producers and novelists all know the power and fascination the unknown has for people.

But a rational person is soon going to ask about evidence, as did Hume.

Evidence for miracles

Knowing whether something has happened or not depends on the gathering and validation of evidence. If you are told that something highly implausible has happened, the most you can say to express your doubt is 'I believe you may have been mistaken.' The grounds on which you say this is that the event described does not fit into your existing view of the world.

The more unlikely the event, the more evidence you would need if you were to accept it as true. Also, the more unreliable you judge the person who gives the account of the unusual event, the more likely you are to believe that he or she was mistaken.

This is the basis of the famous argument about miracles put forward by David Hume in the tenth book of his *Enquiry Concerning Human Understanding*. He starts by making the point that a wise man, in assessing the truth of a report, weighs the evidence with which he is presented. So, if all the evidence points in one direction, that is what he will be inclined to believe. If, on the other hand, the evidence for and against something is almost equal, he will consider his judgement on the matter to be tentative. He (or she) will also take into account the reliability of any witnesses. Thus Hume sets up the issue rather like assessing evidence in a court of law.

He defines a miracle as an event which goes against the laws of nature – on the grounds that an event which conforms to the laws of nature is unlikely to be called a miracle, since an alternative explanation for it can be given. But the difficulty with any evidence for a miracle is that it will always be outweighed by the evidence on the basis of which the laws of nature have been framed.

He therefore argues:

> ‘A miracle is a violation of the laws of nature; and as a firm and unalterable experience has established these laws, the proof against a miracle, from the very nature of the fact, is as entire as any argument from experience can possibly be imagined.

> Why is it more probable that all men must die; that lead cannot, of itself, remain suspended in the air; that fire consumes wood, and is extinguished by water; unless it be, that these events are found agreeable to the laws of nature, and there is required a violation of these laws, or in other words, a miracle to prevent them? Nothing is esteemed a miracle if it ever happen in the common course of nature... The plain consequence is... That no testimony is sufficient to establish a miracle, unless the testimony be of such a kind, that is falsehood would be more miraculous, than the fact, which it endeavours to establish. ❜
>
> (*Hume on Religion* ed. Wollheim, Fontana 1963 p.210)

For Hume, a miracle could be accepted as such only if it would be a greater miracle for all the evidence to be shown to be mistaken. Notice that Hume does not say that, on principle a miracle **cannot** take place, only that there can never be sufficient evidence to **prove** that it has taken place.

In other words:

It will always be more likely that the report of a miracle is mistaken, than that a law of nature has actually been broken. For the evidence against the miracle will always be greater than the evidence for it.

Regularity and miracles

Hume assumes that the world is reliable and regular, and that its regularity may be expressed in terms of 'laws of nature'. Such laws are not apodeictic (in other words, they are not commands issued to nature) but are simply descriptions of what has been observed. If you believe in that sort of world, then there will always be an explanation for whatever happens, even if you do not know it at the moment.

Science is based on this regularity. Without it, the idea of conducting experiments would be nonsense – because you would never know whether the world would decide to operate in the same way on any two different occasions.

Daily life is also based on that reliability and regularity. Imagine driving a car and not knowing whether the laws of physics would work in the same way from one minute to the next! Would turning the steering wheel actually change the direction of the car? It did last time, but perhaps next time it will decide to do something different. If

I fling myself off this cliff, will I fly, or will gravity cause me to plunge downwards? Those who are sane do not inhabit such an unreliable world – and, if they did, they would not remain sane for long!

To accept a miracle, in the sense of a violation of a law of nature, is to believe that the world is selectively unreliable. But this is a very 18th/19th century way of looking at the world. Few today would see the world as a simple machine. If something unusual happens, the tendency is to assume that there is some other factor at work. Thus those who wait for the liquefaction of blood, believe that there are forces at work of which science has as yet no awareness – forces that are acknowledged by religion.

In other words:

The religious believer may want to accept the reliability and regularity of the world, but wants to do so in a way that allows a broader view of causality – a view that allows spiritual agents (God, the devil, angels, spirits) to play a part.

To say that a miracle is a violation of a law of nature is inadequate for serious debate in religion – because those who wish to defend such miracles will simply point to the spiritual realm as providing the cause of that 'violation', and those who do not will simply say that everything has a cause, but not every cause is known at this moment.

There is a further fundamental problem here for the philosophy of religion. The idea of special providence or 'miracle' seems to go against the cosmological and design arguments for the existence of God. Those arguments present the world as structured in a way that displays an overall purpose. They work on the basis of regularity, for only in regularity does the sense of design and purpose appear. Yet the idea of some special providence or a miraculous event, not available to all, introduces a sense of arbitrariness and unpredictability into an understanding of the world.

Comment:

You can't have it both ways. **Either** God is seen to exist because the world is a wonderful, ordered place, **or** his hand is seen in individual events because the world is an unpredictable, miraculous place. It is not reasonable to argue for both at once, since the one appears to cancel out the other!

Appropriately special?

We saw earlier in this chapter that miracles are generally only seen to be such because they are *appropriate*. Nothing would be deemed a miracle unless some good came of it. You may consider someone to be saved by a miracle, but are unlikely to think the same person killed by one (unless, of course, he or she was prevented by death from doing some terrible thing).

Just as in chapter one we saw that an experience was deemed religious if it had certain qualities in terms of giving insight or integrity, so an event may be deemed a miracle on the same basis. And just as an experience could be religious even if there were some perfectly rational account of it, so also an event might be termed a miracle even if it could be fully explained.

Comment:

Religion is a way of interpreting the world; a miracle is a way of interpreting an event. However inspiring that interpretation may be, it is always optional.

There is a Buddist story which tells of a Tibetan Buddhist who, about to leave on a pilgrimage to the holy sites in India, is asked by his mother to bring back with him a relic of the Buddha or one of his holy followers, so that she can use it as a devotional aid on her personal shrine. He is about to arrive back home when he suddenly realises that he has forgotten about the relic. Hoping that she will be fooled by it, he picks up a bone of a dog from the side of the road, wraps it up and delivers it to his mother, who believes it to be the genuine article. As a result of her devotions, many great healings and other wonders are performed by the holy/doggy relic.

The implication of this – and the purpose of the story – is to emphasise the point that (for Buddhists) there is no automatic or magical force in operation, but that all benefits come from human attitudes and striving. The 'miracles' were performed by the dog's bone simply because it became a vehicle for devotion, and the positive feelings and energies developed as a result of it were able to effect cures. Clearly, the significant point here is that at the physical or mechanical level a relic is of no particular significance. The saint's bone and the bone of the dog are equally effective. What matters is the devotion of the person concerned. It is that devotion that is said to produce the fortunate karma.

Note:

- Both Western science and Buddhism have universal causality. 'Whatever arises, does so in dependence upon conditions' is the basis of Buddhism, but it could equally be seen as a Western scientific creed. The whole debate about miracles in the West has come about because the rationalist has said that every event (even the one claimed as a miracle) must have arisen in dependence on a particular set of causal conditions, even if the causes are not known. Buddhism would not argue with this.

Hume and other religions

In his E*nquiry Concerning Human Understanding*, Hume sets out one argument that we are most unlikely to consider seriously today. He notes that all religions report miracles, and use those miracles to support their own beliefs. But he argues that if one religion is correct, then the others must be false. The miracles of each religion, if accepted, disprove the truth of the other religions, and therefore destroy the credibility of the miracles of those other religions.

In other words, miracles – taken as a basis for validating religious beliefs – are mutually destructive across religions.

If you take the view that there can be only one absolute truth and one correct way of interpreting it, then you might try to show that the miracles of 'incorrect' religions could not have taken place, or, if the reported events did take place, the way of interpreting them offered by the 'incorrect' religion must be wrong. Hume's view simply highlights the problem of trying to use miracles as the basis for validating religious beliefs. An event is termed a miracle because it is interpreted through religious beliefs. It cannot be used at the same time as independent evidence for those beliefs.

To sum up on miracles:

- If a miracle is simply the violation of a law of nature, then (according to Hume) there can never be sufficient evidence to command its acceptance.
- A miracle is an interpretation of an event: if the event has no significance, it cannot be a miracle.
- The whole concept of miracle may be seen as conflicting with the cosmological and teleological arguments for the existence of God,

since the arguments presuppose regularity whereas miracles presuppose a suspension of the very laws that sum up that regularity.

Summary

We have been looking in this chapter at causes, providence and miracles. We have seen the dilemma of the scientific and logical claim that we live in a world determined by laws by which everything is explained. In such a world it is difficult to see where there can be room for God, for providence or for miracles.

Neither is there scope in such a world for my own experience of freedom. It is a world that denies the very basic features of human creative life – we have no power to choose to act, only to watch the world act through us. Yet it is in the area of human choice and freedom, human hopes and morally significant actions, that religion lives.

Within the parameters of his own particular debate, Hume was, of course, perfectly right. There is no evidence sufficient to prove that a violation of a law of nature has taken place. But that should not, however, be of much concern to us, for it is clear that the term 'miracle' implies much more than that a particular event is inexplicable – it becomes the vehicle for religious insight and devotion. Those who watch for the blood to liquefy are not concerned with scientific laws, but with a sense of hope and religious and civic pride.

David Hume (in his *Natural History of Religion*) having come to the conclusion that there was no way to establish religious belief rationally, commented:

> ‘We may conclude that the Christian religion not only was at first attended by miracles, but even at this day cannot be believed by any reasonable person without one. Mere reason is insufficient to convince us of its veracity; and whoever is moved by faith to assent to it, is conscious of a continued miracle in his own person, which subverts all the principles of his understanding, and gives him a determination to believe what is most contrary to custom and experience.’

In other words, Hume concludes (with the hint of a smile, I sense) that it really is quite miraculous how people are willing to suspend their rationality in order to continue to embrace religion.

In this, too, Hume may be right. But we then need to ask about why people do indeed continue to be religious, and what that says about the limited place of rationality in the whole scheme of human experience.

7
SUFFERING AND EVIL

Human beings are fragile and short-lived. They are liable to accidents and diseases, and those who escape these still have to face the inevitable prospect of old age and death. The world is not a safe place in which to live, but it is the only place in which to live.

Human beings add to this suffering by their treatment of one another. From world wars to domestic unhappiness, people cause one another pain, whether deliberately or accidentally.

These two features of life are generally referred to as natural (or metaphysical) evil and moral evil respectively. All religions have to face and interpret these facts of suffering and evil, since they are an inescapable feature of life, and no attempt to give an overall view of the meaning and purpose of life can be credible if it overlooks them.

Suffering and evil create for religions both a challenge to which they can respond and also a problem.

The challenge and the response

A frequently described feature of religious experience is a sense of oneness with the rest of the world and an awareness of its suffering and fragility. This generally gives rise to feelings of compassion towards all who suffer. Some articulate this in terms of a God of love, or a God who is all-merciful and all-compassionate. Even Buddhism, which does not tend to make statements about God or gods, responds to this basic awareness in terms of the four 'divine dwellings' – loving kindness, compassion, sympathetic joy and equanimity. These are said to be the qualities through which one is joined with Brahma, or the divine.

The challenge for religion is how to respond to suffering and evil in a way that can express this basic sense of love and compassion. Generally speaking, religions do so in two ways:

- To counter natural suffering, they may promote compassion towards those who are in need. All the major religions have, in various ways, created organisations, structures and rules to help develop this concern for those who suffer. In other words, religion recognises, but aims to reduce, the natural consequences of human frailty.
- To counter human cruelty, they promote moral principles. This may take the form of rules to deter followers from doing those things that are likely to inflict pain on others, or spiritual exercises (like prayer or meditation) which seek to promote a view of life in which deliberate cruelty has no part.

Examples:

- The Sikh *langar*: sharing food together as equals.
- The Hindu principle of *ahimsa*: non-violence.
- The Muslim practice of *Zakat* and *Ummah*: charity, and the principle of unity and equality within the Muslim community.
- The Jewish *Torah*: including commandments to prevent human exploitation and cruelty.
- The Christian concept of love: including the idea of love being expressed even through suffering, as in the case of Jesus on the cross.
- The Buddhist principle of *Karuna*: compassion towards all living things.

These are all ways in which the religions respond to the challenge of suffering and cruelty. They provide the background against which we shall examine the specific 'problem of evil'.

Why consider these responses?

As we shall see, within the philosophy of religion, evil and suffering are usually considered simply as a problem for those who believe in God. But if there is any truth at all in the later Wittgenstein's argument that meaning is found in the context within which words are used, then to understand the meaning that suffering and evil have within the religious language game, we should examine their context, and that will include the responses that have been presented above, for religious people often see themselves as engaged in the task of overcoming suffering and evil. (Whether or not they succeed in doing so is another matter, but not one that is relevant for the purpose of this discussion.)

In the major theistic religions, the task of overcoming evil is something in which God is seen as active, mostly using humankind as his agent, but occasionally acting directly (as we saw in the case of the ideas of providence and miracles).

In general, it would appear that the 'problem of suffering' only emerges when the degree of evil is such that it threatens to overwhelm the whole concept of a loving God. At this point there is a switch in the overall structure of thinking – from engaged and unquestioning cooperation with God to overcome suffering, to one in which belief in a loving God is questioned.

But what is implied in such a switch? Clearly, while God is seen as aiding and inspiring the challenge of overcoming suffering, the implication is that God is *not* the deliberate author of that suffering. Rather, given that the world is such that there is suffering, he works to alleviate it. The switch occurs at the point at which God does not seem to be taking his fair share in the task – the point at which he is seen as an agent separate from human agents, a potentially victorious agent (if he is believed to be omnipotent), and yet an agent who seems content to allow suffering to continue. Once that point is reached, there would seem to be only two options:

- To abandon the concept of God as separate or external agent.
- To try to understand why an omnipotent God should choose not to use his power to eliminate suffering and evil, and why (if he is the creator) he should allow it to exist in the first place.

If the first option is taken, 'God' simply becomes a word that describes a source of inspiration for those who seek to overcome suffering. If the second option is taken, you have 'the problem of evil'.

The problem

If a religion teaches that there is an overall meaning and purpose to the world and that everything that happens is known to and under the absolute control of God, then the implication is that God must be responsible for natural suffering and human cruelty.

In its simplest form, the problem can be stated like this:

- **If** God is all-loving, he would want to do away with suffering and evil.
- **If** God is omnipotent, there is nothing he cannot do. He is therefore able to overcome suffering and evil.
- **But** there is evil and suffering in the world.

The philosopher David Hume can generally be relied upon to state a problem directly. Here is what he says in Book XI of his *Dialogues*. It is the point at which he turns the argument from design on its head, and presents a world that is far from a comfortable, reassuringly designed machine:

> ❛ Look round this universe. What an immense profusion of beings animated and organized, sensible and active! You admire this prodigious variety and fecundity. But inspect a little more narrowly these living existences, the only beings worth regarding. How hostile and destructive to each other! How insufficient all of them for their own happiness! How contemptible or odious to the spectator! The whole presents nothing but the idea of a blind nature, impregnated by a great vivifying principle, and pouring forth from her lap, without discernment or parental care, her maimed and abortive children! ❜

The conclusions to be drawn from this problem would seem to be:

- **Either** God is not all-powerful;
- **Or** God is not all-loving;
- **Or** Suffering is either unreal, necessary, or a means to a greater good;
- **Or** The whole idea of an all-loving and all-powerful creator God was a mistake in the first place.

Note:

It could be argued that all suffering and moral evil is caused entirely by natural processes and that therefore there is no need to implicate God. But that will not do, for the fact is that God did not **intervene** to prevent evil from happening (whatever its immediate cause) which (if omnipotent) he might reasonably be expected to do. Also, a God who creates *ex nihilo* is presumed to be absolutely responsible for creating and sustaining the laws of nature, and with them the limitations that give rise to suffering.

Therefore, for the purposes of this argument, it does not matter exactly **how** evil has come about, it is enough **that** it has come about.

Let us start with this last option. The whole 'problem of evil' is based on some basic religious assumptions:

- that the world is capable of being understood rationally;
- that there is an overall meaning and purpose in everything that happens;
- that there is a single underlying reality (God) rather than two or more basic realities in conflict;
- that the underlying reality can be described (even if not literally – see chapter two) as in some way 'good' and 'loving';
- that this underlying reality is such that it has a direct and absolute control over individual events.

Now, the problem only really applies to theism – the belief in one God who is the creator of the world, infinite, perfect, omnipotent and omniscient. Let us therefore look first at the possibility of side-stepping the problem by limiting God's power.

It is possible to hold that there was a creator God who started the world, but, having established its structures, had no ongoing influence over it (this is known as *Deism*). Equally, it is possible to take a dualistic view that God is limited by the matter out of which he has created the world. Some religions (e.g. Zoroastrianism) have gone further in their dualism and have argued that the world is a battleground between opposing forces of good and evil.

If God is limited in this sort of way – either by facing an independent and opposing force, or through the material within which he works – then suffering and evil are at least partially out of his control.

In other words:

If you insist that there is a God who is both free and able to do anything, and is the sole cause of all that happens, then the problem remains. On the other hand, if God is less than that, any limitation imposed on him by independent forces or matter will serve as his excuse.

If we stay with the idea of a loving, omnipotent God, then suffering and evil need to be explained as part of his intention for the world. They need to find a place within an overall scheme which can still be seen as the intention of an all-powerful and loving God.

The attempt to find this is called a *theodicy* – an attempt to show that God is right and just.

Throughout this chapter we need to distinguish between two things:

- Suffering that results from the nature of the universe in which we live and the effect this has upon fragile human life. This would include diseases, earthquakes and all other forms of 'natural evil'. This is sometimes called 'metaphysical evil', since it is a form of evil that is built into our whole understanding of the world.
- Moral evil, which results from the free choice of individuals to inflict suffering. Warfare, torture, inequalities that lead to suffering, emotional pain – all these can come under the general heading of moral evil.

But we need to keep in mind that these two forms of evil are not equally balanced, for the following reasons:

- **If** everyone behaved perfectly, there would still be natural evil. Disease and death do not depend upon moral wickedness, but are the result of the way the world is made.
- **But if** there were no natural evil – that is, if everything were created perfect – then it could be argued that there would be no moral evil either, since moral evil results from an inadequate or defective understanding of self and world. The murderer is not a perfect being who just happens to choose to kill an innocent person, but a human being who, because of his or her imperfections and/or the imperfections of at least one other person, chooses to kill.

Therefore 'natural' or 'metaphysical' evil is the greater problem for theism. If suffering results from an act of deliberate wickedness by a human individual, it is logical to blame that individual for the suffering, but there is a more fundamental question to be asked: Why is the world such that people can choose to perform deliberate acts of wickedness?

There have been the two traditional lines of approach to the problem of evil – the Augustinian and the Irenaean. They were set out by John Hick in *Evil and the God of Love*, and they have been taken up by many other writers, including Peter Vardy in *The Puzzle of Evil*. These books deal with this important subject in greater depth than is possible here.

The Augustinian approach

The Augustinian approach is named after St Augustine of Hippo (354–430) and reflects the influence of Plato on his thought. For

Plato, particular things are imperfect copies of their 'Forms'. Imperfection is a feature of the world of everyday things.

Augustine argued that evil is not a separate force opposing the good, but is a lack of goodness, a deprivation (his term for which is *privatio boni*). Human fallibility and human free will can lead to suffering and evil, for the world as we experience it is full of imperfect copies, and suffering and evil are bound up with that imperfection.

For Augustine, evil first came into the world through the 'fall' of the angels. In books XI and XII of his *City of God*, he argues that all angels were created perfect, but that some received less grace than others, and were able to 'fall'. This fall is then repeated in human terms in the Garden of Eden, following the temptations of Satan (himself the chief of the fallen angels) which meant that humankind would, from that point on, be imperfect.

Notice that this theory does not imply that evil is a separate reality, it is merely an indication that the world has fallen short of its intended perfection.

The Augustinian view has been particularly influential because it was taken up by Thomas Aquinas (1226–1274), and through him has dominated Catholic thinking on this topic.

In other words:

The world is good, but it is not as good as it was designed to be. Goodness is a perfection after which we may strive. Evil is not a thing or substance in itself, but a falling short of an intended perfection.

Another way of looking at this approach would be to say that suffering and evil are the result of our taking too narrow a view of the world.

For example:

We may believe that the colours of autumn are beautiful, inspiring and therefore good. But those colours are simply the result of the dying of leaves. If a leaf were conscious, would it welcome the beauty of autumn? Would autumn not be an evil to be avoided, an inexplicable denial of all the rising of sap and nourishing that the leaf had known since the spring? You might say: 'But that's just a leaf! That's what a leaf is. It grows in the spring, dies in the autumn and ends up as leafmould.'

> We have become conscious of the shape of our lives, but in other respects are we really that different from leaves? Might not the autumn and winter of our ageing and dying be viewed as equal in beauty to the young shoots of our spring?

A central question to ask of the Augustinian approach is this:

Evil may be a lack of goodness, but why is there a lack of goodness? If God were all-powerful, could he not have organised the world such that there were no fall from perfection?

There is a further underlying problem, as pointed out by Peter Vardy. It runs rather like this:

- **If** goodness is the same thing as completion (or perfection), then, in order to know if something is good or evil, you have to know what its true nature is.
- **But** do we, for example, know what perfect or complete human nature is like? Is it a matter of being natural? If it is, then there may be many things (like rape or violence) which may seem 'natural', in the sense that they arise out of deep seated natural urges that are not restrained by reason. Does this therefore make them 'good'? Clearly not; so the final judge of what is good or evil is reason, applied to our observation of the world.
- **But that is the problem**: when reason assesses what it sees, it is confronted with both good and evil, happiness and suffering. It cannot see perfection, so how can it judge?

But even if we do not know what perfection is like, we certainly know that this world is – from a human perspective – far from perfect. Need it have been so? If it is believed that this is the only world that God *could* have created, then he is limited. If, on the other hand, it would have been possible for God to create different worlds, then he could have created one that did not have the imperfections of this one. He therefore chose to create a world with imperfections, and must therefore be held responsible for those imperfections.

In other words:

Even if evil and suffering are simply a lack of perfection, that does not excuse God from choosing to create a world that is less than perfect.

Aquinas (in *Summa Theologiae*) presents the issue in another rather stark way. His argument starts with the fact that God and evil are incompatible:

- God is believed to be both good and without limit, so there is nowhere that God is not present.
- In that case, evil cannot exist; there is no room for it, since it cannot arise where God is present, if God is good.
- But we know that evil exists.
- Therefore there cannot be an infinite and good God.

Clearly, for Augustine and then Aquinas, the way out of this dilemma is to say that evil exists only as a limitation of good. But does this Augustinian approach actually solve that problem?

Can, for example, the torture of an innocent child be regarded simply as a *lack of goodness* in the torturer? Is there not a very definite act of evil in such situations?

Comment:

If evil is defined as a lack of goodness, is it not equally the case that goodness is simply a lack of evil? You could argue that, in a world created by a psychopath, where nature forces its way forward only by means of suffering and death, there is a 'problem of goodness'.

The clue to unknot this particular problem is that 'good' and 'evil' are not entities (things) but qualitative judgements. There is no such 'thing' as evil, only things which are judged to be evil. Describing the world as fundamentally good or fundamentally evil is a choice that reflects personal values – it doesn't change the facts.

Extreme cases of goodness or evil are almost universally acknowledged. The problem is with the middle ground of ambiguous actions, and with the overall balance between good and evil. It is here that the most obvious element of interpretation and choice come in. We are all familiar with the attempt to change one's perception of the facts in the marketing of products: my 'small' carton of fries or drink is now termed 'regular', my medium becomes 'large' and my large is now 'giant', or some other superlative. The cartons remain the same size, only the marketing image has changed! In the case of the world, there is only one carton – we choose to call it what we will, but the choice we make will influence how we habitually interpret what happens within it.

If there is a God, and if he chose to create a less than perfect world, then it is logical to seek a reason for his doing so. That brings us to the second of the traditional ways of answering the problem of evil – that set out by Irenaeus.

The Irenaean approach

The Irenaean approach is named after Irenaeus, Bishop of Lyons (c.130–c.202). It does not deny that suffering and evil exist, or that they are permitted to exist by God. Rather, it seeks to show that God chose to allow these things to exist in the world in order to bring about a greater good – human freedom and the ability of human beings to have a relationship with God.

This approach admits that human life is imperfect but, having been made in the image of God, men and women should have the opportunity to grow and develop into what God intended them to be. As they encounter the sufferings of life, people have an opportunity to grow and to learn. Without the existence of both good and evil, that would be impossible:

> ❛ How, if we had no knowledge of the contrary, could we have had instruction in that which is good? ... For just as the tongue receives experiences of sweet and bitter by means of tasting, and the eye discriminates between black and white by means of vision, and the ear recognises the distinctions of sounds by hearing; so also does the mind, receiving through the experience of both the knowledge of what is good, become the more tenacious in its preservation, by acting in obedience to God... But if any one do shun the knowledge of both kinds of things, and the twofold perception of knowledge, he unaware divests himself of the character of a human being. ❜
>
> (Irenaeus *Against Heresies* iv. xxxix.1 quoted in Hick p. 220; Fontana, 1968)

Hick's approach to the problem of evil follows from this. He sees evil as something to be tackled and overcome, but with the hope that, ultimately, it will be seen as part of an overall divine plan. In this sense, evil is a necessary evil, without which there can be no spiritual growth:

> ❛ A world without problems, difficulties, perils, and hardships would be morally static. For moral and spiritual growth comes through response to challenges; and in a paradise there would be no challenges. ❜ (op. cit. p.372)

Hick describes the world as 'a vale of soul making' – an environment within which people can grow.

Comment:

Notice that belief in some sort of life beyond death is important for this approach. The world may give people an opportunity to grow – but why should they bother to do so? Clearly, they will be motivated only if present hardships can be justified in terms of something better for which this life is a preparation.

If belief in God and life beyond death are removed, it might still be possible to say something like this:

- When we consider life, we cannot avoid acknowledging that human beings are fragile and fallible, liable to practise cruelty as well as kindness, liable also to seek goals that are limited and which may cause them suffering. People may seek excitement through driving dangerously fast or taking drugs; some will die as a result. Relationships may fail, and hatred between people may fester. That is the sort of world we live in.
- The fact that we call some things good and others evil shows that we are able to stand back from them and interpret them in terms of an overall view of human life and its place in the universe.
- Whether we like it or not, we therefore find ourselves in the sort of world in which we are forced to be creative in personal terms – we have to make choices and live with the results.
- A person who acknowledges personal responsibility, who reflects on the consequences of the choices that he or she makes, is already using the world as 'a vale of self making' (to remove the rather loaded term 'soul'). That is what intelligent life is about.
- We don't get a choice in the matter – we cannot take our world back and exchange it for another! We either live creatively, or we complain at the fundamental injustice of a world that we naively had assumed was fashioned solely for our benefit.

The free will defence

Might it not have been possible for God to have created a world in which there was no moral evil, because everyone freely chose to do what was right? If such a world were a logical possibility, then God stands accused of not having made a possible world in which there was no moral evil.

God's position is defended by what is generally called 'the free will defence'. It runs like this:

- If you are to be free to choose to do good, then it must be possible for you to choose to do evil.
- If the world were to be such that moral evil were made impossible, then it makes no sense to speak of having a free moral choice.

- **But** having free will is an essential condition of all moral life.
- **Therefore** there needs to be the possibility of moral evil in order for people to have free will and to live morally.

This argument has been presented very starkly by Swinburne. He points out that, for a moral choice to be real, you need depravity, in other words, you need to *want* what is wrong and then decide to reject it. But he then makes an important distinction between the *possibility* of evil and the *fact* of evil:

> ❛ This depravity is itself an evil which is a necessary condition of a greater good. It makes possible a choice made seriously and deliberately, because made in the face of a genuine alternative. I stress that, according to the free will defence, it is the natural possibility of moral evil which is the necessary condition of the greater good, not the actual evil itself. Whether that occurs is (through God's choice) outside God's control and up to us. ❜ (p.101)

One possible way of countering this is to claim that God, if he is all-powerful, should be able to make people freely choose what is good. Both alternatives are there, but the evil one will never be taken. But is that freedom?

A greater good?

The implication of the 'free will defence' (and, indeed, the Irenaean approach that lies behind it) is that it is better to have a world in which people are free to choose evil, rather than a world in which they are not free at all. Human freedom is the greater good, for the sake of which we have to cope with mass murder, abuse of children, torture and the like.

The implication is that an all-knowing God weighed the evil of all these horrendous things against the benefit of human freedom, and chose freedom. Can that be justified?

A classic example of the argument against such a choice is given in Dostoyevsky's *The Brothers Karamazov* (Book 5, Chapter 4). There is a gruesome story of a child who, for a minor misdemeanour, is punished by being torn apart by hounds in front of his parents. Dostoyevsky presents the case for saying that no end can ever justify such means. Whatever benefits might come from it, nothing could ever justify the torture of an innocent child. Ivan Karamazov says to Alyosha:

> ❛ ...if the sufferings of children go to swell the sum of sufferings which was necessary to pay for truth, then I protest that the truth is not worth such a price. ❜

In other words, Dostoyevsky is challenging the morality of a God who would allow evil no matter how good the end result of allowing it might be. Some challenge this approach. Swinburne says:

> ❛ Being allowed to suffer to make possible a greater good is a privilege, even if the privilege is forced upon you. ❜ (p.102)

An example might be the situation of conscripts killed in war to save their country from foreign oppression.

For reflection:

Generally speaking, the problem of evil has focused on the impact of suffering and evil on human life, but other species also suffer from 'natural evil' and in some cases (like that of a cat playing with a mouse) they may be thought to choose to inflict unnecessary pain – which would be the equivalent of 'moral evil'. What then of these other species? What of the situation on Earth before the appearance of human beings? Nature would have been cruel to many species; how might that be justified?

The argument used by Swinburne above, and the Irenaean approach in general, requires the possibility of human development as justification for the way the world is. How can it deal with the fact that humankind has only emerged very recently on Earth? What of all the suffering experienced by the non-human species that came before? Has life changed significantly? If it hasn't, then how can human development be its justification? And if the possibility that the world should be a 'vale of soul making' is the reason for all the suffering of all the species since the first appearance of life on the planet Earth, does that not reinforce the horror and anthropocentric arrogance of such a therory?

Was such a divine sledgehammer really necessary to crack the human nut?

Revealing the nature of God or good?

Notice that the problem of evil, as it has been explored so far, assumes that we have a knowledge of good and evil that is independent of any knowledge of God. If that were not the case, then we would have no reason to challenge the goodness of God.

Let us put this in philosophical terms. As we saw earlier (see p.48) an analytic statement is one in which its truth can be known simply by defining the terms. 'A triangle has three sides' is analytic; you don't have to examine triangles to show that it is true. A synthetic statement is one that can be shown to be true or false on the basis of evidence. 'The cat is sitting on the mat' can be affirmed or denied only by looking.

Now the question to be considered is this: is the statement 'God is good' analytic or synthetic?

If it is analytic, anything God does is good by definition (that is what 'good' means). If he allows the torture of children, then – within the whole scheme of things – that must be good.

Comment:

It is the revolt against this view that leads to the 'problem of evil'. If there is a genuine problem here – if in any way suffering and evil challenge the idea of a good creator God – then we cannot accept the simple identity of 'God' and 'good'. That may have implications for how we understand good and evil (and we shall look at that a little later) but it is equally significant for how we understand the word 'God'.

If, on the other hand, the statement 'God is good' is synthetic, the implication is that we have some idea of goodness that is over and above our idea of God, and by which we can assess both individual things and events and also God.

But this would suggest that the concept of God is limited, and that there is something greater, namely a sense of 'the good'. But here there is another problem, for the ontological argument for the existence of God (see above p.89) argued that God was that than which a greater could not be conceived. The 'problem of evil' suggests that over and above any concept of a creator God, there is a fundamental sense of the 'good', by which that concept may be judged.

Comment:

Plato might well be smiling and nodding his head at this point. The trouble set in when Christian theologians took too much notice of young Aristotle, and started to neglect his own idea of the 'Form of the Good'.

The argument presented above suggests that the image of God that dominates the 'problem of evil' debate is inadequate and manipulative. It is of a god who is external to events, who permits but is not within the suffering. But if God is thought of as being fully immanent as well as transcendent (see chapter three), then he might well be thought of as active within suffering, and as actually suffering alongside the individuals in and through whom he lives.

A suffering God, working through particular situations to bring about healing and good, is an idea that may find echoes in the day-to-day experience of religious people, but it seems at odds with the idea of a creator who chooses to permit suffering as part of his greater scheme.

And this, of course, was one of the great stumbling blocks in developing and presenting the Christian concept of God – since the idea that God could suffer in and through the person of Jesus went against the more absolute transcendence of the Jewish idea of God. Equally, for Islam, the absolute transcendence of Allah means that he can be seen as merciful and compassionate, but not as actually becoming immanent in the person who is suffering. Jesus is hailed as a prophet, but he cannot be divine.

This highlights the dilemma of believing in a god who is both transcendent and immanent. Take the example of a child dying of disease. If it happens just because that is the natural fragility of human life, then it is sad, but must be accepted. People may be helped by the idea that God, through Christ, understands and shares in the suffering of this child, giving courage and strength to all who are involved.

But how does this square with the idea that the suffering of the child, far from being an accident of human frailty, is actually part of a divine plan, that the Creator decided in his inscrutable wisdom that this particular child should die in order that he can fulfil his overall plan for the world? It is particularly difficult to square the idea of an overall designer with that of the immanent suffering God. The problem is not one that can be solved by some form of logic, it concerns the fundamental ideas of God that are being employed.

If God remains literally the designer for whom everything has its chosen place, then the price of his design is too high. However good his intention, his method of bringing it about seems disastrously bad – such a God appears like an army commander who, having freely allowed the enemy to take up positions, sends wave after wave of unarmed troops towards their lines!

In other words:

If God is the omnipotent creator of the world, shaping the whole creative process but deliberately permitting suffering and evil, how can he be called 'good'? But if God is immanent within the suffering, sharing and helping and identifying with those who suffer (as in the image of Jesus on the cross) then how can he be an omnipotent creator God? And in any case, we seem to have an intuition about what is 'good' that does not depend upon our concept of God. Within this argument, 'Good' becomes a god beyond God.

Suffering has the effect of negating inadequate images of God. When Job is brought face to face with the wonders of the created world he is awe-struck and no longer able to complain that God should not have allowed his suffering.

Modern science, and in particular the recognition of the genetic process in the production and development of life, has brought a new factor into this discussion. The very process of mutation that leads to examples of natural or metaphysical evil is necessary for the development of life.

> ❛ The chance disorganisation of the growing human embryo that leads to the birth of a defective human being and the chance loss of control of cellular multiplication that appears as a cancerous tumour are individual and particular results of that same interplay of 'chance' and 'law' that enabled and enables life to exist at all. ❜
>
> (A Peacocke *Theology for a Scientific Age* p.126)

Comment:

This may give some comfort to those who need to see natural suffering as a necessary part of the creative process in order to justify the idea of a good creator God. But it might still be difficult to square this with the actual response of religion in showing compassion towards those who suffer. Can a believer really be committed to helping overcome cancer and at the same time see the cancer as a necessary side-effect of the purposes of God?

God as moral agent

Brian Davies (in *An Introduction to the Philosophy of Religion* p.22f) points out that much of the argument presented by John Hick and others depends on the idea that God is a moral agent – that the things he does (or permits individuals to do) can be labelled good and bad, just as if he were a human agent. Now, for classical theism (see above p.64) God creates *ex nihilo* and is therefore involved with everything that comes into being. God cannot be one being among others (see above p.33 for Tillich's description of God as 'being itself'). But to describe something as a moral agent implies that it is an individual being, for it must be able to act and have effects external to itself, which can be called good or bad. But nothing is external to God – so how can he have effects, and without them how can he be called a moral agent?

The second point that Davies makes is that to be a moral agent one must have duties and obligations. But how can one describe God in this way? If God is changeless, it makes no sense to speak of him choosing to do one thing or declining to do another.

> ❛ The notion of God's changelessness means that God just does what he does, or, as some would prefer to say, that he just is what he is. ❜ (Davies op. cit. p.24)

Now Davies makes another important point. Moral agents can either succeed of fail, and which of these is judged to be the case depends on comparing their actions with those of others. There has to be some external standard against which action can be judged. But there is no external standard in the case of God; no alternative God creating alternative worlds with which our own may be compared. Davies concludes:

> ❛ But what is the background for judging the Creator *ex nihilo*? There cannot be any, in which case the God of classical theism cannot be said to be even capable of succeeding or failing. And in that case he cannot be a moral agent, for such an agent must be able either to succeed or to fail. ❜ (op. cit. 24)

An issue to ponder:

- Classical theism may take the idea of God beyond the world of beings and therefore beyond the possibility of individual good or evil actions or intentions. But if that is the case, then as far as morality and suffering are concerned, God becomes irrelevant.
- That which is everywhere, is perceived nowhere. That which has no boundaries cannot be seen and compared with others. That which does everything equally, takes responsibility for nothing in particular.

- In which case, what has this sort of God to do with the deepest intuitions of religious people, who, in the face of life's fragility and cruelty, sense a moral and spiritual challenge and proclaim a fundamental goodness and compassion?

– Suffering and the major religions –

There is no scope here to go into the details of how each of the major religions attempts to deal with the challenge and the problem of suffering and evil. We have already noted that they all offer moral guidelines in order to attempt to curb the tendency for people to inflict suffering on one another. They also offer spiritual practices in order to help people to cope with suffering and loss. But each religion has particular experiences and a particular approach.

Judaism

The event which now dominates the Jewish way of thinking about suffering is the holocaust – the murder of six million Jews under the Nazis. The fundamental question, in the face of such extreme evil is 'Where was God?', and all subsequent Jewish theology has had to take this into account.

In an article about suffering Rabbi Dan Cohn Sherbok refered to the book of Job:

> ❛ The message of the Book of Job is that human beings are unable to understand God's ways and that it is futile to question divine providence. This solution to the problem of evil transcends all theological speculation. Here we are reminded that human beings are finite, whereas God is infinite. What appears unjust is part of God's unfathomable plan. There is therefore no untidy scheme of reward for the righteous and punishment for the wicked that operates in everyday life. Instead we must be confident that God in His mercy exercises concern for His creatures, even though we cannot understand His purposes. ❜
>
> (*Daily Telegraph* 22.7.95 p.10)

Islam

Here a dominant theme is 'the will of Allah' – since it is paramount in Islam that God has absolute control over everything. There is no doubt here but that suffering is allowed by God, even though his purpose in doing so is beyond human understanding. In terms of moral evil, however, there is a recognition of human freedom to either accept or reject the teachings of Allah, and Islam has never been soft on the punishment of what it sees as human wickedness in deliberately turning away from the path set by Allah. As with Judaism, an absolute and transcendent God cannot be questioned. On the other hand, Allah is always described as merciful and compassionate, so he is certainly not seen as indifferent to human suffering.

Christianity

The central image of the Christian religion is the figure of Jesus on the cross. Although most Christians would say that we cannot know the purposes of God, the arguments presented earlier in this chapter have largely come from within the Christian tradition and show a serious concern to present a theodicy (the general term for an attempt to justify belief in God in the face of suffering and evil) that is logical and coherent. On the other hand, there is the general recognition in theology and also in the practical and pastoral concerns of the Church, that God in some way suffers with people and works to alleviate that suffering. The image of Jesus on the cross represents the immanent aspect of God, suffering alongside human beings, and also – through the person of Jesus – forgiving those whose moral evil has inflicted suffering.

The tension within Christianity on this issue is between this image of God in Jesus, healing, suffering and forgiving, and the God of 'natural theology' presented as the uncaused cause etc.

Notice that the idea of a suffering and forgiving Jesus being God incarnate is the point at which Christian thought parts company with the more strictly monotheistic systems of Judaism and Islam. Christianity deliberately sets this image of the suffering Jesus at the very heart of its creed. Its answer – the 'resurrection' – of good triumphing over evil, presents a potent image of hope, rather than a logical answer to the problem.

Hinduism

It is difficult to ascribe a single theory of evil to Hindu thought, simply because Indian religious traditions are so diverse. In general, the fact that – at the popular level, at least – there is a diversity of gods and goddesses means that no single deity is required to account for everything that happens, so the typical 'problem of evil' faced by Western monotheism does not really apply. A key concept to understand the Indian approach to suffering is *karma*. At its simplest level, karma is the result of action. Good deeds bring favourable results, either in this lifetime or in future lives (since Indian thought includes the idea of reincarnation). This has the effect of giving a balance to moral evil (since the person who does evil will have to bear the consequences in terms of the bad *karma* that it generates). It also serves as an explanation of natural evil, for moral and natural evil are linked through the idea of karma: those who suffer natural evil are experiencing the result of *karma* generated in former lives.

Buddhism

Buddhism offers a path to overcome suffering, a path that includes morality, spiritual development through meditation, and the wisdom to take a radical look at the world as it is, with all its imperfections. Unlike the other religions, it does not work on the basis of a creator God, whose existence needs to be defended. Buddhists believe that natural suffering occurs because everything is in a constant state of change, and individual things do not exist independently of the conditions that bring them about. We are fragile, limited and very vulnerable things. Why should we expect to be free from natural suffering, old age, sickness and death? That is simply what life is like. The task of the Buddhist path is to help understand and overcome suffering, in the sense of being able to find happiness even in a world which is recognised as fragile and fleeting.

When it comes to moral evil, Buddhism teaches that actions have results (*karma*). Any action which Buddhism sees as morally wrong (e.g. the deliberate taking of life) has immediate harmful consequences for the victim, but also, in the longer term it diminishes the person who performs it. Some Buddhists present this in terms of reincarnation – so that the good or bad karma accumulated in one life determines how one will be born in the next. Others speak in more psychological terms, with one's present state determined to a large extent by one's earlier choices.

In terms of the challenge of suffering, compassion (along with wisdom) is seen as a key feature of the Buddhist path. Helping those who suffer both improves their situation, and also generates more good *karma* for the helper.

Sikhism

Sikhism is a monotheistic religion, and therefore faces the 'problem of evil' as do other monotheisms. Where it differs from the three Western religions, however, is that it is devotional rather than intellectual in its approach.

From its earliest days the Sikh community suffered persecution, generally at the hands of Muslim rulers. Its response was to seek justice for all, to celebrate martyrdom as a triumph of truth and justice over oppression, and to emphasise self-respect, both for individuals and the community.

In terms of a response to physical suffering, Sikhs place great importance on service to the community and the relief of suffering and want. This is symbolised particularly in the *langar*, the free kitchen which is attached to every Sikh place of worship (*gurdwara*). All are welcomed, and all sit together as equals to share food.

Without entering into the philosophical debate, Sikhism, in its symbols of carrying a *kirpan* (a small sword or dagger) and sharing food in the *langar*, proclaims a struggle for justice and right and also a homely compassion for all in need.

Comment:

All too often, the philosophy of religion considers the logic and coherence of propositions in a kind of religious vacuum. It seeks logical answers and points out where claims are self contradictory, but seldom takes into account the various ways in which religions actually respond to the problem. By introducing some very brief comments on how the world's great religions have responded to the fact of suffering and evil, the intention has been to show the narrowness of presenting only a logical answer. This is particularly clear in the cases of Christianity and Buddhism. Christianity, without achieving a logical answer to the problem of evil, nevertheless explores it in the person of Jesus, and in what it understands by 'dying and rising to life again'. Within that religion, the idea of resurrection is a symbol of hope, which is affirmed in the face of suffering. It is less an answer to a logical problem, more a way of affirming a religious experience.

Buddhism, again focusing centrally on the problem of suffering, considers how it may be overcome, rather than speculating on its cause. In the well known Buddhist image of the man who has been shot, he is concerned to have the arrow removed from his body, not with the details of how the arrow was made. In Buddhist terms, the Western 'problem of evil' is merely an exercise in arrow analysis, and it does nothing to remove the dart or bind the wound.

— Coming to terms with suffering —

Funeral rites and the process of mourning show how many religious believers come to terms with suffering and loss. It would therefore be instructive to look at the language used at funerals in order to see how it relates to the problem of evil. Let us, by way of example, consider the implications of the Church of England's Book of Common Prayer service for the Burial of the Dead.

Arriving at the graveside, the priest is instructed to say:

> ❛ Man that is born of woman hath but a short time to live, and is full of misery. He cometh up, and is cut down, like a flower; he fleeth as it were a shadow, and never continueth in one stay. ❜

> ❛ In the midst of life we are in death: of whom may we seek for succour, but of thee, O Lord, who for our sins art justly displeased? ❜

In the first there is a recognition of the fragility of life, and in the second there seems to be a shift towards the idea of a God who is displeased, and rightly so. But does that imply that it is the sins that have caused the death?

> ❛ Yet, O Lord most holy, O Lord most mighty, O holy and most merciful Saviour, deliver us not into the bitter pains of eternal death. ❜

> ❛ Thou knowest, Lord, the secrets of our hearts; shut not thy merciful ears to our prayer; but spare us, Lord most holy, O God most mighty, O holy and merciful Saviour, though most worthy

> Judge eternal, suffer us not, at our last hour, for any pains of death, to fall from thee. ❞

Here there is to be a contrast between the eternal life or death of the soul and the natural death of the body – with all the implication for an understanding of the self that were explored in chapter five. God is still seen as Judge and as one to whom one should plead, as though he were totally in charge. And if so, might he not have decided that, in the overall scheme of things, this death was beneficial? That, of course is what follows...

> ❝ Forasmuch as it hath pleased Almighty God of his great mercy to take unto himself the soul of our dear brother here departed.... ❞

Here again there is the contrast between the temporal and the eternal. The point remains, however, that God is believed to have designed this world in which a person does well to escape from this body into something better, as is then reinforced...

> ❝ We give thee hearty thanks, for that it hath pleased thee to deliver this our brother out of the miseries of this sinful world... ❞

Again, notice the Augustinian approach here. The world of suffering is also the world of sin, and the implication here is that the two are inextricably linked. Through sin came death and all that goes with it.

Of course, few people now choose to use the traditional forms of the Book of Common Prayer, but it does throw into stark relief the various approaches to the problem of suffering. At one and the same time, it affirms God as sovereign and almighty, and also seems to absolve him from any accusation of evil, by saying that his decision to cause this death is simply in order to allow the person to pass from this world to something better.

Furthermore – and this relates to the whole idea of God, creation, and a sense of value – the implication of the Prayer Book service is that the world, through the Fall of Adam, is judged negatively. There is more evil in it than good, and people would do well to escape.

For reflection:

The Prayer Book service presents a world of suffering from which the person who has died has escaped to something better. This might provoke the question: Is religion escapist or does it face reality?

Marx saw religion as the cry of the oppressed, the voice of the voiceless and the opium of the people, at a time when opium was widely used to alleviate suffering of many kinds. He saw in religion's promise that one might be released out of this world into an eternal one, a form of escapism, to be contrasted with his own demand that people take responsibility for the improvement of their situation here and now.

- Was Marx right? Is religion an opiate that people administer to themselves rather than face the harsh reality of the world in which they live, and the death that they must one day face?
- Was he fundamentally Buddhist in the demand that people face reality?
- Was Marx taking a kind of self-help Irenaean approach – that the suffering of people here and now are the spur they need to develop themselves and improve their material conditions?

The Devil and Hell

Within the philosophy of religion, the idea of a devil, or evil force, is part of the overall question about evil and suffering. If there is an all powerful God and if he is good, then where do evil and suffering come from? The idea of a force against God, personified in the figure of the devil, is one way to express such an origin of evil.

Religious experiences may include elements of unworthiness and guilt. There may be a sense that certain actions deserve punishment, and where that punishment is not obviously forthcoming in this life, a natural sense of justice suggests that (if the world is controlled by God, and he wishes to act justly towards it) then there should be some punishment for those who do wrong – hence the idea of hell as a place of post-death punishment.

During part of its history, particularly in the medieval period, Christianity used images of hellfire to warn people of the consequences of evil actions. Islam too has a concept of hell, in contrast to the joys of heaven, and Buddhism has a whole variety of hells, both hot and cold. In Buddhism it is generally emphasised that the hells describe a self-created state of unhappiness to be experienced within life, rather than seeing them literally as places to enter after death.

The same is generally true of Christianity – although whether the Devil and Hell exist in any real sense is a matter of debate between those of a more literal and those of a more liberal interpretation of Christian doctrines.

In general, the matter of hell – literal or otherwise – is connected with morality. At its crudest, the threat of hell is an incentive to do good rather than evil. At a more subtle level, it is a reminder that evil actions can have painful consequences. It may also serve as a mirror on experience – a person who is violently cruel may, in the images of hell, enter imaginatively into what it is like to suffer from violent cruelty.

For further reflection:

- If the world is believed to be ordered by a just God, then a place or state such as 'hell' might well be thought to exist. Although, if God is thought of as loving, he might in fact decide to spare everyone from actually having to experience it.

Summary

The problem of evil, in the many forms in which it has been considered, remains the major obstacle to monotheism. Any understanding of the world which includes evil will be at odds with the literal acceptance of the concept of an all-loving God who has the power to order everything according to his will. This is shown very starkly in terms of traditional theism in which God creates the world *ex nihilo* – in other words that he does not merely shape and influence something that exists outside himself, but is the sole ground and origin of everything. He is thus absolutely responsible for everything, hindered neither by external matter nor external agency. If he permits human freedom, knowing that evil will result, he is therefore responsible for that evil – the supposedly 'free' human beings are simply the agents through which he has permitted the evil to come about. The only way out of this dilemma is in terms of the value that we place on that freedom and on the possibility of human growth through the challenge of evil and suffering. But even Swinburne (see above p.179) has to admit that prolonged suffering must count against belief in a good God.

There have been many different ways to try to find a place for evil within an overall positive view of the world:

- evil as a necessary contrast to good
- evil as a just punishment (and Augustinian approaches)
- that, on balance, we may agree with Leibnitz that this is the best of all possible worlds, and that, for example, compassion is made possible by suffering, thus balancing good against evil
- that all is (or will be) well from God's perspective (including Irenaean approaches in terms of the world including suffering and evil as a necessary environment within which humans can grow).

And yet all of these together still have to face the challenge of Dostoyevsky – that no final result can be worth the price of the suffering of even one innocent child.

Comment:

All three Western monotheistic religions (Judaism, Christianity and Islam) accept that, to some extent, God's purpose in allowing suffering and evil is a mystery. It is something that is deemed to be beyond the power of human understanding. But from a rational point of view, assessing all the arguments, it would seem most unlikely that there can be a god who is literally both omnipotent and loving.

8
RELIGION AND SCIENCE

Science is the systematic attempt to understand the world through observation, analysis and deduction. It seeks to formulate theories by which observations may be understood, and which may then be used to predict events and their consequences.

An important feature of science is that it is always changing and throwing up new ideas. Its theories are provisional; they represent what scientists see as the best way of making sense of observations. They are constantly being tested out and modified. For a time they may become established and normative for understanding the world, but later they are likely to be discarded as new theories, which may be more comprehensive, or more successful in predicting what will happen, emerge to take their place.

Science is a process based on *observation* and *reason*. It produces a growing and changing body of knowledge. It should not be identified with any one particular theory, but with the process by which that theory emerged, and by which it may eventually be superseded.

Science seeks two things:

- **Understanding** In this it reflects the natural curiosity that has always led human beings to wonder about the nature of the world in which they live.
- **Control** As a result of increased understanding, it is possible to develop technology which may seek to improve the quality of life.

For reflection:

Life in the developed world today is quite inseparable from the knowledge and technology make available by science: we take it for granted. You may have bought this book in a bookshop equipped with electric light, air conditioning and a computer to check stock, identify titles and place orders. You may have paid by credit or debit card – digital information being exchanged instead of hard currency, in a way that would have been unthinkable a generation ago. Even the book itself – from the methods used in paper production, the typesetting and printing technologies, the binding storage and distribution process – is a product of modern technology. None of these things would have been possible without basic scientific research.

Technology has the effect of illustrating the effectiveness of science. If something works in practice, you may generally assume that the theory upon which it is based is correct. We know that modern science has transformed many aspects of life, and are therefore predisposed to say that the scientific method of understanding the world is 'correct'; if it were not, none of this technology would have been possible.

In other words:

- Through technology, science is seen to be effective, and therefore its approach is generally believed to be 'true'.
- That does not imply that any one particular scientific theory is correct, for part of the process by which science progresses is the critical re-evaluation of existing theories, but that the scientific approach offers a sound, pragmatic basis for understanding the world.

The problem science poses for religion

Most forms of religion have teachings which claim to give knowledge about the nature of the world and the place of humankind within it. We have already looked at some of the implications of this: belief in the existence of God, providence and miracles. In examining them, we saw how they were related to the philosophical ideas of the period during which they were formulated (e.g. when looking at Aquinas' arguments for the existence of God, we needed to consider the way in which he was influenced by the rediscovered interest in Greek thought, and particularly in the work of Aristotle).

But we have also seen that religion is to do with commitment as well as discernment. The view of the world offered by religion is not simply a passing hypothesis waiting to be replaced, it is held as an eternal truth.

This is where science causes difficulties for the religious believer. The scientist examines the evidence and may find an existing hypothesis inadequate. If that is a scientific hypothesis, there is (relatively speaking) no problem: if the evidence for the adoption of the new theory is established, then it replaces the old. But if it is a religious belief (e.g. that a miracle has taken place) then, in the face of much evidence to the contrary, the religious person may seek to continue in his or her belief – and will (if necessary) change the meaning of 'miracle' or 'God' in order to accommodate the inescapable evidence provided by the scientific method.

For reflection:

Much human thought is given to problem solving. Life throws up problem after problem, and we gradually learn the most effective ways of dealing with them. Sometimes, of course, we simply stand and enjoy or admire or indulge. Sometimes (as in a mystical experience) our mind is taken out of its normal mode of operation and gains some profound intuition that had previously defied rational thought. But such moments are the exception, rather than the rule. Most of the time our minds are concerned with 'What is this? What are its implications for me? How do I deal with it?'

This is where the religion and science dilemma comes in – for the scientific method offers a very effective way of dealing with many of life's problems. It requires no act of faith, but simply a willingness to examine, consider and formulate theories. It gets things done!

When we look at the twin aims of science – -understanding and control – we see that each poses particular problems for religion:

- The **understanding** of science challenges the literal understanding of many traditional religious doctrines, which were formulated in a pre-scientific age and make assumptions about the world that science cannot endorse (e.g. the literal notion of the world being made in six days).
- The **control** that science makes possible poses moral problems for

religious people (as well as for non-religious). So, for example, nuclear technology offers an effective way of harnessing energy, which is theoretically less damaging to the environment than the use of fossil fuels, but it can also lead to nuclear accidents and the manufacture and use of nuclear weapons. Genetic engineering is another area where the possibilities available through science raise moral issues.

There may appear to be some 'quick' ways out of the science and religion issue:

- science is concerned with facts, religion with values
- science looks at life in an impersonal way, religion in a personal way.
- Religion is a left-over from a pre-scientific age. It will diminish as science reveals more and more about our world.
- Religion does not depend on reason, but on faith. What science has to say about the world is therefore quite irrelevant.

None of these does justice to either religion or science; the situation is far more complex than that.

The psychology and sociology of religion

In a book on the philosophy of religion there is a tendency to see religion mainly in terms of a set of ideas and values which are held by believers. Not only is this too narrow a view of religion, it also overlooks the fact that religion is also a phenomenon like any other. It may be studied and analyzed scientifically. It is possible to ask not just 'is religion true?' but 'why are people religious?'

Psychology and sociology are disciplines that examine such human phenomena, and each from its own perspective gives an explanation of the origin and continuing phenomenon of religion.

- Psychology examines religious beliefs and practices mainly from the standpoint of the individual psyche, seeing them as external expressions or projections of internal psychological impulses. This may lead to a positive or negative evaluation. Freud, for example, called religion the 'universal obsessional neurosis', in that he saw parallels between the desire for forgiveness through religious rituals and the obsessional behaviour (e.g. repeated washing of hands) in some of his patients. On the other hand, Jung saw in religion a way of giving life an overall pattern of meaning, without which people could only experience it as pointless, and which helped them to relate to some of the deepest images (archetypes) within the collective unconscious.

- Sociology approaches religion from the point of view of the role it plays within society. In general, it is seen as giving a sense of coherence and group identity. A society without a religious basis is more likely to fragment, for it lacks the facility offered by religion to express shared values and beliefs.

In other words:

Psychology and sociology do not ask 'is it true' but 'what does it do?' Just because they come up with an answer to the second question, does not mean that the first is not worth asking. Just because a society maintains the structures of an established religion in order to hold itself together, or an individual prays fervently in order to cope with a problem of deep-seated guilt, does not mean that the religion is **nothing but** a means of solving those problems. Its teachings **may** also be true – but that is quite another matter.

The key issues

The interaction between science and religion is a vast subject, and much of it could be related to topics covered within the philosophy of religion. However, for the purposes of this book, we need to limit ourselves to a number of key issues. They are:

- the changing world-view in Western thought
- the contrasting methods of science and religion
- the implications of science for a religious understanding of the origin of the universe
- the implications of science for a religious understanding of the nature of humankind and its place within the universe.

The first two of these provide the background to any discussion of science and religion. The second two show how they impinge on important features of religious belief.

Science and Buddhist thought:

In general this chapter will deal with the science and religion issues that occur within Western religion. This is because it is within Western culture that the rise of modern science has created a 'problem' for the literal acceptance of some religious beliefs. By contrast, Buddhism, with its undogmatic and open exploration of reality, its emphasis on the interconnectedness of all things, and its recognition of impermanence, has no problem whatever with modern science. The view of the world presented in its teaching is very similar to that of modern physics, and where it uses traditional images (e.g. heavens and hells) it has little problem interpreting these in symbolic or psychological terms.

What is even more crucial is the fact that clinging on to a fixed doctrine or a set form of words is, for Buddhists, a hindrance rather than a help on the spiritual path. Teachings are like a raft used for crossing a river – you leave it on the far bank and walk on; you do not carry it with you as a burden. This attitude has parallels with modern science's willingness to let previously useful hypotheses go when a new situation presents itself.

The changing world-view

In order to understand the religion and science debate, it is important to appreciate something of the historical context within which it has taken place. In Western thought, there have been two major shifts in the overall way in which people have viewed the world. (These are sometimes referred to as 'paradigm shifts' – a paradigm being the overall model of reality, around which various theories are clustered.) Without becoming involved with the history of science, we should at least note the impact of these, for each has had a profound effect on the interpretation of religious beliefs.

From the medieval world to Newton

The first paradigm shift gained momentum during the 16th and 17th centuries, causing the medieval world-view to give way to one based on Newtonian physics. This is the period to which is generally ascribed the rise of modern science. Although some features of later science are found before this time (for example the attitude to evidence and experiment taken by Roger Bacon at the end of the 13th century) it was the period leading up to Newton that saw a decisive shift in thinking.

Medieval Christianity had a view of the world that was based partly on biblical imagery, and partly on a mixture of Aristotle (384–322BCE) and the cosmology of Ptolemy of Alexandria (2nd century CE).

As we saw earlier, Aristotle argued that everything we know about the world comes from experience – and that experience is interpreted by reason. In this, Aristotle was at one with modern science. But Aristotle also considered that everything had both an **efficient cause** (which we would normally think of as a cause: that which produces an external effect) and also a **final cause**, which is the intended result.

An example:

If a baby grows, the efficient cause of that growth is the food and drink and oxygen that it takes in, and the final cause is the adult human being into which it is growing. If the growth were not controlled and shaped by a final cause, individual tissues would grow wild, and not fit the overall system of the body.

For Aristotle, there was an unmoved mover who constituted the final cause of everything (see above chapter four). In the medieval world-view, this was linked to Ptolemy's view of the Earth at the centre of the world, surrounded by ten glassy spheres. Seven of these spheres were thought to carry the seven heavenly bodies, the eighth carried the stars, a ninth was invisible, but turned all the others, and a tenth was the abode of God. Everything that happened on Earth was thought to be controlled by the movement of these spheres, and they, in turn, were controlled by God.

It is important to realise that this way of thinking was *deductive*. A person would consider the ideas of perfection, or of biblical revelation, and come to a conclusion about what the world should be like. Observations of the actual world were intended to confirm this idea, but not to challenge it.

For example:

Everything above the sphere of the Moon was considered to be perfect. The circle is a perfect shape, therefore the motion of the planets must be circular. If observation suggests otherwise, it must be accounted for in terms of a planet moving round one circle, whose centre was simultaneously moving round another (an epicycle), hence an elaborate system of such epicycles was devised in order to account for planetary motion and at the same time remain true to the tradition of circular perfection.

It is unlikely that there was ever a single, universally accepted view of the universe. What was believed religiously was a combination of some ancient near-Eastern views with Greek philosophy. The idea of the heavenly perfections, or the uncaused cause, so vigorously defended at a later date by the Church, would have been quite meaningless to the characters described in the scriptures.

In practice, different people accepted different views. For the uneducated majority, the more primitive view of a three-decker universe, centred on the Earth, with hell below and heaven above, was portrayed in Church murals and probably accepted with varying degrees of literalness. Depicting the joys or heaven and miseries of hell was regarded as beneficial for promoting morality.

Natural philosophy (as science would have been known at that time) was based on the authority of Aristotle and on divine revelation. But in spite of more than a thousand years under such authority, reinforced by the work of Aquinas in the 13th century, in which he interpreted and integrated Aristotle into Christian thinking, there was a gradual move towards the examination of evidence. This is illustrated by the work of Copernicus (1473-1543), a Polish priest. He wrote *De Revolutionibus Orbium Coelestium* – 'On the Movement of the Heavenly Bodies' – in which he appeared to claim:

- that the Sun (rather than the Earth) was at the centre of the universe;
- that the Earth rotated once every day and circled the sun once every year;
- that the stars were further away from the Earth than was the Sun, since there was no shift in their relative positions from different viewpoints on Earth.

Although unremarkable claims by modern standards, they broke new ground because:

- they were based on observation rather than on an interpretation of authoritative texts, scriptural or otherwise;
- they therefore challenged the authority of Aristotle;
- they displaced the Earth from its central position.

On its publication, the book was prefaced by the Lutheran theologian Osiander, who claimed that it was no more than a hypothesis, and did not challenge the traditional view. Later, his work was brought very publicly into the religion and science debate by Galileo (1564–1642) who, in 1632, published a book comparing Copernicus' system with the traditional one, and concluding that Copernicus was correct. Galileo was put on trial and forced to recant his views. Thus we see a growing desire to look at evidence and formulate theories – in other words, to develop a new body of knowledge – in the face of opposition from religious authority.

The full flowering of this new approach to natural philosophy, based on reason and observation, came with the work of Isaac Newton (1642–1727), and particularly in his *Philosophiae Naturalis Principia Mathematica* (1687). He devised a system of physical laws, using concepts of mass, force, velocity and acceleration. To put it crudely, Newton saw the universe as a huge machine, the operation of each part of which was controlled by fixed laws. These laws could be discovered by observation, there was no need to seek either authority or supernatural revelation. God might be the creator, but he had devised a creation which was capable of being understood on the basis of rational observation.

A monolithic system of ideas does not crumble overnight. The medieval world-view was shaken by the scientific discoveries of the 16th and 17th centuries, but its authority base was also weakened by the Reformation.

The implications of this shift for religion were:

- Authority was challenged by reason and observation. Sadly, the Church found itself largely on the side of authority, and fighting a losing battle.
- Newton, and many others who contributed to the rise of science, were themselves religious, and certainly did not see their work as undermining religion. God was seen to have written two books – scripture and nature – both of which could be studied profitably, and both offered a reflection of his glory.
- The very regularity of the universe, as set out by Newtonian physics, became an argument for the creative and providential work of God – as we saw in chapter four (the teleological argument).

A religious basis for the scientific quest?

Four features of the Christian religion encouraged the rise of science in the 16th and 17th centuries. They were the beliefs:

- that the world has been created good, and is therefore worth examining
- that God created the world in a rational and orderly way, and that it is therefore capable of being understood
- that nature itself is not to be worshipped (which would be pantheism) and people are therefore free to examine it critically
- that humankind has been given authority over the earth to subdue it. This allowed the rise of technology without the sense that this would automatically constitute a violation of God's world.

It should also be remembered that many of the great scientists of the past were religious. They saw the attempt to understand the world as an expression of their religious convictions. In particular, the idea that the world was capable of being understood rationally implied (to them) that it was the product of an intelligent creator.

Into the twentieth century

Two major scientific theories – relativity and quantum theory – formulated early in the twentieth century, brought about another fundamental change in the understanding of the universe, and the old world of Newton was suddenly seen as rather parochial, covering the physical laws that operated only within a limited set of conditions.

For Newton, space, time, matter and energy had been discrete, *a priori* concepts. They formed the framework of his whole view of the world. And of course, within the range of observations and experiments within which Newton worked, they served well enough.

With the formulation early in the twentieth century of Einstein's theories of relativity, Newton's concepts proved inadequate. Central to the change in perspective was the recognition of the interplay between concepts which, for Newton, had been separate:

- The theory of Special Relativity (1905) stated that matter and energy were linked, such that – using the famous formula $e=mc^2$ (where e represents energy, m mass and c the speed of light) – the destruction of a small amount of matter could release a large amount of energy. Matter is no longer 'solid'; it is energy locked into a physical form.
- In the theory of General Relativity, published in 1916, time, space, mass and energy are all related to one another. Time and space are no longer fixed, but relative to one another, and both are influenced by gravity.

For reflection:

As I look out through space, I am also looking back through time. I do not see what is now, but what has been. I observe a galaxy as it was thousands of years ago, and an observer within that galaxy now, observing the earth, would see a planet upon which human life had not yet developed.

What sort of world is this? How does it relate to traditional arguments for the existence of God?

The other dramatic area of change is at the atomic and sub-atomic level. In Newtonian physics, bodies obey fixed laws, and their behaviour is therefore predictable. But with the discovery of the electron and the subsequent development of particle physics and of quantum theory, it came to be recognised that, at a fundamental level, the component parts of matter could not be predicted accurately.

In other words:

If the certainties of fixed concepts of space and time had vanished with relativity, so too the idea of solid and predictable matter seemed to be challenged by the very unpredictability of its smallest component parts.

So we have a universe in which space and time, energy and matter are all bound up with one another. What is more, we know that there are four basic forces – gravity, electromagnetism, and the strong and weak nuclear forces. One of the aims of physics is to find a theory which will link all four to one another (a Grand Unified Theory or GUT) and eventually see how this would relate to relativity and particle theory (thus providing a Theory Of Everything or TOE).

The universe also reveals many different levels of complexity. We see it most obviously all around us in the physical, chemical, biological and social levels. Complex wholes tend to behave in a way that is different from their component parts.

In other words:

Nothing is 100% certain – that is the implication of much of this new view of the universe. The very act of making observations will influence what is being observed. Equally, it is unrealistic to isolate one thing from everything else in the universe. Everything influences

> everything else, but you cannot take everything into account. What you end up doing therefore is settling for an approximation.

The implications of this shift for religion

In a world controlled by predictable mechanical processes, God may be relegated to the realm of 'before' or 'outside' (Deism); he is no longer required within the machine, even if its original design and creation is ascribed to him. But the more complex and integrated view of the world that came in with relativity and quantum theory rendered a simplistic deism incredible (which was no bad thing, since from a religious perspective 18th century deism is quite inadequate).

The more holistic approach of modern physics also goes against the earlier tendency for religion to regard science as reductionist – in other words, to accuse science of reducing every complex thing to its physical component parts and then claiming that, since those parts obeyed fixed laws, this constituted a sufficient explanation of the activity of the more complex whole.

> *In other words:*
>
> Recognising that complex entities behave in different ways from simple ones prevents the idea of the mind, for example, being seen as 'nothing but' individual brain cells, or a game of chess being equated with a list of the moves that each piece is allowed to make.

Summary:

- Most Christian doctrines and arguments were formulated at a time before the rise of modern science. They can best be under stood against the background of Biblical imagery and Greek philosophy.
- The rise of science was the result of knowledge gained through evidence and rational thought. This approach challenged authority, and was seen by some religious people as a threat to traditional beliefs.
- The world revealed by twentieth century science suggests that both the Newtonian world-view, and the religious arguments that developed alongside it, are limited.

The methods of science and religion

Both science and religion claim to be exploring and making claims about what is 'true'. But what counts as truth depends on the way in which it is arrived at. So, for example, the truth of 2+2=4 is quite different from the truth about what I did last Thursday morning. The one is shown to be true by definition, the other by evidence, or the reliability of my memory. But what about religious claims? If someone says 'God is within my heart' or 'Everyone has a Buddha nature', we may well ask whether such statements could be shown to be true or false, and if so, what sort of evidence would count for or against them.

With scientific statements, however, the matter is rather more straightforward. In his *History of Western Philosophy*, Bertrand Russell makes the following comment:

> ❛ ...it is not what a man of science believes that distinguishes him, but *how* and *why* he believes it. His beliefs are tentative, not dogmatic; they are based on evidence, not on intuition. ❜

Now, part of this may be challenged: for example, it is a matter of debate to what extent the formulating of hypotheses from evidence is a matter of systematic deduction and how much depends on intuition. Seeing a possible explanation for a previously mysterious phenomenon may be an act of intuition, which is then confirmed or rejected on the basis of available evidence. But, in general, he has highlighted the central feature of science – which is that it is characterised by method and not by results.

If a scientist and a religious believer (even if they are one and the same person) believe the same thing, they do so on different grounds. So, in order to appreciate the different sorts of claim to truth that religion and science may put forward, it is necessary to examine the methods they use.

The scientific method:

Science works through *rational empiricism* – in other words, it is the rational examination of evidence. The process may involve the following:

1 observing and collecting data

Scientists try to make sure that the information they collect is influenced as little as possible by their own particular assumptions, and that in evaluating it they eliminate those factors that are not relevant to their enquiry. Thus, for example, drug trials involve the use of a 'control group' of patients suffering from the same condition, who are not given the drug, but whose progress is monitored. Without such a group, it would be impossible to know if the patients receiving the drug would have recovered anyway.

2 forming a hypothesis based on that data

This is where imagination and even intuition may come in, since there may be many possible hypotheses suggested by the same data.

3 performing experiments to test the hypothesis

If the hypothesis is correct, similar data should produce similar results.

4 working out a theory to account for the experimental results

This is termed induction, and there are limits to the degree of certainty that it can achieve (see below).

5 making predictions based on the theory

If a theory is correct, then certain things should follow from it. Checking out these secondary results is an important check on the truth of the original theory.

6 verification – testing out the theory by devising further experiments

This is often a long-term process of checking a theory against new experiments and perhaps new evidence, as a result of which it may need to be modified.

Nothing is claimed with absolute certainty. The more a theory is confirmed, the greater the statistical likelihood of its being correct. It is expected that every theory will eventually be superseded, or will be shown to apply only within a limited range of circumstances.

Induction

It might be tempting to argue that you can simply gather facts and, by a process of induction, be able to establish an absolute truth from them.

Hume pointed out (in his *Enquiry...* section four) that induction can never in itself be adequate to establish truth. His reasoning is very straightforward: however many examples of something you check, there will always be the possibility that the next example will prove you wrong. Thus, having checked a considerable number of pieces of evidence, a person has to presuppose a basic *orderliness* in nature, and frame a hypothesis accordingly. But that orderliness remains a presupposition: it is not something that can be proved.

A delightful example of this is given by Bertrand Russell in his *Problems of Philosophy* (page 63 of 1952 edition) where he points out that the chicken, having been fed every morning, expects the same thing to happen on Christmas Eve, only to have its head chopped off! We never know, in going through evidence, whether the next piece we examine will not prove to be our Christmas Eve!

Interpreting data

In the early part of the 20th century, the Vienna Circle of philosophers (see above p.49) argued that the only meaningful language was that which pictured reality. They emphasised the analytic/synthetic distinction – whatever was not simply a piece of logic, needed to be based on empirical evidence and verified with reference to it. In taking this view, they were deeply impressed with the success of the scientific method.

However, this view worked largely on the assumption that there was a simple, literal way of perceiving and describing reality – that the information gathered by scientists was free from their particular interpretations and prejudices. This view (that you can gather uninterpreted data) has been challenged by some modern philosophers, including Quine and Popper. Popper argued, for example, that all observation was impregnated with theories, and that there are no uninterpreted facts. Even the basic selecting of data involves interpretation; the process of interpreting and shaping is there from the start.

Popper pointed out that scientists do not progress by concentrating on indubitable facts (i.e. not by induction) but by constantly putting forward theories and testing them against the facts to see if they work (see Karl Popper *The Logic of Scientific Discovery*, written in 1934, but published in the UK in English in 1959). Two very basic features of traditional empiricism are challenged by the idea of all data being interpreted:

- Locke's view that the mind starts as a *tabula rasa*, and gradually is filled with information. Instead, the mind is constantly creating images in order to enable it to interpret information brought by the senses. To experience something is therefore to interpret it.
- Witgenstein's early view (in *Tractatus*) of language as providing a straightforward image of the external world. Instead, language is already shaped by the way we perceive things – in other words, our use of language is creative, and part of the interpretive process.

Neither experience nor language therefore works in the simplistic way that the earlier positivists had thought – both are creative activities.

Note:

The creative role played by the mind in shaping and testing out theories reflects a philosophical view that goes back to Kant. Kant pointed out that concepts like space, time and causality were a necessary part of the way in which we experience the world – we impose them on our experience.

So, whether we are looking at the creative use of 'language games' in the work of the later Wittgenstein, or Popper's recognition of the imaginative and creative use of theories, there is a general movement away from a simple gathering of indubitable facts or literal picturing of the world.

Understanding the world is a complex and creative activity – and that applies as much to science as it does to religion.

Images

As part of the process of interpretation, scientists use models – analogies drawn from something familiar – in order to explain theories. These models are simply convenient ways of conceptualising things, and are always subject to change.

An example:

- Originally, an atom was thought of as a very small but solid piece of matter.
- Later the model used for the atom was that of a solar system, with the nucleus as a sun and the electons circling it like planets.
- Now even that model breaks down, since sub-atomic particles are not locatable objects in orbit. Particles can be described as 'waves', but that too is an analogy.

- A quantum entity can be considered either as a wave or as a particle – but it cannot be both things at once.

We should not think of scientific language as uniform and totally empirical. It can be as rich as any other, full of imagery and interpretation.

Religious method:

Religion does not have a systematic method of arriving at its beliefs. In general, however, it draws upon three sources:

- Revelation: the belief that God has revealed truths direct to humankind. These may be embodied in scriptures, or learned directly from inspired teachers.
- Personal experience: we saw in chapter one that there is a whole range of religious experiences, many of which lead a person to make claims about what has become known.
- Natural theology: the argument for particular beliefs based on reason and an observation of the world.

The third of these comes closest to the scientific method. The key difference, however, is that (for most religious people) their religious tradition provides the concepts and words through which everything is experienced anyway. Also, because those beliefs are held on grounds that are not simply rational, religious people may be less willing than scientists to see them replaced.

Faced with the challenge of the scientific method, religious thinkers tend to respond in one of two ways:

- To minimise the factual content of belief claims;
- To argue that religion is a matter of faith, to which human reason had little to contribute.

The second of these is sometimes argued in Christian terms by referring to the 'Fall' in Genesis, with the implication that a fallen humanity therefore had no more than a fallen rationality and that therefore the only way to receive salvation was by faith. This approach had in any case been taken by the more Protestant thinkers (typified in the 20th century by the work of Karl Barth and in the nineteenth by Kierkegaard), whilst natural theology – as expounded by Aquinas – was officially approved by the Catholic Church.

In other words:

- A key feature that distinguishes the scientific and religious methods is that, for religion, trust is placed in a **particular view** of the world, whereas for science, trust is placed in **the process by which views of the world are formed, evaluated and modified**.
- Science is method: religion is commitment to a view.

How? and why?

Because of the difference in method, it may be tempting to say that science asks 'how?' questions and religion 'why?' questions. In other words, that one deals with facts and causality, the other with meaning and purpose.

It is not quite that simple, however, for science appears to be asking 'how?' in order to gain the best overall way of understanding the world – the best set of models by which things may be understood and their future predicted. In a way, religion too is seeking a best overall way of understanding the world. A significant difference, however, is that science attempts to eliminate the personal response to what is being examined, whereas for religion that response is an essential feature.

Reductionism

A complaint regularly made by religious philosophers about the scientific method is that it tends to be reductionist. Reductionism is a term used for a process which analyses complex entities into their component parts and then claims that it is the component parts that are 'real' rather than the original complex whole. It is commonly characterised by the tendency to say that the complex wholes are 'nothing but'.

Examples:

- A symphony is 'nothing but' sets of vibrations in the air.
- A painting is 'nothing but' arrangements of particles of pigment on canvas.
- You are 'nothing but' the sum total of all the cells in your body.

This is less true today than it was during the period dominated by Newtonian physics, since there is now a wider examination of the operations of complex structures and chaos theory.

In terms of human evolution, however, the issue has been raised again by the publication of Dawkins' book *The Selfish Gene*. To put it crudely, the argument is that the behaviour of human beings is genetically motivated. Genes struggle to survive and propagate, and people are really just their survival suits. The reductionist issue is about which level of activity you consider to be primary and which secondary. Are we here for our genes, or are our genes here for us?

The problem is to strike a balance between looking at those things that take place at a simple level (e.g. cell reproduction) and those that involve the whole complex organism (e.g. learning to play a physical game). The complex entity makes no sense apart from its constituent parts, but neither does it make sense to explain a game in terms of particular neurones firing in the brain and muscles contracting in the arms and legs!

In terms of evolution, the limitations of a reductionist approach are clear from the work of Karl Popper (*The Open Universe*, 1982). He argues that evolution is indeterminate and unpredictable, since at a higher level there are developments that could not be predicted at a lower one.

Comment:

For both philosophers and scientists, there is a tendency to analyze things into their simplest component parts in order to discover what is 'real'. For Locke, Hume and the whole empirical tradition in philosophy, the real is known through the basic building blocks of sense experiences. For Descartes, experience cannot be trusted, and so he starts with the fact of his own thinking. For a nuclear physicist, atoms give way to sub-atomic particles and then quarks – everything is 'really' a collection of tiny quanta of energy.

But since the time of Plato, there has been the recognition that reality comprises both substance and form. He went beyond the earlier Atomists in trying to express what it meant for substance to take on character, to have a shape. For Plato, the 'forms' were eternal – they defined the reality of individual things.

Reductionism is a process by which form gradually gives way to formless substance. Its logical end is a vision of a single universal reality – perhaps such as existed in the first milliseconds of the 'big bang', before our universe expanded, cooled, differentiated out its components and took on character. As such, it is a valid quest, but it is not the only way to view reality. The universe has been moving away from that simplicity for 15 billion years – and, as we encounter it now, it is shaped and known only through its 'forms'.

In other words:

In a world of constant change, the reductionist asks 'What has made this come about?', always looking to the past. The more interesting questions are 'What may this become?' and 'In which direction is this going?' always looking to the future.

The origin of the universe

Scientists seek theories which give the most comprehensive explanation possible; the wider the successful application of a theory, the greater its acceptability within the scientific community.

This assumes that there is a fundamental unity within the universe. In other words, laws which appear to work only in one part of the universe are regarded as special cases of a broader law operating throughout. Thus, Newtonian physics is valid for a limited range of conditions (those within which Newton worked, of course) but cannot be applied to the sub-atomic or the cosmic dimensions.

Hence the quest for a TOE (Theory Of Everything), and the drive for explanations that are simple and universally applicable.

In other words:

Science assumes a fundamental unity and coherence within the universe – that beneath different special conditions there is a basic truth of which all else is an outworking.

This fits neatly with the overall religious desire for a single explanatory theory – generally seen in terms of belief in God. It is the attempt to interpret religious experience within a single overall coherent view of the universe which makes the questions asked by theology parallel to those asked by science.

Let us examine the most fundamental of questions. Why is our universe as it is? Why does it exist at all? Can there be other universes, or is that a contradiction in terms? What does it mean to claim that God created the universe?

We have already seen in chapter four that the cosmological and teleological arguments move from the fact of the world's existence and the appearance of purposeful design of things within it to the idea of an overall creator God. How does science deal with these two things?

The generally held view is that the world that we observe now began about 15 billion years ago, expanding outwards in what is termed the 'big bang' from a spacetime singularity – in other words, from a point at which all known space is compressed into an infinitely small point.

It is impossible to ask what happened before the big bang, since time is related to space, and therefore time began in the same singularity out of which the world unfolded. Looking out through space and back in time, we probe the earliest phases of the universe, but beyond that is the singularity, the point beyond which our faculties can no longer probe.

Logically, that does not mean that there is nothing beyond a singularity, but that to say that something exists means that it exists in time and space. Everything that can be said to exist therefore exists within this world. To describe anything as 'outside' the world is a rather crude image – for the whole concept of 'outside' implies existence in space and time.

In other words:

We cannot get outside or beyond or before the universe that has exploded outwards from that original hot big bang. Our faculties and our concepts work only within the world.

In terms of scientific cosmology, it therefore makes no sense to 'locate' a God literally outside the world. Creation is an ongoing event, the gradual unfolding of that big bang. If God is described as 'creator' then that is his sphere of operation – but how might one relate the idea of God to the fundamental constants set up in the earliest phase of that outward explosion?

Science shows relationships between phenomena; one thing may be caused by another; one set of conditions is necessary for something else to come about. It may even show how a particular phenomenon relates to the universe as a whole. What it does **not** say, however, is that any of these relationships are deliberately brought about for some **purpose**. Religion on the other hand (at least, in so far as it is represented by the teleological argument – see page 102), seeks to find purpose in the design of the world, and in particular seeks to express a purpose for humankind.

If the fundamental features of the early universe had been different, things would not have evolved in the way that they have. If the size of planet Earth, or its distance from the Sun, or its atmosphere, or the prevalence of carbon and water, or any of a multitude of other conditions were other than they in fact were, then humankind would not have evolved.

So much is obvious. But this argument is sometimes given a twist – and one which may be grasped by someone who is looking for evidence of God's design and purpose in the universe. The twist is called '**the anthropic principle**' – and it simply claims that all the fundamental features **had** to be as they were, in order for human life to have appeared, therefore we can start from the fact that human life exists, and work backwards in showing a chain of necessary conditions.

The believer in God may then take this 'anthropic principle' and use it to show that, without God's guiding hand, it would have been highly unlikely that – with all the billions of possible worlds that could have emerged – the world did actually evolve in exactly the right way for humankind to develop.

Comment:

Fundamentally, the anthropic principle achieves nothing more than to highlight the simple fact of interconnectedness – everything is as it is because everything else is also as *it* is, and human beings are part of that world. If you use the anthropic principle to argue that the world was designed specially to produce humankind, then every other species can argue the same. Had the universe been any different, spiders would not be spiders. And, indeed, on a rather larger scale, galaxies would not be galaxies!

Design and purpose is only meaningful if you can stand back and see both the designed object and the designer. You also need some prior knowledge of what constitutes 'design' to recognise that the object has certain 'design' qualities. Without an awareness of these three things, saying something is designed is nonsense. This, of course, was considered (with reference to Hume and others) in looking at the teleological argument for the existence of God.

The problem of considering the origin and nature of the universe as a whole, from a religious point of view, is that you are constantly pushing up against the limits of what **can** be known. To say that the universe appears to have started from a single point (at the 'big bang') or that it has physical features that are absolutely necessary for the development of intelligent life, is to say **just that, and nothing more**. To try and say more is to go beyond anything that can be justified by the evidence.

Having said that, however, we might acknowledge that science goes some way in the direction of the religious impulse. The quest for a TOE – a single explanatory theory – is not so far from the religious quest for an uncaused cause, or for a god who will include the whole universe in a single purposeful act.

Summary:

Whatever the facts about the origin or 'design' of the universe, **nothing in the evidence requires us to go beyond the fact that the world exists and is as it is**. Even if we imagine that other worlds might exist, this is the only one we can ever know.

Evolution and humankind

The very notion that humans have evolved from other species contradicts a literal interpretation of the Book of Genesis, in which God creates Adam and Eve as a separate and distinct species and gives them authority over the rest of creation. Hence the long and colourful story of the debates between those who insist on a literal interpretation of Genesis and those who see such ancient literature as poetic and symbolic, and who therefore have no problem in principle in accepting the truth of a scientific theory about the evolutionary origin of species.

However, there seems little point in going through those debates in the brief space available here. Instead, we shall look at some of the ways in which the idea of evolution impinges upon religion.

Darwin

At its crudest level, the argument about Darwin's *Origin of Species* concerned whether humankind was a unique and special creation, or whether it was descended from apes. Opposition to all theories of evolution was fuelled by two things:

- the desire to give humankind a special position with respect to all other species;
- a belief in the literal truth of the biblical account of creation.

But beneath this – and of greater interest from the perspective of the philosophy of religion – was a threat posed by Darwin's theory to beliefs about the action of God.

The teleological argument had presented God as the designer and creator of the world – the watchmaker, whose mechanisms went infinitely beyond human mechanical abilities. Each creature, it was argued, had a unique and effective design, and even parts of creatures (e.g. the human eye) seemed so perfectly adapted to their particular use, that there seemed no way to account for it other than as a special action of God.

The central feature of Darwin's argument was the mechanism by which evolution worked – **natural selection**. In this theory, those creatures which are better adapted to their environment than others are more likely to survive to adulthood and breed. In the next generation, there will therefore be more members of that species with the particular characteristics of those breeding survivors. As time goes on, this self selecting of beneficial characteristics will cause the species to 'evolve'.

The theological problem posed was that this theory, if correct, could account for exactly those features in creatures that had previously been ascribed to the designing agency of God. Over time, according to natural selection, things would design themselves.

In other words:

Natural selection did not remove the element of design from the world, but gave a purely natural explanation for how it had come about; an explanation which appeared to render God redundant.

Note:

Darwin himself was religious, and he certainly did not see his theory as undermining belief in God. Equally, Christian folk at that time were divided in their views on evolution – so this debate should not be seen as one with scientists on one side and religious people on the other. It was simply a matter of whether or not the discovery of a mechanism by which species could self-design over long periods of time would in itself threaten the idea of a creator God.

Neo-Darwinian approaches

Genetic theory has clarified the way in which the random variations, which form the basis for Darwin's natural selection, come about. Random damage to genetic material leads to these variations which are either to the advantage or disadvantage of the individual members of the species.

Richard Dawkins (in *Climbing Mount Improbable*, 1996, but see also his earlier book *The Blind Watchmaker*) examines the apparent improbability that scattered atoms and molecules (at the foot of the mountain) could ever, by themselves, come together to form complex entities like an eye (representing the peak of this mountain of ascending complexity).

His argument is that, because natural selection preserves advantageous gene mutations and discards disadvantageous ones, there is a gradual path up the back of that mountain. In the end, one comes to the conclusion that – far from being improbable – it is quite inevitable that complex forms will arise that are particularly well adapted to their environments. Using computer simulations, Dawkins shows that it is possible, using just a few variables, to produce a wide range of complex shapes.

Aided by genetic theory and by computer simulation, the modern exponents of natural selection can show the mechanisms by which all those phenomena, which previously have been ascribed to God's design, can be brought about.

By contrast, John Polkinghorne (see *Science and Creation*, 1988) argued that the likelihood of any individual thing happening is so remote that he cannot see how the universe can be controlled by 'blind chance', and therefore postulates an overall intelligence to account for it.

The problem with this argument is in the relationship between 'chance and necessity' (itself the title of a famous book on the subject by Jaques Monod, published in 1972 in which he said 'pure chance, absolutely free but blind, is at the very root of the stupendous edifice of evolution'). The need to posit an external intelligence to account for each individual improbability arises only once individual things are removed from their setting:

- In a complex world where everything is interconnected, each thing comes about because of a practically infinite number of chances.
- If any one thing were to be different, then everything would be different.
- In retrospect, everything seems very improbable, but equally, everything seems absolutely necessary and predictable.

The mistake is in trying to extricate something from its causal connections, and then trying to find out how it came to be as it is, and – failing to find a path through the infinite number of chances in life – positing an external influence.

For example:

In a lottery, someone has to be a winner. An almost infinite number of chances produce a particular combination of numbers. The probability of that particular number coming up is very low. But that does not imply that some external intelligence is influencing the falling of the lottery balls!

Comment:

There seems no doubt that Richard Dawkins is correct. Life can develop and organise itself into more and more complex forms. It is therefore logical to reject any idea of an external designer God.

Fine – the external watchmaker bows out. But what has gone? Consider the discussion in chapters three and four. Is an external watchmaker really an adequate concept to account for what religious people mean by 'God'?

The implication of Mount Improbable is that life is creative. The world is not a heap of dull matter waiting for an external spark. That spark is within it – taking up every opportunity afforded by genetic mutations. Life is opportunist, pushing forward to develop and adapt as best it may. And we, as human beings, both take part in that process, and are also capable of recognising that process all around us.

Except – isn't that what creation *ex nihilo* is about? Was there not a long tradition of seeing God as the creative power within matter, not some external mechanic?

Surely, what Dawkins has demolished is the case for deism – a concept that was never religiously adequate. Religion does not require a 'celestial conjurer' who interferes with natural laws (see for example, Polkinghorne, *Science and Creation*, p.56).

Life is essentially a creative process. But is that not (stripped of its imagery) what belief in a creator God is really about?

Teilhard de Chardin

Teilhard de Chardin argued in a number of books (the best known being *The Phenomenon of Man*) for a religious vision which not only included the idea of evolution, but which made it a key feature. In describing the process leading from atoms up through cells to simple life forms and finally to humankind, he noted that it was one of increasing complexity and rising consciousness – the more complex a being, the more conscious it became. In terms of simple observation, this was hardly controversial, since a very basic creature has little scope for perception, thought and action, whereas more developed life forms are increasingly observed to take on character and to show signs of emotion and thought.

Looking to the future, Teilhard saw humankind converging, with a growing network of communications spreading and deepening over the limited surface of planet Earth. Where could such a process of increasing complexity and consciousness lead?

Having the Christian conviction that all things would find their fulfilment in Christ, he claimed that all things would eventually converge on a single point in the future – a point Omega. That point, the culmination of the whole process of evolution, he identified with the Cosmic Christ.

His whole scheme can therefore be expressed in terms of a cone, with simple atoms at the base, rising up to Christ Omega at the apex. This scheme enabled him to integrate his religion and his science. Previously, he had felt torn between development of the earth and a religious aspiration that had nothing to say about the terrestrial future of mankind. Now, since all that helped the further evolution and convergence of humankind would be a step in the direction of the fulfilment of all things in Christ, he could incorporate his science into an overall religious vision.

In such a scheme, the whole movement of evolution is 'pulled' from above – from the final goal of Omega (rather like the final cause of Aristotle). For Darwin and neo-Darwinians, the process is more like Aristotle's 'efficient causality' – evolution is pushed from the present into the future, not pulled from that future.

Teilhard de Chardin effectively took a scientific hypothesis (the rise of complexity/consciousness towards a single point in the future) and overlaid it with Christian imagery. In a way, he 'baptised' an evolutionary structure, much as earlier Christian theologians had 'baptised' the philosophy of Plato and Aristotle. The problem is that, if one adopts a particular hypothesis and makes it a vehicle of religious convictions, it has to be defended on religious grounds. For Teilhard, the future Omega is not merely a provisional deduction from present observations, but an act of faith.

Such an approach is vulnerable on two counts:

- Science may show its factual basis to be flawed, and religion would then be fighting a losing battle if it felt obliged to defend an indefensible hypothesis.
- The scientific theory may have religiously undesirable consequences. Teilhard de Chardin found himself arguing in favour of the racial and cultural superiority of Europe, and even welcoming the atomic bomb as a sign of humankind's triumph over nature! In short, having identified his religious vision too closely with a particular evolutionary theory, he finds that the theory rather than the religious tradition determines what he can believe.

But however flawed the attempt at integrating a scientific hypothesis and a religious vision may be, it does have the advantage of integrating the religious impulse with an overall structure for understanding the world.

Comment:

One of the great problems for religion – particularly since the time of Newton – has been the separation (either by externalising God through 'deism', or by making religions exclusively concerned with emotions and values) of the religious vision from an overall scientific and philosophical grasp of reality.

Some conclusions

If we look back to the time before the rise of modern science, we find a world in which the intellectual claims of religion and those of natural philosophy fitted together. Both had been influenced to a great extent by Greek thoughts, both used the same language. Particular views may have been wrong in terms of what we understand now – but at least they were consistent with the generally accepted understanding of the world at that time.

With the rise and success of science and technology in providing an effective and useful view of the world, the tendency has been for religion to retreat from making statements about the world that might conflict with science. It has emphasised meanings and values rather than facts. This in turn has encouraged a caricature of science as giving a literal, factual and precise account of everything.

Now, although nobody can deny that religion does deal with the affective side of life, exploring the moral and spiritual responses of individuals to their experience of the world, that does not mean that religious people cannot make claims about the nature of the world – claims based upon their own religious experience. Such claims can be examined in the same way as those of science, to see if they give a reasonable account of what is experienced, whether they are widely applicable, and whether they are fruitful in helping people to interpret other aspects of life.

But we have seen in this chapter that science too uses models for interpreting its data. It too creates general views about how the world is, views that must always be open to revision.

Arthur Peacocke, in *Theology for a Scientific Age*, took a critical realist view of science. That is, he saw it as depicting – as well as it can – actual structures and entities in the world. He then sought to apply this same critical realist position to theological claims. In other words, religion took that which was encountered in terms of religious experience and tried to find models to explore and describe it. Given that both science and theology were using this same process of finding and modifying models used to describe reality, he was able to say:

> ❛ From a critical-realist perspective both science and theology are engaging with realities that may be referred to and pointed at, but which are both beyond the range of any completely literal description. Both employ metaphorical language and describe reality in terms of models, which may eventually be combined into higher conceptual schemes (theories or doctrines). ❜

In other words, he accepts that both science and religion make cognitive claims, and both should therefore be judged in terms of their reasonableness. Both, equally, should always be open to examine and modify the concepts they use.

Value and purpose

Looking at the complexity and richness of life – the amazing way in which a great variety of forms seems to develop on the basis of a simpler underlying structure – it is tempting to give such value to those things which are closest to us that we assume that the whole universe exists for their benefit. Hence, when we contemplate the fact that our planet will one day cease to exist, we may be tempted to ask what, then, is the purpose in the whole exercise? Why should life develop if only to be extinguished?

Such a view implies that value is given in terms of the future, not of the present. If the whole meaning, purpose and value is seen now, then it is not diminished if it subsequently ceases to exist. Only if the present state is made subservient to some future state is its present value negated and conditional.

In looking at the idea of God in chapter three, we noted the distinction between eternal and everlasting. The one was encountered only in the present moment, and was completely outside the framework of space and time. The other was about endless extension within that framework. Now it may be useful to bring the same distinction to bear here. If a sense of purpose operates only within the space-time framework, then my purpose in being what I am now will only become apparent later, when I have become something else. But that in turn will depend on what happens after that. In a world that goes on everlastingly, we can never therefore know what, if anything, is our purpose – because whatever final state we visualise, its purpose will still lie beyond it. On the other hand, if purpose and value are related to that which is *outside* the space-time framework (the Eternal, to use traditional terminology) then value is entirely in the present instant (the only point when our experience is *outside* the space-time framework of subsequent reflection) and is not dependent upon the future or the past.

The goals of science and religion

One could argue that the ultimate goal of science is to develop 'a theory of everything' – a rational understanding of the whole of experience. In practice, it is difficult to see how one could ever know that such a theory had been achieved, for in practice, new evidence is always being examined to assess whether it confirms existing theory or requires it to be modified. Special cases are the stuff of which new theories are made.

What then is the overall goal of religion? In part – and certainly in so far as religion is regarded as a set of beliefs about the nature of reality and the place of humanity within it – religion has much the same goal. Aquinas' unmoved mover or uncaused cause, giving coherence and meaning to the whole of his view of the world, was the basis of just such a 'theory of everything'.

What is more, the basic assumption that the world is ultimately able to be understood by human reason is shared by 'natural theology' and science, and we have seen that it is this assumption that aided the rise of modern science.

An amazing vista opened up by modern science is that of the universe as a structured field of energies – as something dynamic and interconnected. It comprises a pattern of relationships in which everything is in some degree dependent upon and related to everything else. The whole of the universe is in some degree present in every part, and equally that part is only understood fully in the context of the whole.

Comment:

This view is similar to mystical experience and to the Buddhist philosophy of interconnectedness. At that level, religion and science both express the same deep longing to understand and experience both the universe and our place within it.

In the 1996 Richard Dimbleby lecture, Richard Dawkins attacked what he saw as an epidemic interest in the paranormal, and argued that science, if properly taught, could satisfy the 'appetite for wonder.' He pleads for reason in the face of superstition:

> ❛ Let's not go back to a dark age of superstition and unreason, a world in which every time you lose your keys you suspect poltergeists, demons or alien abduction. ❜

His argument against such superstition is the economy of explanation – if there is a straightforward reason why something happens, why should one choose to believe something elaborately improbable instead?

Comment:

It is crucially important, in assessing the relationship between science and religion, not to allow religion to be identified with superstition. When Aquinas or Newton spoke of God, they were not setting aside their rational faculties, but attempting to integrate their knowledge into a single vision of reality.

9
RELIGION AND ETHICS

In looking at the various philosophical issues that are raised by religious beliefs, we have seen that religion offers both a way of understanding the world and also a way of evaluating it. It does not give an objective, detached view of how things are, but a view that embodies both value and commitment.

That being the case, it is clear that a person's religious beliefs will influence his or her moral choices, and that a society is likely to reflect the values of its dominant religion, even if these are not made explicit in each and every individual moral choice, or in each piece of social legislation.

Ethics is the examination of the grounds on which individuals and societies make moral decisions. It is clear therefore that there will be quite a close link between religion and ethics.

Descriptive and normative ethics

Descriptive ethics simply offers a description of what is done in a particular society at a particular time: this or that tribe is cannibalistic, this or that religion insists on monogamy. There is no attempt to make an evaluation of what is described.

Now, you can give a descriptive study of the moral attitudes taken by the world religions. Some general principles – not taking innocent life, or not stealing – are held by all the major religions; on other issues, for example on sexuality or wealth, there is a variety of views.

By contrast, normative ethics examines the principles upon which moral choices are made. In terms of the philosophy of religion, we are therefore particularly interested in **normative ethics** – since it is in the area of fundamental principles that morality and religion have common ground.

Natural law

Aristotle distinguished between efficient causes and final causes. Efficient causes were those things which existed prior to something happening and which were perceived as agents in bringing it about (e.g. the sculptor and his chisel are the efficient causes of a piece of marble becoming shaped into a bust). Final causes are those things which lie in the future but which give direction to what happens in the present (e.g. the idea of the bust is the final cause of the work of the sculptor). The final cause of a thing defines its true or ultimate character.

In other words:

A baby takes in food, drink and oxygen as efficient causes of its growth, but its final cause is the adult human being into which it is growing. Final causes give purpose and direction to change. Therefore, if you want to know what is right for that baby, do not consider it simply as the product of food, drink and oxygen, but as a potential adult human being.

This theory was taken up by Aquinas, and became the basis of the *natural law* theory of ethics, which has dominated Roman Catholic ethical thinking. According to natural law, everything has a purpose for which it has come about. (In a Christian context, of course, that is seen as the purpose given by God, its creator.) An action is morally right if it is in line with that purpose, wrong if it frustrates it.

Example:

A clear example of the application of the natural law theory is the Roman Catholic opposition to contraception. It is argued that the conception of a child is the natural purpose of the sexual act. That act may also be enjoyable and strengthen the relationship between the partners, but – however positive these things may be – they arise in the context of an act which has as an essential purpose the conception of children. Therefore, anything which deliberately frustrates that outcome must be morally wrong, and every sexual act should at least be open to *the possibility* of the conception of a child.

The conception of a child remains, of course, a possibility rather than a certainty. Nature itself certainly does frustrate that outcome – since the vast majority of sperm never make it to the egg, fertilised eggs do not always implant successfully, and miscarriages can end the process at a later stage. But such things are outside moral control, and since they are part of the natural order it might be argued that God had used them for some particular purpose.

By contrast, anal intercourse, oral intercourse, homosexuality and masturbation cannot lead to the conception of children, and are on that basis considered to be against nature and therefore morally wrong.

From the above example, it is clear that something can be considered morally wrong, and yet be perfectly 'natural' in the usual sense of that word. Masturbation, oral sex, homosexual acts and so on are the result of 'natural' desires. The nature considered by natural law is **nature as interpreted by reason**. More specifically, it is nature as seen as having a sense of purpose, in which each event looks for its justification to its 'final cause'.

Here, the link with religion is clear. Natural theology – the whole attempt to argue for belief in God on the basis of a rational understanding of the world – is an attempt to make sense of the world, and to give an overall coherence to our understanding of it, a coherence which is centred on the idea of 'God'. When we looked at the arguments for the existence of God in chapter four, we saw that the cosmological argument linked the existence of God to the structures of the world (as uncaused cause etc), and the teleological argument linked him with a sense of design and purpose (as the designer of the world).

The natural law approach to morality is the ethical equivalent of that natural theology; it is the attempt to understand and evaluate each action in the light of a some universal purpose and direction.

Utilitarianism

The next major theory we need to consider is **utilitarianism**. This is the attempt to justify a moral action in terms of its expected results, and is associated particularly with the work of Jeremy Bentham (1748–1832) and John Stuart Mill (1806–1873).

In its simplest form, this argues that we should aim to do that which gives the greatest happiness to the greatest number of people.

There are various forms of utilitarianism – act utilitarianism (which concentrates on looking at the results of individual acts), rule utilitarianism (which accepts the need for rules, but only on the grounds that those rules could be justified by the anticipated benefits to society as a whole), and preference utilitarianism (in which the preferences of those involved are to be taken into account, so that morality is not just decided upon results, but on the sort of results that people choose).

All of them, however, are based on the general principle that people seek happiness for themselves, and therefore need to take into account that others will seek it too. But clearly, the attempt to maximise one's own happiness at the expense of others is likely to be frustrated by the desire of other people to do the same. Utilitarianism, in seeking the maximum happiness for the maximum number, aims at a compromise in which everyone ultimately benefits.

In other words:

Utilitarianism is enlightened self-interest. It is based on hedonism – the theory that everyone seeks happiness – but recognises that, in a competitive world, happiness is most likely to be achieved by fostering a cooperative spirit.

Utilitarianism is a very practical and commonsense approach to ethics, but from a religious perspective it does not probe deeply enough into its own presuppositions. What utilitarianism cannot show is how to **achieve** happiness; it merely offers the possibility of happiness, by dissuading people from doing those things that will frustrate the potential happiness of others. This was recognised by 'preference utilitarianism' – you cannot prescribe what happiness will be for individual people, for not everyone will want the same thing; it has to be a matter of choice and preference.

In other words:

If everyone could get together and decide exactly what would make them happy, **then** utilitarianism would give a practical method of deciding right and wrong on the basis of what is most likely to achieve the greatest happiness for the greatest number. What utilitarianism does not provide is a fundamental examination of what makes people happy, other than the satisfaction of their basic human needs.

The actions of individuals have results which affect other people. To act without taking these results into account, and to encourage others to do the same, would be a recipe for chaos and mutual frustration. All the world's major religions have something to say to this effect, since all recognise the inter-connectedness of people's lives.

The difference between the religious view and the utilitarian is that the former attempts to explore the ultimate source of happiness, whereas the latter is mainly concerned with its subsequent distribution through society.

Note:

Nietzsche contrasted the morality of slaves with that of masters. The former were likely to promote a morality which gave them a more equitable share of life's good things – and Nietzsche saw that exemplified particularly in the Christian morality of love and compassion towards those who suffer. By contrast, masters are more likely to seek what is noble, to want to develop themselves to the limit. His fear was that the Christian slave morality would weaken society, depriving it of its nobility and striving. He did not want to see the strong held back on account of the weak. Nietzsche therefore presents us with the fundamental question – Why be utilitarian? Why seek a fairer sharing of happiness? Why not seek for a higher goal?

However utilitarian it might be in practice, a religious morality is therefore likely to want to underpin the utilitarian theory either with a natural law argument of some kind, or with some statements about the meaning and purpose of life.

Absolute ethics

In chapter four (see page 111) we looked at the way in which Kant used the sense of absolute moral obligation (the categorical imperative) in his argument for the existence of God based on the pure practical reason. If we feel an absolute moral obligation to do something, we actually believe at that moment that we are free to choose to do it, that we are immortal (in the sense that the implications of what we do go beyond the expected results in this life) and that there is a God (who will ensure that virtue will lead to happiness).

An example:

Someone risks his or her own life by rushing into a burning building to try to rescue a stranger who is trapped inside.

- At the moment of making that rescue bid, the person must feel that the outcome is not settled, something can be done (freedom).
- By risking his or her life, there is a sense of life being more important than simple physical existence (immortality).
- There is also a sense that in the end, life is such that one's own happiness, even if one dies, is based on doing that which is right – that one cannot be happy if one ignores the cries for help coming from that burning building.

This does not imply that, before rushing in, a person will weigh up all three issues and conclude that, because he or she believes in freedom, immortality and God, it is worth risking everything to try to save a stranger. Rather, by rushing in, that person shows a belief in some form of freedom, immortality and God.

In other words:

Kant provides a very close link between morality and religion. Religious concepts are seen as the presupposition of a sense of absolute moral obligation.

Morality and facts

In the early part of the twentieth century, the theory known as Logical Positivism suggested that language was basically descriptive and that its meaning could only be justified with reference to evidence of those things that it purported to describe (see above, chapter two). Clearly, moral statements could not be justified in this way, since the values and obligations they described were not 'things' to be examined independently. They were therefore branded, along with religious statements, as 'meaningless'. But if moral language could not give a picture of values and obligations, since these were not objects 'out there' to be described, what could it do? Clearly, it must describe something else. There therefore developed a number of theories about ethical language which sought to give it meaning.

- **Emotivism** argued that moral statements were really just statements about how one felt about something. If you like something, you call it right and good, if you dislike it, you call it wrong and bad.
- **Prescriptivism** suggested that to say something was morally right was to prescribe it as a recommended course of action. To say 'that is wrong' is just another way of saying 'don't do that'.

Comment:

These theories were an attempt to separate moral statements and empirical 'facts'. They are really saying that morality is not based on what *is*, but on *what we would like*. It reflects our choices, and does not need to be justified by reference to facts. When it comes to religion, the same could apply: that religion supplies values, expresses our hopes and fears, gives outlet for our emotions, but that it cannot be justified with respect to empirical facts. Against this approach, we may set the whole 'natural theology' attempt to show that religious ideas are based on the nature and structure of the universe; that they are not ideas and values picked at random, but expressions of the way the world *is*.

Another way out of the dilemma posed by Logical Positivism had already been provided by G E Moore in his *Principia Ethica* (1903), who argued that goodness could not be defined because it was quite unlike any other quality. You simply knew it by intuition. His analogy was with descriptions of colour – you can't describe what yellow is, you just need to point to it and say 'that's what I mean by yellow'. The same, he claimed, applied to goodness – you simply point to it, for you cannot express its meaning by trying to define it or reduce it to its constituent parts. It just is. This theory is generally called **intuitionism**. This approach does not deny the reality of goodness (or of God) any more than it denies the reality of 'yellow', but says that these things can only be known by intuition.

Comment:

In a mystical experience (see chapter one) there are things that are 'known', but cannot be described. Also, Otto argued that the mysterium tremendum (see above, p.29) can be evoked, but can only be described in terms of a 'schema' of analogies and hints.

Religion might well claim that intuition is important, not because when we fail to analyze and describe something literally we have to fall back on intuition as a lesser form of knowledge, but because intuition harnesses both the conscious and the unconscious mind to transcend the limits of what can be understood by reason alone.

How are religion and morality related?

We have looked briefly at some ethical theories, and noticed that they have implications for religion, either because they share an overall structure of thought with religion (e.g. natural law), or because they recognise the limitations of what can be said of either religion or morality (e.g. intuitionism). Other theories either did not examine the source of the values on which they were based (e.g. utilitarianism) or saw religious concepts as lying behind practical moral reason (e.g. Kant's categorical imperative).

What we need to do now is to explore how ethics (which is, after all, an independent branch of philosophy) relates to religion.

The section that follows is taken from Teach Yourself Ethics, pages 197 – 200.

There are three possibilities:

autonomy Morality may be autonomous if it is based on reason alone, without any reference to religious ideas. If its values are the same as a particular religion, that is seen as purely coincidental.

heteronomy Morality may be said to be heteronomous (i.e. rules coming from outside itself) with respect to religion if it depends directly upon religious belief, or upon a set of values given by religion.

theonomy Morality is theonomous (i.e. comes from God) if both it and religion are thought to come from a common source of inspiration and knowledge – a source which religion might refer to as 'God'.

Some arguments in favour of autonomy:

- Responsible moral choice depends on freedom and the ability to choose rationally. But some religions have inculcated rules that should be obeyed out of fear of punishment. Rewards and punishments may be offered after this life – either in terms of heaven or hell, or in terms of rebirth into higher or lower forms of life. With such religious pressure, can a person be truly free or moral?

- Different religions (or even different sects within a single religion) often take different approaches to moral issues. There is no clear guidance. In order to choose between conflicting religious views, a person has to use his or her reason as the ultimate deciding factor – which is autonomy!
- If I subscribe to one of the theistic religions (i.e. I believe in God), then I will believe that God already knows what I will choose to do before I myself choose to do it. If he is all-powerful, he should be able to prevent me from doing what is wrong. If he does not do so, he is responsible for the consequences of my action, aiding and abetting me through divine negligence! In which case, I lose my moral responsibility.

Thus it would benefit ethics if it acknowledged and cut free from religious influences. Morality would then be based on reason and experience alone.

Some arguments in favour of heteronomy:

- People cannot escape from the influence of religious values and attitudes. They have an unconscious effect, even for those who reject religion. Better, then, to acknowledge that influence than try to deny it.
- As soon as you try to define moral terms (such as 'goodness' or 'justice') you are using language which has been shaped by the prevailing religions. Natural law, for example, may have come originally from Aristotle, but today it is understood largely through the use made of it by Aquinas and the Catholic Church. Religion has largely supplied the language of ethical debate.
- It is one thing to understand what is right, quite another to have the courage or conviction to put it into effect. It can be argued that religion is the source of such courage and conviction, and that it provides a society within which values and moral attitudes can be shared and reinforced.
- Philosophers often assume that everyone is reasonable. Religions, by contrast, are well aware of human selfishness and unreasonableness. Religion is likely to offer a more realistic view of human nature than philosophy, and therefore be better able to guide moral choice.

Thus it is inevitable that ethics will depend on religion, and also that it is beneficial for it to do so, since religion gives a broader and more realistic view of human nature than does pure reason.

Some arguments in favour of theonomy:

- Intuitionism was right in saying that there are certain things that are known, but cannot be described. We have an intuitive sense of the meaning of the word 'good' – and this intuition lies behind both the ideas and practice of religion, and also the impulse to understand ethics.
- It can be argued that religion and morality have a common source in 'mystical' experience – moments of intuitive awareness of a sense of meaning, purpose of wholeness in life, of wellbeing and acceptance. This is a basic feature of religious experience, and also gives the impetus to act in a purposeful and moral way.
- Metaphysics – the rational exploration of meaning and purpose in the world – can be seen as a basis for morality (as in Greek thought, in the 'natural law' tradition, and as explored today by, for example, Iris Murdoch in *Metaphysics as a Guide to Morals*) and also as fundamental to religion.
- Ideas like 'categorical imperative' and 'conscience', imply the personal awareness of obligation and meaning that are also fundamental to religion.

In other words, forget 'religion' as a separate part of life, and just concentrate on the fundamental ideas and values that it expresses. Those ideas and values also serve as the basis for morality.

Values and choices

All the world's religions offer systems of values which influence moral choice, and very often go on to set out the implications of these in very specific terms, either as sets of moral rules, or as general principles upon which the lifestyle promoted by that particular religion is to be based. For an outline of these, see the chapter on 'Religion and Moral Values' in *Teach Yourself Ethics*.

The areas where religion and morality come together most often are those concerned with sexuality, marriage and family life, and also with the issues of life and death. These are spheres of human experience where ultimate values come closest to the surface of conscious decisions. Euthanasia, suicide and abortion all raise fundamental questions about the inherent value of life. Equally, sexuality and family life raise fundamental questions about relationships and the overall purpose of human life for individuals and for society as a whole.

All of these topics are regularly explored in books on morality and religion, and there is no room here even to outline the main arguments. Let us, however, take a single current issue, and look at the values implied in it, and the relationship between these fundamental religious ideas.

The Human Genome Project

The Human Genome Project, based in the United States but involving scientists from all over the world, seeks to identify the function of each of the 100,000 or so genes that are found in cells of human beings. Particular genes and combinations of genes not only define physical characteristics, but also show susceptibility to certain life-threatening illnesses. Eventually, it is hoped that the knowledge provided in this way will lead to the elimination of a large number of diseases.

Although the project is far from complete, the present state of knowledge is such that a genetic test can predict the likely onset of a number of diseases. It is estimated that about 10% of the population have genes which indicate that they have a significant chance of developing a life-threatening disease at some point. The move from the identification of those at risk to effecting a cure is still a long way off. At this stage, genetic testing can point out the problem, but cannot supply the answer. This raises many practical, moral problems.

In February 1997, the Association of Insurance Brokers announced that it would not provide life insurance cover of more than £100,000 for those who had genetic tests predicting the onset of a fatal disease. All insurance, and ordinary choices concerning the future, are based on a balance of risks. Heavy smokers, drinkers and drug-takers, or those who take part in dangerous sports, or have dangerous occupations, know that their chances of a long and healthy life are thereby reduced. They take that into account in the choices they make. What will be the effect on those choices if people know from birth what diseases they are liable to get later in life?

- Should you abort foetuses who show genetic abnormalities?
- What is abnormal, anyway? Height? Colour of eyes? Sexual orientation? A susceptibility to heart disease or cancer?
- What would be the implications of trying to eliminate all but those who conform to some genetic norm?
- Should genetic information be confidential? Who should hold it, and under what circumstances should it be revealed?

- Genetic identification is already used by the law in order to identify offenders. Should one be forced to submit to a genetic test?

We can move from these practical questions to those of a more religious or philosophical nature:

- What gives you your identity as an individual? Most of the cells in your body are constantly dying and being replaced; physically you are very different now from a few years ago. The common thread, the thing that enables those cells to reproduce and maintain continuity, is the genetic code. You might perhaps express it by saying that your genetic code is you, expressed digitally!
- Your future is predicted in your genes. How does that relate to freedom? How does it relate to the idea of a God who makes things happen?

The project has set aside 5% of its funding to study the ethical, legal and social implications of genome research, and (even from the questions mentioned above) it is clear that such implications are profound.

The Genome Project is exploring the most fundamental feature of life. It is relating what actually happens (in terms of disease or behaviour) to a basic genetic code. That relationship is not so different from the 'natural theology' approach, examining particular causes of events here and now and relating them back (or outwards) to the ultimate cause of everything. Both processes seek to relate the particular to the whole. Genetic research, as it shows the particular functions of individual genes, will be able to spell out the implications of routine and random damage to genetic material – damage which, by altering the genetic make up of living things, may influence the process of evolution.

There are fundamental questions here:

- Who am I?
- What is life for?
- What does it mean to create something, or have responsibility for it?
- Do we have the right (or obligation) to interfere with the natural process of which we are a part?

These questions are essentially philosophical and religious; they cannot be answered from within the parameters of the scientific method. To resolve the various moral tangles involved with genetics, it will be necessary to tackle these basic questions, and without some working understanding of them, there is unlikely to be a general agreement over the values which should determine the practical moral safeguards that are needed.

How might this relate to the three possible relationships between ethics and religion given above?

Clearly, the ethical issues connected with the Human Genome Project cannot be considered as autonomous. We cannot pretend that they can be solved logically without also probing the fundamental issues of meaning and value that lie behind them.

Equally, a heteronomous abdication of moral value – waiting for various religions to determine the principles that will govern what should be done – is unlikely to be satisfactory, particularly in a global, multi-faith context.

The most fruitful approach here would seem to be the theonomous one, in the sense that the practical moral issues raise the same fundamental questions as are considered by religion. There is therefore the possibility of a genuine exploration in which religious traditions have a contribution to make without detracting from a logical and coherent approach to the moral dilemmas raised by the availability of human genetic information.

Comment:

Ethics is a huge and fascinating subject. It relates to every area of life in which there can be significant choice. But just as scientific advances require to be considered in the light of their ethical implications, so ethics also needs to be considered in the light of its fundamental assumptions about the nature of the universe and of the place of human life within it – and such questions have always been at the heart of religion.

Conclusion

This chapter has been no more than a brief attempt to make links between ethics and the philosophy of religion. Historically, it is clear that much ethical debate has been (consciously or unconsciously) **heteronomous**: it has been based on values given by religion, rather than on pure reason. On the other hand, in an increasingly secular or multi-faith society, it is important that ethical decisions which affect everyone should be taken on rational grounds that in some way transcend the values of any one particular religion. In this sense, ethics might become increasingly **autonomous**.

But in the end, even the most secular process of reasoning, in exploring the fundamental structures of life and the values that it is reasonable to hold in the light of them, will find that it is examining exactly that sense of ultimate purpose and meaning which is the bedrock of religion. In this way, even if the word 'God' is never used, it is likely that secular ethics will be seen by the religious people as **theonomous,** recognising a common source of inspiration.

POSTSCRIPT

All too often, philosophy of religion has simply considered propositions (e.g. the existence of God; the immortality of the soul) based on what it takes to be Christian belief (although with relatively little concern to address what the Christian faith actually teaches, for example, the Trinity or the resurrection of the body) and has subjected them to rational analysis.

It has therefore been a precise discipline, but a curiously unreal one; reaching rational conclusions which seem to be faultless but make little difference to anyone's views. Its detailed arguments sometimes appear like the tracery in a medieval window – fascinating and sometimes beautiful, but quite irrelevant to anything other than itself.

Some of the arguments presented in books on the philosophy of religion can then appear to be a logical game setting out the case for or against what nobody believes! Such an approach also fails to address the issue of why it is that people are religious, or why they continue to hold beliefs that rational argument has long ago shown to be absurd.

What I hope we have shown in this book is that the impulse towards religious belief – as found in religious experience, and as subsequently lived out as a particular way of interpreting and valuing life – inevitably goes beyond the rational. Religious beliefs come from within the experience of religion; that is their context, and only within that context can their meaning be fully appreciated. They are not grounded in logic but in tradition and personal intuition.

But philosophy is about logical argument, about evidence and the way in which we draw conclusions from it, about the nature and validation of the language we use. If philosophy attempts to deal with religion in the same way that it deals with, for example, science, politics or language, it is bound to come up against one of two crises:

- *Either* a failure to reach logically coherent conclusions, simply because the material with which it deals is not able to be fully appreciated through a process of logical analysis,
- *Or* a failure to have such conclusions as it reaches accepted by those who practise religion, simply because they do not take account of the more intuitive and experiential elements in religion.

In other words:

Either you fail to fit religion into a neat, logical scheme. Or you define exactly what a religious person can or cannot logically accept, only to find that, in the real world, religious people simply continue believing as before, oblivious to your arguments.

This should not surprise us. Does anyone really think that the personal hopes and fears of an individual can be encompassed within the parameters of rational thought alone?

Reasoning takes place when we stand back and look. Our process of weighing evidence, examining logic, and coming to conclusions on any matter is – as with science – a phenomenon which follows on behind the elusive, moving 'now' of experience. But religious experience (along with love, hate, fear and other immediate and powerful experiences) happens when we no longer stand back, but launch into the most immediate awareness of the present. Of course, there can be nothing more infuriating for a rational person than to be told that nothing can be examined, but that everything belongs to the feelings of the present moment. There can be a kind of anarchy of the 'now' that is profoundly egocentric and out of touch with the rest of the world. But equally, there can be few things more irritating for the feeling and acting person than to have every scrap of his or her life analyzed as though, in order for it to be real, is has to be set within an overall rational structure. Life's not like that!

Comment:

Hopefully, the balance which enables personal integrity to flourish is one in which immediate feelings and responses are not denied, but are allowed to inform one's whole awareness of life, and to be integrated subsequently into an overall pattern of understanding.

We started the book with a chapter on religious experience, on the grounds that if there were no religious experience there would be no religion, and therefore no philosophy of religion. What I hope has become clear in the intervening chapters is that the raw experience of that which is ultimate in our lives – whether or not it is considered in overtly religious terms – cries out for reflection, understanding and integration into an overall view of life. The process by which this takes place is the Philosophy of Religion.

SUGGESTIONS FOR FURTHER READING

Classic texts, available in a variety of translations and editions, not only present important arguments for the Philosophy of Religion but also provide a sense of the background and style of each of the thinkers. The following are particularly valuable:

Anselm *Proslogion and Monologion*

Aquinas *Summa Theologiae*

Descartes *Meditations*

Hume *Dialogues Concerning Natural Religion*

James *The Varieties of Religious Experience*

Kant *Critique of Pure Reason*

Kierkegaard *Philosophical Fragments* and *Concluding Unscientific Postscript*

Otto *The Idea of the Holy*

Plato *The Republic*

Schleiermacher *On Religion: speeches to its cultured despisers*

Also, *Historical Selections in the Philosophy of Religion* ed N Smart (SCM Press, 1962) offers a most valuable selection of passages along with biographical and philosophical notes on each of the thinkers.

The following is a small personal selection of books, all referred to in the text, for those who want to follow up these issues in greater depth:

Craig, W L and Smith, Q *Theism, Atheism and Big Bang Cosmology*, 1993 (Clarendon, Oxford, pbk. 1995)

Davies, Brian *An Introduction to the Philosophy of Religion*, OUP, 1982 (second edition 1993)

Dawkins, R *The Blind Watchmaker*, Penguin Books, 1988

Dawkins, R *Climbing Mount Improbable*, Viking, 1996

Firth, R *Religion: a humanist interpretation*, Routeledge, 1996

Griffiths, Bede *A New Vision of Reality*, Collins, 1989

Hick, John *Evil and the God of Love*, Macmillan & Co, 1966 (Fontana, 1968)

Hick, John *God and the Universe of Faiths*, Oneworld, 1973/93

Kenny, A *Reason and Religion*, Basil Blackwell, 1987

Kenny, A (ed) *The Oxford Illustrated History of Western Philosophy*, OUP, 1994

Kung, Hans *Does God Exist?* Collins, 1978

Mackie J L *The Miracle of Theism*, Clarendon Press, Oxford, 1982

Peacocke, A *Theology for a Scientific Age*, Basil Blackwell, 1990

Peterson, M; Hasker, W; Reichenback, B and Basinger, D *Reason and Religious Belief*, OUP, 1991

Polkinghorne, John *Science and Creation*, SPCK, 1988

Rorty, Richard *Philosophy and the Mirror of Nature*, Basil Blackwell, 1980

Stanesbury, D M *Science, Reason and Religion*, Croon Helm, 1985

Swinburne, Richard *The Existence of God*, Clarendon Press, Oxford, 1979 (a shortened version of which is available as *Is there a God?* OUP, 1996)

Vardy, Peter *The Puzzle of Evil*, HarperCollins (Fount), 1992

Within the *Teach Yourself* series there are:

Teach Yourself Philosophy
(This gives more general background material on philosophy. Its chapter on The Philosophy of Religion has material which appears in expanded form in this book.)

Teach Yourself Ethics
(This provides a more detailed outline of the ethical theories touched on in chapter nine of this book.)

And for those who wish to follow up with further study on the response of particular religions to these issues, there is *The Teach Yourself World Faiths Series*, which includes volumes on Buddhism, Christianity, Hinduism, Islam, Judaism and Sikhism.

INDEX

Other related titles

Other related titles

PHILOSOPHY

Mel Thompson

- What can we know for certain about the world or ourselves?
- Can we prove the existence of God?
- How is the mind related to the body?
- What is justice?
- How should society be organised?

This book is an introduction to the way in which these and other questions have been explored by some of the greatest minds in the history of Western thought. From Platonism to post-modernism, Anselm to Ayer, it examines the central themes in philosophy that have shaped the way in which we think about the world.

Teach Yourself Philosophy explains philosophical terms, such as epistemology, metaphysics, or existentialism in a straightforward way, providing an accessible outline of Western thought for the student or general reader.